ADVANCED HINDI GRAMMAR

ADVANCED HINDI GRAMMAR

USHA R. JAIN

CENTER FOR SOUTH ASIA STUDIES
UNIVERSITY OF CALIFORNIA, BERKELEY
2007

Library of Congress Cataloging-in-Publication Data

Jain, Usha R.
    Advanced Hindi grammar / by Usha R. Jain.
        p. cm.
    In English and Hindi.
    "A follow-up to Introduction to Hindi grammar (1995) and is recommended for
    second- and third-year Hindi students learning Hindi as a foreign language"--Pref.
    ISBN 0-944613-42-X (alk. paper)
    1. Hindi language--Grammar. 2. Hindi language--Textbooks for foreign
    speakers--English. I. Jain, Usha R. Introduction to Hindi grammar. II. Title.

PK1933.J338 2007
491.4'38242--dc22

                                                                    2006052130

To my husband Santosh

TABLE OF CONTENTS

PREFACE

Advanced Hindi Grammar is a follow-up to *Introduction to Hindi Grammar* (1995) and is recommended for second- and third-year Hindi students learning Hindi as a foreign language. As with the first-year book, the material for this text grew out of my experiences teaching intermediate and advanced Hindi at the University of California, Berkeley. My objective here has been threefold: (1) to write a Hindi grammar textbook that provides in-depth explanations of grammatical points necessary for the advanced Hindi student; (2) to make these explanations accessible to students of all disciplines by using non-technical language; and (3) to provide drills and exercises for the lessons. [1] In creating the drills, I have focused on common patterns and grammatical points while using a simple vocabulary so as not to obstruct grammar comprehension. Instructors should introduce more advanced vocabulary through readings and other audio-visual sources. I have been testing and revising these grammatical lessons and their accompanying drills in my own classrooms for several years now. I have found that the combined use of clear and thorough explanations with drills and exercises in the classroom has proven an effective pedagogical tool in reinforcing both old and new grammatical concepts.

The book is divided into twenty-five chapters and is meant to be used in conjunction with readings and audio-visual materials chosen by individual instructors. Many or most of the grammatical aspects covered in this book will be required to fully comprehend advanced readings and audio-visual materials. I have organized the chapters based on the degree of difficulty of each lesson and the occurrence of grammatical points in the course materials I have chosen, as well as my own students' needs in the classroom. However, instructors may choose to rearrange the lessons to emphasize specific grammatical points that correspond to their own course materials. In addition, both a glossary and appendices have been provided. The glossary covers all new vocabulary introduced in this text. The appendices, which also include words not used in the text, provide extensive lists of common adverbs, postpositions, and conjunctions.

I would like to thank all those who have helped with this project in its various stages. Preeti Chopra and Sujata Mody helped me with my research

---

[1] Chapters 24 and 25 are exceptions. As these chapters explain the rules that govern the formation of word pairs and affixes, they do not need accompanying exercises. Just understanding the rules and seeing multiple examples will better equip students to analyze and understand new words they encounter in their readings and conversation.

of the field, helped edit my existing teaching materials, provided insightful comments and feedback throughout the project, and entered part of the manuscript on the computer. Chris Plummer provided technical support and entered part of the manuscript on the computer. All three deserve my special thanks.

The Center for South Asia Studies at UC Berkeley has provided financial support for this project, for which I am grateful. Were it not for this support, I could not have embarked on such an extensive and demanding project.

Finally, I would like to thank my husband Santosh, my daughter Amita and her husband Niteen, and my son Sharad for their constant support, understanding, and encouragement. I would also like to thank my grandchildren, Neha and Vivek, for cheering me up when I was under pressure to finish this book.

Berkeley, California   Usha R. Jain
January 2007

ABBREVIATIONS

A	adjective
Adv	adverb
Conj	conjunction
F	feminine noun
FPl	feminine plural
FS	feminine singular
Ind Intr	indirect intransitive verb
Intr	intransitive verb
M	masculine noun
MPl	masculine plural
MS	masculine singular
MSO	masculine singular oblique
pl	plural
Post	postposition
Pro	pronoun
sg	singular
Tr	transitive verb
Tr (non-ने)	transitive verb that does not use the ने construction in perfect tenses

1. THE OBLIQUE INFINITIVE + देना CONSTRUCTION

The verb देना, when preceeded by the oblique infinitive of the main verb, means "to allow (someone/something) to do (something)," "to let (someone/something) do (something)," "to permit (someone/something) to do (something)." In this construction the main verb always remains in the oblique infinitive form, and only देना shows the changes due to number, gender, person, and tense agreement. Since देना is a transitive verb, in the perfect tenses the subject of this construction is marked by the postposition ने.

Examples:

मैं बहुत थका हूँ, मुझे सोने दो ।	*I am very tired; let me sleep.*
क्या माँ तुम्हें अमरीका जाने देंगी ?	*Will mother let you go to America?*
पिता जी ने उसको पार्टी में नहीं जाने दिया ।	*Father did not let her go to the party.*
सब्ज़ी (को) कुछ और पकने दो ।	*Let the vegetable(s) cook some more.*
फूलों को मत छुओ । उनको वहीं खिलने दो ।	*Don't touch the flowers. Let them bloom right there.*

Notes

1. In a negative sentence, the negative particles (नहीं, न or मत) can either precede the oblique infinitive or follow it.

Examples:
बच्चों को सड़क पर मत खेलने दो ।
       OR
बच्चों को सड़क पर खेलने मत दो ।
Don't let the children play on the street.

उसने मुझे नहीं जाने दिया ।
       OR
उसने मुझे जाने नहीं दिया ।
She/He didn't let me go.

2. The words इजाज़त (F) and आज्ञा (F) both mean "permission." Thus for

अब मुझे जाने दीजिये ।	*Please let me go now.*

one can also say:

अब मुझे जाने की इजाज़त दीजिये ।	*Please give me permission/allow me to go now.*
अब मुझे जाने की आज्ञा दीजिये ।	*Please give me permission/allow me to go now.*

But the much more common expression is the first example above -- i.e., the one the with the oblique infinitive + देना. The subtle difference in meaning is the same as seen in the English translations above. The use of इजाज़त or आज्ञा makes the statement more formal. As permission is given only to people, इजाज़त and आज्ञा are not used when "letting" inanimate nouns "do something." In such cases, only the oblique infinitive + देना should be used.

Examples:

गरमी बहुत है । पंखा चलने दो ।	*It is very hot. Let the fan run.*
कपड़े धूप में सूखने दो ।	*Let the clothes dry in the sun.*

3. Note the following common expressions in which the oblique infinitive + देना construction is frequently used.

रहने दो ।	*Let it be.*
जाने दो ।	*Let it pass; forget it.*
जो हो रहा है, होने दो ।	*Whatever is happening, let it happen.*

2

Oblique Infinitive + देना Construction: Exercises

1. Substitution drill

Please let me read now.
अब मुझे पढ़ने दीजिये ।

>sleep
>speak
>play
>eat
>listen to the music
>go inside
>rest
>work

2. Substitution drill

Ram didn't let us go.
राम ने हमें जाने नहीं दिया ।

>didn't let us study
>didn't let us rest
>didn't let us play
>didn't let us play the sitar
>didn't let us work
>didn't let us smoke cigarettes
>didn't let us sleep
>didn't let us read the book
>didn't let us drink wine

3. Complete the following sentences with an appropriate clause
(Use different subjects in the second clause.)

He wanted to go home, but we didn't let him go.
वह घर जाना चाहता था लेकिन हमने उसको घर जाने नहीं दिया ।
वह सोना चाहता था लेकिन ...
वह रेडियो सुनना चाहता था लेकिन ...
वह टेलीविज़न देखना चाहता था लेकिन ...

वह उपन्यास पढ़ना चाहता था लेकिन ...

वह बाँसुरी बजाना चाहता था लेकिन ...

वह भारतीय संगीत सुनना चाहता था लेकिन ...

वह आराम करना चाहता था लेकिन ...

वह शतरंज खेलना चाहता था लेकिन ...

4. Transformation drill

He will go.   Will Father let him go?
वह जाएगा ।   क्या पिता जी उसको जाने देंगे ?

वह यह किताब पढ़ेगा ।

हम इस होटल में रहेंगे ।

हम यह नई फ़िल्म देखेंगे ।

वह हिन्दी सीखेगा ।

मैं नये कपड़े ख़रीदूँगा ।

वह विदेश जाएगा ।

हम सुबह को दस बजे तक सोएँगे ।

वह रात को पार्टी में जाएगी ।

मैं शराब पिऊँगा ।

5. Translation exercise

1. Please let me go home now.
2. My father will never let me smoke a cigarette.
3. Because of the fever, his mother didn't let him go to school.
4. I let my son watch television only one hour every day.
5. He is very tired. Please let him sit down.
6. Why did you let him drink so much wine?
7. They didn't let me work.
8. He wanted to go to America, but his mother didn't let him go.
9. They didn't let the students speak.
10. Who let you come in?
11. Mr. Sharma lets his wife go to India every year.
12. Don't let him go.

2. IMPERFECTIVE PARTICIPLES

Definition of a Participle

A participle is a verbal form that has the qualities of both a verb and another part of speech (e.g., adjective, adverb, noun, or conjunction). This chapter and the following chapter will cover the adjectival and adverbial uses of imperfective and perfective participles. Conjunctive participles will be covered in Chapter 11.

Hindi uses imperfective and perfective participles, both of which can function adjectivally or adverbially. Whereas an imperfective participle denotes an *action in progress* or an unfinished activity, a perfective participle denotes a *past completed action* or a past action resulting in a state.

Formation of Imperfective Participles

Imperfective participles are formed by adding the suffix -ता, -ते, or -ती to a verb stem.

Infinitive	Verb Stem	Imperfective Participles
रोना	रो	रोता (MS), रोते (MPI), रोती (FS/FPI)
खेलना	खेल	खेलता (MS), खेलते (MPI), खेलती (FS/FPI)

Note that imperfective participles are often strengthened by the addition of a perfective form of the verb होना. The addition of the perfective form of the verb होना can avoid confusion between the use of a verbal form as a participle (e.g., चलती (हुई) गाड़ी *the moving train*) and its use as part of the main verb (e.g., गाड़ी चलती है *the train moves*).

Examples:

खेलता	खेलता हुआ लड़का	*the boy who is/was playing…*
खेलते	खेलते हुए लड़के	*the boys who are/were playing…*
खेलती	खेलती हुई लड़की	*the girl who is/was playing…*

5

| खेलती | खेलती हुई लड़कियाँ | *the girls who are/were playing…* |

Usage

Adjectival use of imperfective participles

An imperfective participle can be used as an adjective modifying a noun. An adjectival participle always precedes the noun it modifies and agrees with it in number and gender. Here, the noun modified is in the process of performing the action of the participle. Sometimes a Hindi imperfective participle can be rendered in English by "verb + —ing" or by a phrase (e.g., "the moving train" or "the train that is moving"). Often, however, it is more appropriate to translate the adjectival participle from Hindi into English as a phrase (e.g., "the man who is singing," rather than "the singing man").

Examples:

भागता हुआ आदमी	*the man who is/was running*
लड़ते हुए आदमी	*the men who are/were fighting*
हँसती हुई लड़कियाँ	*the girls who are/were laughing*
उड़ती चिड़िया / उड़ती हुई चिड़िया	*the flying bird*

Note that a predicative use of the imperfective participle (e.g., लड़की पढ़ती हुई है) is not standard Hindi. In such cases, it is better to use the progressive tense (लड़की पढ़ रही है).

Adverbial use of imperfective participles

An imperfective participle can also be used adverbially. In such cases, the subject or the object performs the action of the participle at the same time as the action of the main verb (e.g., "Smiling, she looked at me," or "She saw her brother while he was working").

An imperfective participle used as an adverb is *generally* in the invariable masculine singular oblique form (ए form) and is strengthened by the use of हुए.

6

Examples:

Imperfective participle referring to the subject:

उन्होंने हँसते हुए मुझसे यह कहा ।   They said this to me while
                                      laughing.

रोते हुए, उस आदमी ने यह कहानी सुनाई । That man told the story [while
                                      he was] crying.

Imperfective participle referring to the object:

मैंने उसको गाते हुए सुना ।   I heard him [while he was]
                                      singing.

पिताजी बच्चों को खेलते हुए देख रहे थे । Father was watching the
                                      children while they were
                                      playing.

Duplication of imperfective participles

An imperfective participle used as an adverb can be duplicated in order to emphasize the extended duration or the repetitiveness of an action. Note that duplicated participles are never strengthened with हुए.

Examples:

वह पढ़ते पढ़ते सो गया ।   He fell asleep while reading.
मैंने रेडियो सुनते सुनते अपना काम किया । I did my work while listening
                                      to the radio.
मैं रोज़ रोटी पकाते पकाते थक गई ।   I got tired of cooking rotis
                                      every day.

Notes

1. *Word order*

The adjectival use of imperfective participles is straightforward. The participle always precedes the noun it modifies.

In the adverbial use of an imperfective participle, the participle may refer to the subject or the object of a sentence. If the subject of a sentence performs the action of an adverbial imperfective participle, then the participle should follow the subject. Sometimes, however, the participle may precede the subject; in this situation a comma must follow the participle. If it is the object of a sentence that performs the action of the participle, then the imperfective participle should follow the object.

Examples:

मैंने घर जाते हुए उस लड़के को देखा ।	*I saw that boy while I was going home.*
घर जाते हुए, मैंने उस लड़के को देखा ।	*I saw that boy while I was going home.*
मैंने उस लड़के को घर जाते हुए देखा ।	*I saw that boy while he was going home.*

When the participle follows the subject and precedes the object, then it may be unclear whether it is being used as an adverbial participle referring to the subject or as an adjectival participle modifying the following object. In such cases, only context can clarify the exact meaning.

Example:

मैंने घर जाते हुए लड़के को देखा ।	*I saw the boy while I was going home /I saw the boy who was going home.*

2. Agreement

When a participle is used as an adjective, it always agrees in number and gender with the noun it modifies.

When used adverbially, a participle may refer to the subject or the object of a sentence or clause. If it refers to the subject and the subject is followed by a postposition (generally ने), it blocks agreement of the participle with the subject and the participle will be in the masculine singular oblique form.

Example:

उसने मुस्कुराते हुए कहा ।	*He/she said [it] while smiling.*

Similarly, if a participle refers to the object and the object is followed by a postposition (generally को), it blocks agreement of the participle with the object and the participle will be in the masculine singular oblique form.

Example:

मैंने लड़की को नाचते हुए देखा ।   *I saw the girl as she was dancing.*

In situations where there is no postposition blocking the agreement of a participle, then it can either agree with the noun to which it refers (either subject or object) or it can take the masculine singular oblique form.

Examples:

वह हँसता हुआ (हँसते हुए) बोला ।

He said (it) while laughing.

वह गाता गाता (गाते गाते) अपना काम कर रहा था ।

He was doing his work while he was singing.

मैंने आसमान में हवाई जहाज़ उड़ता हुआ (उड़ते हुए) देखा ।

I saw the airplane flying in the sky.

If there is any question or doubt regarding agreement, students can use the masculine singular oblique form for any adverbial use of the imperfective participle and it will always be correct.

3. *Nominal use of imperfective participles*

In addition to functioning as adjectives and adverbs, imperfective participles can also be used as nouns.

Examples:

मरता क्या न करता ?   *What wouldn't a dying person do?*

गिरतों को उठाओ ।   *Uplift the fallen [people].*

Imperfective Participles: Exercises

1. Substitution drill

I saw the girl who was laughing. (I saw the laughing girl.)
मैंने हँसती हुई लड़की को देखा ।

रोती हुई

मुस्कुराती हुई

पढ़ती हुई

सोती हुई

आती हुई

काम करती हुई

खेलती हुई

गाती हुई

2. Transformation drill

The girl was smiling. I saw the girl.
लड़की मुस्कुरा रही थी । मैंने लड़की को देखा ।

I saw the girl who was smiling.
मैंने मुस्कुराती हुई लड़की को देखा ।

लड़के घर जा रहे हैं । लड़कों को बुलाओ ।

बच्चा रो रहा है । बच्चे को उठाइये ।

लड़की सो रही है । लड़की को न जगाओ ।

बच्चा दौड़ रहा था । बच्चा गिर गया ।

बस चल रही थी । वह बस से उतरा ।

बच्चे खेल रहे थे । मैंने बच्चों को देखा ।

लड़की हँस रही थी । मैंने लड़की को बुलाया ।

लड़के लड़ रहे थे । मैंने लड़कों को रोका ।

चिड़िया उड़ रही थी । मैंने चिड़िया को देखा ।

3. <u>Transformation drill</u>

The girl was reading a book. The girl was laughing.
लड़की किताब पढ़ रही थी । लड़की हँस रही थी ।
The girl was laughing while reading a book.
लड़की किताब पढ़ते हुए / पढ़ती हुई हँस रही थी ।

वह खाना पका रही थी । वह गा रही थी ।
मोहन हँस रहा था । मोहन ने दरवाज़ा खोला ।
लड़की गा रही थी । लड़की जा रही थी ।
छात्र रेडियो सुन रहा था । छात्र ने अपना काम किया ।
पिता जी घर लौट रहे थे । पिता जी उससे मिले ।
मैं बगीचे में काम कर रही थी । मैंने आपको देखा ।
बच्चा रो रहा था । बच्चा माँ के पास आया ।

4. <u>Transformation drill</u>

I heard you. You were singing a song.
मैंने आप को सुना । आप गाना गा रहे थे ।
I heard you singing a song.
मैंने आपको गाना गाते हुए सुना ।

लड़की ने माँ को देखा । माँ खाना पका रही थी ।
छात्रों ने शिक्षक को देखा । शिक्षक आ रहे थे ।
हमने उसको देखा । वह पढ़ रहा था ।
राम ने मुझे देखा । मैं काम कर रही थी ।
मैंने डेविड को सुना । डेविड हिन्दी बोल रहा था ।
मेरे दोस्त ने तुम्हें देखा । तुम नाच रहे थे ।
मैंने उसको देखा । वह मुस्कुरा रही थी ।
मैंने बच्चे को देखा । बच्चा सो रहा था ।
मैंने रेलगाड़ी देखी । रेलगाड़ी चल रही थी ।

मैंने आसमान में बिजली देखी । बिजली चमक रही थी ।

मैंने इश्तहार देखा । इश्तहार हवा में उड़ रहा था ।

5. <u>Transformation drill</u>

The girl was crying. The girl arrived home.
लड़की रो रही थी । लड़की घर पहुँची ।

The girl arrived home crying.
लड़की रोते रोते / रोती रोती घर पहुँची ।

मैं किताब पढ़ रही थी । मैं सो गई ।

चोर भाग रहा था । चोर वहाँ पहुँचा ।

बच्चे खेल रहे थे । बच्चे थक गए ।

वे लड़ रहे थे । वे मेरे पास आये ।

मैं सो रही थी । मुझे याद आया ।

मैं सारा दिन काम कर रहा था । मैं थक गया ।

मरीज़ पलंग पर लेटा था । मरीज़ ऊब गया ।

वह नेता जी का भाषण सुन रहा था । वह सो गया ।

6. <u>Translation exercise</u>

1. He jumped off the moving train.
2. I stopped the boys who were fighting.
3. The woman asked [while] looking at me.
4. She came into the office crying.
5. I got tired of [continuously] talking.
6. The child fell asleep while listening to the story.
7. I saw him going with John.
8. She saw the burning fire.
9. The girl who is sleeping there is my sister.
10. We heard you singing a Hindi song.
11. Laughing, she told me about this incident.
12. She came home running.

3. PERFECTIVE PARTICIPLES

Imperfective vs. Perfective Participles

Whereas an imperfective participle describes an action that is *in progress* (e.g., food that is being cooked), a perfective participle describes a *state* that is the result of a completed action (e.g., cooked food).

<u>Imperfective</u>

पकता हुआ खाना
food that is being cooked (cooking food)

खिलता हुआ फूल
the blooming flower

<u>Perfective</u>

पका हुआ खाना
cooked food

खिला हुआ फूल
the bloomed flower

Example:

वह कुरसी पर बैठते हुए गाना गाने लगी ।
While sitting down on the chair, she began to sing a song.

वह कुरसी पर बैठे हुए गाना गाने लगी ।
While seated on the chair, she began to sing a song.

Formation of Perfective Participles

Perfective participles and the perfective forms of a verb are similar in appearance. They are both formed by adding the suffix आ, ए, or ई to a verb stem.

Infinitive	Verb Stem	Perfective Participles
रहना	रह	रहा (MS), रहे (MPl), रही (FS/FPl)
पढ़ना	पढ़	पढ़ा (MS), पढ़े (MPl), पढ़ी (FS/FPl)

If a verb stem ends in आ, ए, or ओ, the consonant य is inserted before the suffix आ and is also frequently inserted before the suffix ए. It is only rarely inserted before the suffix ई.

Infinitive	Verb Stem	Perfective Participles
आना	आ	आया (MS),आये / आए (MPl), आई / आयी (FS/FPl)
खाना	खा	खाया (MS), खाये / खाए (MPl), खाई / खायी (FS/FPl)

If a verb stem ends in ई, it is shortened to इ and य is inserted before adding the masculine singular and plural endings. In the feminine forms, the verb stem and the ending coalesce, forming a long ई.

Infinitive	Verb Stem	Perfective Participles
पीना	पी	पिया (MS), पिये (पिए) (MPl), पी (FS/FPl)
सीना	सी	सिया (MS), सिये (सिए) (MPl), सी (FS/FPl)

The following verbs have somewhat irregular perfective forms:

Infinitive	Perfective Participles		
होना	हुआ(MS)	हुए (MPl)	हुई (FS/FPl)
जाना	गया	गये (गए)	गई
करना	किया	किये (किए)	की
लेना	लिया	लिये (लिए)	ली
देना	दिया	दिये (दिए)	दी

Note that like imperfective participles, perfective participles are often strengthened by the addition of perfective forms of the verb होना.

बैठा	बैठा हुआ लड़का	*the boy who is sitting (seated)*
थके	थके हुए आदमी	*the tired men*
सोई	सोई हुई लड़की / लड़कियाँ	*the girl/girls who is/are sleeping*

Usage

<u>Adjectival use of perfective participles</u>

Like an imperfective participle, a perfective participle can be used attributively (i.e., it precedes the noun it modifies). In such cases, it agrees with this noun in number and gender.

Example:

वहाँ बैठी हुई लड़की मेरी बहन है ।　　*The girl who is seated there is my sister.*

A perfective participle can also be used as a predicate adjective (i.e., it follows the noun it modifies).

Example:

मेरी बहन वहाँ बैठी हुई है ।　　*My sister is sitting (seated) there.*

When a perfective participle is used as a *predicate adjective*, it indicates that the subject is in a certain state described by the participle. The basic structure of such a sentence is:

subject + perfective participle + हुआ/हुए/हुई + appropriate form of होना

लड़का + बैठा + हुआ + है ।　　*The boy is [in the state of] sitting.*

When a perfective participle is being used as a predicate adjective, if the participle does not have its own object, it agrees with the subject of the sentence in number and gender.

Examples:

वह लेटा हुआ है ।　　*He is [in the state of] lying down.*

लड़की सोई हुई है ।　　*The girl is [in the state of] sleeping.*

मेरा नाम यहाँ लिखा हुआ है ।　　*My name is written here.*

If the perfective participle has its own object, then it will take the invariable masculine singular oblique form (ए form).

Examples:

वह हाथ में बटुआ पकड़े हुए था ।	*He was [in the state of] holding a wallet in his hand.*
औरत चश्मा पहने हुए थी ।	*The woman was [in the state of] wearing glasses.*
हमारे दोस्त ख़ूब (शराब) पिये हुए थे ।	*Our friends were [in the state of being] very drunk.*

Adverbial use of perfective participles

A perfective participle can also be used adverbially. In this usage, it refers to either the subject or the object of a sentence or clause and is *generally* in the invariable masculine singular oblique form (ए form).

Examples:

Perfective participle referring to the subject:

वह हाथ में फूल लिए हुए आया ।	*He came holding flowers in his hands.*
बैठे हुए, मैंने उससे पूछा ।	*While sitting, I asked him.*

Perfective participle referring to the object:

मैंने उसको वहाँ खड़े हुए पाया ।	*I found him standing there.*
डॉक्टर ने मरीज़ को लेटे हुए देखा ।	*The doctor saw the patient lying down.*

The duplication of perfective participles

A perfective participle when used adverbially can be duplicated in order to emphasize the extended duration of a past action resulting in a continuous or repetitive state. Note that duplicated participles are never extended with हुए.

Examples:

हम उसके इन्तज़ार में खड़े खड़े थक गये ।	*We got tired of standing around and waiting for him.*
क्या आप सारा दिन लेटे लेटे ऊब गये ?	*Are you bored with lying around all day long?*
कपड़ा ज़मीन पर पड़ा पड़ा गंदा हो गया ।	*Lying on the ground [for so long], the cloth became dirty.*

Notes

1. *Word order*

When the adjectival perfective participle is used attributively, it precedes the noun it modifies. When used as a predicate adjective, the perfective participle comes after the noun it modifies and before the verb "to be."

Examples:

उस जली हुई रोटी को न खाओ ।	*Don't eat that burned bread.*
मेरी किताब वहाँ रखी हुई है ।	*My book is [kept] over there.*

In the adverbial use of a perfective participle, the participle may refer to the subject or object of the sentence. If the subject of a sentence performs the action of an adverbial perfective participle, then the participle should follow the subject. Sometimes, however, the participle may precede the subject; in this situation a comma must follow the participle. If it is the object of a sentence that performs the action, then the perfective participle should follow the object.

Examples:

मैंने खड़े हुए उसको देखा ।	*I saw him while I was standing.*
खड़े हुए, मैंने उसको देखा ।	*While standing, I saw him.*
मैंने उसको खड़े हुए देखा ।	*I saw him while he was standing.*

When the participle follows the subject and precedes the object, then it may be unclear whether it is being used as an adverbial participle referring to the subject or as an adjectival participle modifying the following object. In such cases, only context can clarify the exact meaning.

Example:

मैंने खड़े हुए आदमी को देखा ।	*I saw the man while I was standing/ I saw the man who was standing.*

2. *Agreement*

When a participle is used as an attributive adjective, it always agrees in number and gender with the noun it modifies. When used as a predicate adjective, the participle will agree with the subject unless it has an object of its own, in which case it will take the invariable masculine singular oblique form.

With adverbial use, the participle may refer to the subject or the object of the sentence. If it refers to the subject and the subject is followed by a postposition (generally ने), it blocks agreement of the participle with the subject and the participle will be in the masculine singular oblique form.

Example:

उसने लेटे हुए अपनी किताब पढ़ी ।   *He read his book while lying down.*

Similarly, if the participle refers to the object of the sentence and the object is followed by a postposition (generally को), it blocks agreement of the participle with the object and the participle will be in the masculine singular oblique form.

Example:

हमने आपको वहाँ खड़े हुए देखा ।   *We saw you as you were*
standing there.

The participle will also take the masculine singular oblique form if it has its *own* object.

Example:

बच्चा हाथ में खिलौना लिये हुए बैठा था ।   *The child was sitting with (holding) a*
toy in his hand.

In situations where there is no postposition blocking the agreement of the participle with the noun to which it refers (either subject or object) *and* the participle does not have its own object, it can either take the masculine singular oblique form or agree with the noun to which it refers.

Examples:

लड़की बैठी हुई (बैठे हुए) अपना काम कर रही थी ।
The girl was doing her work while seated.

वह बिस्तर पर पड़ा पड़ा (पड़े पड़े) गाना सुन रहा था ।
He was listening to the song while lying in bed.

If there is any question or doubt regarding agreement, students can use the masculine singular oblique form for any *adverbial* use of the perfective participle and it will always be correct.

3. *Nominal use of perfective participles*

In addition to functioning as adjectives and adverbs, perfective participles can also be used as nouns.

Example:

माता-पिता का कहा मानना चाहिये ।   *One should listen to what one's parents say.*

4. Since all actions do not result in states, all verbs cannot be used as perfective participles. The following verbs are often used as perfective participles:

फटना	Intr	to be torn
टूटना	Intr	to be broken
लिखना	Tr	to write
रखना	Tr	to keep; to put, to place
पीना	Tr	to drink
पड़ना	Intr	to fall; to lie (down)
बनना	Intr	to be made
कटना	Intr	to be cut
खिलना	Intr	to bloom, to blossom
थकना	Intr	to be tired
सोना	Intr	to sleep
लेटना	Intr	to lie down
बैठना	Intr	to sit
खड़ा होना	Intr	to stand
पहनना	Tr	to wear, to put on
पकना	Intr	to be cooked; to ripen
लेना	Tr	to take

खुलना Intr	to be opened, to open
धुलना Intr	to be washed
सूखना Intr	to dry up
जलना Intr	to burn
सड़ना Intr	to rot
भरना Intr/Tr	to be filled; to fill
पकड़ना Tr	to hold, to grasp
गिरना Intr	to fall, to fall down
लगना Intr	to be attached/connected to

Perfective Participles: Exercises

1. Substitution drill

Bring the books that are kept in that room.
उस कमरे में रखी हुई किताबें लाओ ।

> pen
> things
> flowers
> clothes
> cup
> tea
> papers
> chairs

2. Substitution drill

I don't need this broken chair.
मुझे यह टूटी हुई कुरसी नहीं चाहिये ।

> यह रखा हुआ खाना
> यह फटी हुई साड़ी
> यह जली हुई रोटी
> ये सूखी हुई सब्ज़ियाँ
> ये सड़े हुए फल
> यह टूटा हुआ प्याला

3. Transformation drill

The flower had bloomed. The flower was looking pretty.
फूल खिल गया था । फूल सुन्दर लग रहा था ।
The flower that had bloomed was looking pretty.
खिला हुआ फूल सुन्दर लग रहा था ।

खाना बाहर रखा था । खाना ख़राब हो गया ।
कुरसी टूट गई है । कुरसी की मरम्मत करो ।
ये कपड़े धुल गये हैं । ये कपड़े पहनिये ।

दरवाज़ा खुल गया है । दरवाज़े को बन्द करो ।

मज़दूर थक गये हैं । मज़दूरों को आराम चाहिये ।

फल सड़ गया है । फल को मत खाओ ।

आदमी थक गया था । आदमी घर आकर लेट गया ।

साड़ी फट गई है । लड़की साड़ी की मरम्मत कर रही है ।

काग़ज़ गिर गया है । काग़ज़ को उठाओ ।

4. Substitution drill

The girl was sitting on the chair.
लड़की कुरसी पर बैठी हुई थी ।

> was lying on the bed
> was holding a pen
> was wearing a blue sari
> was standing there
> was carrying a bag
> was drunk

5. Transformation drill

The girl was lying on the bed. The girl was reading a book.
लड़की पलंग पर लेटी हुई थी । लड़की किताब पढ़ रही थी ।

The girl was reading a book while lying on the bed.
लड़की पलंग पर लेटे हुए / लेटी हुई किताब पढ़ रही थी ।

लड़के बैठे हुए थे । लड़के गपशप कर रहे थे ।

वह आँखें बन्द किये हुए था । वह कुछ सोच रहा था ।

छात्र खड़े हुए थे । छात्र उसका भाषण सुन रहे थे ।

हम थक गये थे । हम घर पहुँचे ।

आया बच्चे को लिये थी । आया बाज़ार गई ।

उसने आँखें बन्द कीं । वह लेटी थी ।

उसने हाथ में किताब ली । वह घर पहुँची ।

हम बग़ीचे में बैठे थे । हमने उसका गाना सुना ।

6. Transformation drill

I saw him. He was standing near the door.
मैंने उसको देखा । वह दरवाज़े के पास खड़ा था ।
I saw him standing near the door.
मैंने उसको दरवाज़े के पास खड़े हुए देखा ।

मैंने आपको देखा । आप कुरसी पर बैठे थे ।
मैंने लड़की को देखा । लड़की साड़ी पहने थी ।
मैंने मरीज़ को देखा । मरीज़ पलंग पर लेटा था ।
मैंने छात्रों को देखा । छात्र किताबें लिये हुए थे ।
मैंने बच्चे को देखा । बच्चा सोया था ।
मैंने मोहन को देखा । मोहन आँखें बन्द किये था ।
मैंने छात्र को देखा । छात्र क्लास के बाहर खड़ा था ।
मैंने उसको देखा । वह हाथ में फूल लिये हुए थी ।

7. Transformation drill

I stood all day today. I became tired.
मैं आज सारा दिन खड़ी रही । मैं थक गई ।
Standing all day today, I became tired.
मैं आज सारा दिन खड़े खड़े / खड़ी खड़ी थक गई ।

माँ कुरसी पर बैठी थी । माँ सो गई ।
लड़का सारा दिन लेटा रहता था । लड़का मोटा हो गया ।
फल बाहर रखे थे । फल ख़राब हो गये ।
मरीज़ को सारा दिन लेटना पड़ा । मरीज़ ऊब गया ।
मैं सारी रात रेलगाड़ी में बैठी रही । मैं थक गई ।
छात्र लेटा हुआ था । छात्र ने कहानी पढ़ी ।
कपड़े फ़र्श पर पड़े थे । कपड़े गन्दे हो गये ।
कुरसी बाहर धूप में रखी थी । कुरसी ख़राब हो गई ।
चाय मेज़ पर रखी थी । चाय ठंडी हो गई ।

8. Translation exercise

1. These tired men want to go home.
2. The boy is wearing a beautiful shirt today.
3. I saw the girl who was sitting in the garden.
4. Don't eat the half-baked roti.
5. Their names are written on the paper.
6. They saw a man standing near your door.
7. Lying in (on) bed all day, he got bored.
8. Can you fix this broken chair?
9. The food that was kept out, got spoiled.
10. Sitting all night, I waited for you.
11. With his eyes closed, he was thinking about his children.
12. The students came into the class carrying books in their hands.

4. MULTIPLE SUBJECTS

We have learned that the verb always agrees with the grammatical subject of a sentence. Sentences in Hindi, however, may often have more than one subject. This may cause some confusion regarding subject-verb agreement. In order to avoid such confusion, there are some general rules of agreement that can serve as guidelines.

When two subjects are connected by the conjunction और (व, तथा, etc.), the following rules apply:

1. If the subjects are either all inanimate or all animate and are of the *same gender*, the verb will take the plural form of that gender.

Examples:
ये मेज़ें और कुरसियाँ यहाँ क्यों पड़ी हैं ?
Why are these tables and chairs lying around here?

मेरे कुरते और पाजामे कल धुलेंगे ।
My kurtas and pajamas will be washed tomorrow.

पिता जी और उनके दोस्त रोज़ यहाँ कसरत करते हैं ।
Father and his friends exercise here everyday.

शीला और उसकी सहेलियाँ शाम को हम से मिलेंगी ।
Sheila and her (girl) friends will meet us in the evening.

2. If the subjects are inanimate and are of *different genders*, the verb usually agrees in gender and number with the *last* of the subjects (i.e., with the noun closest to the verb).

Examples:
यहाँ क़ीमती ज़ेवर और साड़ियाँ मिलती हैं ।
Expensive ornaments and saris are available here.

ये दुकानें और वे बड़े मकान कब बने ?
When were these shops and those big houses built?

25

वहाँ आपको शान्ति और आराम मिलेगा ।

You will get peace and comfort there.

3. If the subjects are animate and are of *different genders,* then the verb will take the masculine plural form.

Examples:
मैं और मेरी पत्नी अगले साल दुनिया घूमेंगे ।

My wife and I will tour the world next year.

ये लड़के और लड़कियाँ यहाँ क्या कर रहे हैं ?

What are these boys and girls doing here?

प्रेमी और प्रेमिका कैसे अलग रह सकते हैं ?

How can a lover and [his] beloved stay apart?

4. To simplify problems of agreement or for the sake of variation, multiple subjects may also be listed and followed by दोनों, तीनों, चारों, or सब with the verb in the masculine plural.

Examples:
यह निबन्ध और वह कहानी दोनों गम्भीर होंगे ।

This essay and that story must both be serious.

रावण, शूर्पनखा और कुम्भकर्ण तीनों बड़े भयानक राक्षस थे ।

Ravan, Shurpanakha, and Kumbhakarna were all three very fearsome demons.

मैं और मेरे दोस्त हम सब इस मैदान में क्रिकेट खेलेंगे ।

My friends and I, we will all play cricket in this field.

अध्यापक, लड़के और लड़कियाँ सब यह समाचार सुनकर ख़ुश होंगे ।

The teacher, boys, and girls will all be happy to hear this news.

Note that the rules for subject-verb agreement discussed above are similar to the rules for the agreement of adjectives modifying two or more nouns (covered in Chapter 3, *Introduction to Hindi Grammar*).

When two subjects are separated by the conjunction या (अथवा, etc.), the verb agrees with the second item in the multiple subject (i.e., with the noun closer to the verb).

Examples:

आपको इस अवसर पर शानदार कुरता या साड़ी मिलेगी ।
On this occasion you will receive a gorgeous kurta or sari.

आपसे मिलने कल मेरा भाई या मैं आऊँगा ।
My brother or I will come to meet you tomorrow.

मुझे अपने दोस्तों के लिए शरबत या लस्सी बनानी है ।
I have to make sherbet or lassi for my friends.

क्या इस प्रोग्राम में कोई मशहूर गायक या गायिका गाएगी ?
Will any famous male or female singer sing in this program?

Multiple Subjects: Exercises

1. Fill in the blanks

These days papayas and oranges _____. (have become expensive)
आजकल पपीते और संतरे _____। (have become expensive)

These days papayas and oranges have become expensive.
आजकल पपीते और संतरे महँगे हो गये हैं।

रवि और सुनील कहाँ _____ ? (are going)
मेरा भाई और उसके दोस्त यहाँ _____। (meet)
कल वह लड़की और उसकी सहेलियाँ _____। (went to the market)
मुझे कुछ पेंसिलें और कापियाँ _____। (should buy)
यहाँ सुन्दर चूड़ियाँ और बिन्दियाँ _____। (are available)
उसने शादी के लिए महँगे कपड़े और जूते _____। (bought)

2. Substitution drill

Foreign newspapers and magazines are available here.
यहाँ विदेशी अख़बार और पत्रिकाएँ मिलती हैं।

> ताज़ा दूध और गरम चाय
> दाल और चावल
> समोसे और मिठाइयाँ
> भारतीय साड़ियाँ और कपड़े
> सूती चादरें और ऊनी कम्बल
> रेशमी कपड़े और महँगी चीज़ें
> बच्चों की किताबें और खिलौने
> महँगे क़ालीन और विदेशी चीज़ें

28

3. Fill in the blanks

Why do your brothers and sisters always _____? (quarrel)
तुम्हारे भाई और बहनें हमेशा क्यों _____? (quarrel)

Why do your brothers and sisters always quarrel?
तुम्हारे भाई और बहनें हमेशा क्यों झगड़ते हैं ?

मेरा नौकर और नौकरानी कल सवेरे आठ बजे _____। (will come)
ये लड़के और लड़कियाँ बग़ीचे में _____। (play)
पति और पत्नी मिलकर खाना _____। (will cook)
मेरा दोस्त और उसकी बेटी कल न्यू यॉर्क _____। (will go)
मेरी बहन और उसके दोस्त रोज़ _____। (swim)
प्रेमी और प्रेमिका रोज़ छिपकर _____। (meet)

4. Fill in the blanks

At the wedding, the bride, bridegroom, and their relatives all _____.
(danced)
शादी में दुल्हिन, दुल्हा, और उनके रिश्तेदार सब _____ । (danced)

At the wedding, the bride, bridegroom, and their relatives all danced.
शादी में दुल्हिन, दुल्हा, और उनके रिश्तेदार सब नाचे ।

मुझे अमरीका और भारत दोनों देश _____ । (like)
रिहर्सल में नायक और नायिका दोनों _____ । (came late)
यह डॉक्टर और नर्स दोनों _____ । (work here)
मुझे अपनी साड़ी और ब्लाउज़ दोनों _____ । (have to wash)
मेरी बहन, उसका पति और बच्चे सब कल _____ । (will come)
मैंने भारतीय संगीत और नृत्य दोनों _____ । (have learned)
शैली, गीता, रॉबर्ट, और समीर चारों मुझे _____ । (know)
प्रिन्सिपल, शिक्षक, और उस छात्र की माँ तीनों दफ़्तर में _____ । (are talking)

5. Fill in the blanks

I _____ a shirt or kurta for him. (have to buy)
मुझे उसके लिए कमीज़ या कुरता _____ । (have to buy)

I have to buy a shirt or kurta for him.
मुझे उसके लिए कमीज़ या कुरता ख़रीदना है ।

मुझे बच्चों के लिए फल या मिठाइयाँ _____ । (have to bring)

यहाँ हमें बढ़िया शर्बत या चाय _____ । (will get)

क्या उस दुकान में जलेबी या समोसे _____ ? (are sold)

स्टेशन पर आपको टैक्सी या ताँगा _____ । (will be available)

आपके घर मैं या मेरी बहन _____ । (will come)

मुझे दोस्त के जन्म-दिन के लिये एक किताब या साड़ी _____ । (have to buy)

6. Translation exercise

1. She bought a necklace and a ring.
2. The woman and her friend (M), both ran after the thief.
3. My grandfather and I want to go to Nepal next year.
4. We saw beautiful trees, mountains, and rivers in that country.
5. I have to buy a blanket or a quilt.
6. Today the teacher and her students will go to see a Hindi play.
7. My husband and I will both come to meet you tomorrow.
8. Lentils, rice, and Indian spices are all available at our shop.

5. EXPRESSING CONTINUITY WITH रहना, जाना, AND आना

There are three constructions (different from the progressive tenses) in Hindi that express the continuity of an action:

1. Imperfective/perfective participle + रहना: to keep on doing something
2. Imperfective participle + जाना: to go on doing something
3. Imperfective participle + आना : to have been doing something since a previous point in time

Imperfective/Perfective Participle + रहना

In order to express "to keep (on) doing something" or "to continue doing something" Hindi uses the imperfective participle of the main verb (without हुआ) followed by the appropriate form of the verb रहना. This construction denotes either the constant or the intermittent repetition of an action over a period of time. Such sentences should not be confused with the progressive tenses.

Examples:

वह काम कर रहा है ।	*He is working.*
वह काम कर रहा था ।	*He was working.*
वह काम करता रहता है ।	*He keeps on working.*
वह काम करता रहता था।	*He used to keep on working.*
वह काम करता रहेगा ।	*He will keep on working.*

Note that in the first two examples above the implication is that the individual is/was working at a specific point in time, but in the last three examples, the emphasis is on the continuation and/or repetitiveness of the action over a period of time.

In this construction both the imperfective participle of the main verb and रहना agree with the subject in number and gender, but the changes due to tense take place only with रहना. As in English, this construction may appear in most tenses with the exception of the progressive tenses. Note that in the perfect tenses this construction will not require the postposition ने with the subject since रहना is an intransitive verb.

Examples:

तुम क्यों झूठ बोलते रहते हो ?	*Why do you keep on telling lies?*
हम हिन्दी पढ़ते रहेंगे ।	*We will keep on studying Hindi.*
वे लोग खेत में काम करते रहते थे ।	*They used to keep on working in the field(s).*
वह उसको देखती रही ।	*She kept on looking at him.*
मैं चाहता हूँ कि वह गाती रहे ।	*I want her to keep on singing.*
काम करते रहो ।	*Keep on working.*

If the main verb is a stative verb (i.e., a verb that expresses an action which can turn into a state), the perfective participle can be used instead of the imperfective participle with रहना. Such usage will indicate the continuation of a certain state or condition (resulting from the completion of the action of the main verb).

Examples:

हम उसके दफ़्तर के बाहर बैठे रहे ।	*We remained (kept on) sitting outside his office.*
मरीज़ सारा दिन पलंग पर लेटा रहता है ।	*The patient continues (keeps on) lying on the bed all day long.*

With the compulsion and obligation constructions *only* the invariable masculine singular oblique (MSO) form of the imperfective/perfective participle is used with रहना (also invariable) before चाहिये, होना, or पड़ना. Thus the basic pattern for the compulsion/obligation construction is:

Subject + को + imperfective/perfective + रहना + चाहिये/होना/पड़ना.
               participle in MSO

Examples:

आपको पढ़ते रहना चाहिये ।	*You should keep on reading/studying.*
हमें हमेशा काम करते रहना पड़ता है ।	*We must always keep on working.*

मुझे रोज़ दवाई खाते रहना है ।	I have to keep on taking (eating) medicine every day.
हमें कल बस में खड़े रहना पड़ा ।	Yesterday we were forced to stand on (in) the bus.

Imperfective Participle + जाना

Like the imperfective participle + रहना construction, the imperfective participle (without हुआ) + जाना also indicates the continuity of an action (literally "to go on doing" an action). While both stress the continuity of an action, the primary difference between these two forms is that the imperfective participle + जाना construction *also* implies that some kind of gradual progress is being made.

Examples:

मेरी चिड़िया बाग़ में उड़ती रहती है ।	My bird keeps on flying around within the garden.
ये चिड़ियाँ दक्षिण की तरफ़ उड़ती जाएँगी ।	These birds will go on flying towards the south.

The rules of agreement and usage are the same as with the imperfective participle + रहना construction. However, the imperfective participle + जाना construction is not generally used with perfective participles (e.g., with stative verbs) because it implies progress, whereas perfective participles express a state or condition that has already been achieved.

Examples:

हम काम करते जाएँगे ।	We will go on working.
आजकल मकानों का दाम बढ़ता जा रहा है ।	These days the price of houses continues to rise/goes on rising.
समय बीतता जाता है ।	Time goes on passing.

Note that as with the imperfective/perfective participle + रहना construction, *only* the invariable masculine singular oblique form of the main verb (verb stem + ते) is used with जाना (also invariable) before चाहिये, होना, or पड़ना.

Thus the basic pattern for the compulsion/obligation construction is:

Subject + को + imperfective participle in MSO + जाना + चाहिये/होना/पड़ना

Example:

हमें मेहनत करते जाना चाहिये ।

We should go on working hard.

Imperfective Participle + आना

Another construction which can indicate the continuity of an action is the imperfective participle (without हुआ) + आना. This construction conveys the continuity of an action starting in the past and continuing into the present or another specified time. This construction has limited use and does not apply to future actions. All other rules of agreement and usage will follow the imperfective participle + रहना construction.

Examples:

मैं बचपन से गुजराती बोलती आई हूँ ।
I have been speaking Gujarati since childhood.

पिताजी दस साल से इस कम्पनी में काम करते आये हैं ।
Father has been working in this company for the past ten years.

यह रिवाज हमारे परिवार में पीढ़ियों से चलता आ रहा है ।
This custom has been practiced (going on) in our family for generations.

Expressing Continuity with रहना, जाना and आना: Exercises

1. Transformation drill

He works.	He keeps on working.
वह काम करता है ।	वह काम करता रहता है ।

वह किताबें पढ़ता है ।

वह गाना गाता है ।

वह संगीत सुनता है ।

वह दोस्तों को पत्र लिखता है ।

वह भारत के बारे में पढ़ता है ।

वह हिन्दी की फ़िल्में देखता है ।

वह दोस्तों की मदद करता है ।

वह अपनी मोटर की मरम्मत करता है ।

2. Transformation drill

She will study at this university.

वह इस यूनिवर्सिटी में पढ़ेगी ।

She will keep on studying at this university.

वह इस यूनिवर्सिटी में पढ़ती रहेगी ।

मेरा भाई इस दफ़्तर में काम करेगा ।

आपकी बहन सितार सीखेगी ।

हम हिन्दी पढ़ेंगे ।

कल भी बारिश होगी ।

मैं कोशिश करूँगी ।

मेरा दोस्त कहानियाँ लिखेगा ।

मैं हर साल भारत जाऊँगी ।

3. Substitution drill

They kept on talking about India.
वे भारत के बारे में बात करते रहे ।

     about America
     about their country
     about their family
     about their friends
     about their village
     about their city
     about the election

4. Transformation drill

Yesterday he worked all night.

उसने कल सारी रात काम किया ।
उसने सारी रात कविताएँ सुनाईं ।
लड़के ने सुन्दर फूल को देखा ।
छात्रों ने उस कहानी के बारे में सोचा ।
कल सारी रात बारिश हुई ।
किसान ने सारा दिन खेत में काम किया ।
मेरे भाई ने कल सारा दिन किताब पढ़ी ।
छोटा बच्चा कल बहुत रोया ।
वे बच्चे पार्क में खेले ।

Yesterday he kept on working all night.

वह कल सारी रात काम करता रहा ।

5. Transformation drill

The girl was lying there.
लड़की वहाँ लेटी थी ।
कपड़े ज़मीन पर पड़े थे ।
लड़की कुरसी पर बैठी थी ।
पिता जी पलंग पर सोये थे ।
लड़का उस लड़की के घर के सामने खड़ा था ।

The girl kept on lying there.
लड़की वहाँ लेटी रही ।

वह हाथ में किताबें पकड़े था ।
वे लोग भाषण सुनने के लिये वहाँ बैठे थे ।

6. Substitution drill

(You) please keep on trying.
आप कोशिश करते रहिये ।

  keep on learning Urdu
  keep on asking questions
  keep on working hard
  keep on telling us about your country
  keep on coming to my house
  keep on saving your money
  keep on helping them

7. Substitution drill

We should keep on studying Hindi.
हमें हिन्दी पढ़ते रहना चाहिये ।

  keep on working
  keep on playing
  keep on laughing
  keep on studying
  keep on trying
  keep on helping our friends

8. Transformation drill

He should study Hindi.

उसको हिन्दी पढ़नी चाहिये ।
आपको सवाल पूछना चाहिये ।
हमें हिन्दी बोलनी चाहिये ।
छात्रों को मेहनत करनी चाहिये ।
उसको खेत में काम करना पड़ा ।
यात्री को सारा दिन चलना पड़ा ।

He should keep on studying Hindi.
उसको हिन्दी पढ़ते रहना चाहिये ।

हमें काम करना होगा ।

छात्रों को आजकल बहुत काम करना पड़ता हे ।

9. Substitution drill

His/her interest in India keeps on/goes on growing.
उसकी भारत में दिलचस्पी बढ़ती जा रही है ।

पैट्रोल का दाम

शहर में ग़रीबी

देश की आबादी

उसकी शोहरत

दुनिया में हिंसा

बच्चे का बुख़ार

10. Transformation drill

He was working hard.　　　　He went on working hard.
वह मेहनत कर रहा था ।　　　　वह मेहनत करता गया ।

मौसम बदल रहा था ।

वह कविताएँ लिख रहा था ।

आप का दोस्त शराब पी रहा था ।

मरीज़ का दर्द बढ़ रहा था ।

वह अपने बारे में बता रहा था ।

नदी का पानी बढ़ रहा था ।

हमारा काम बढ़ रहा था ।

11. Transformation drill

I have been (am) living here for (since) twenty years.
मैं बीस साल से यहाँ रहता हूँ ।

I have been (continuously) living here for (since) twenty years.
मैं बीस साल से यहाँ रहता आया हूँ ।

वह दस साल से इसी दफ़्तर में काम करता है ।

मेरी नानी जी बचपन से साड़ी पहनती हैं ।

मेरे अब्बा बचपन से रोज़ नमाज़ पढ़ते हैं ।

मैं बचपन से लोकगीत सुनती हूँ ।

क्या तुम हमेशा से विदेशी कार चलाते हो ?

दुनिया में हमेशा से लड़ाइयाँ होती हैं ।

12. Translation exercise

1. My friend keeps on buying new things.
2. She used to keep on asking questions in class.
3. They should keep on working.
4. I will keep on trying.
5. These days I should keep on studying.
6. They kept on singing and dancing all night.
7. He sat (kept on sitting) near his ill mother all night long.
8. We had to (were forced to) keep on standing in line for two hours.
9. My friend will go on learning Indian music.
10. Poverty in the world keeps on (goes on) increasing.
11. He went on telling us about his village.
12. I have been hearing about Indian culture since [my] childhood.

6. POSTPOSITIONS

Hindi postpositions, like prepositions in English, serve to indicate the exact relationship of a noun or noun phrase to other parts of a sentence. Thus, in the sentence "शीला घर में है ।" (*Sheila is in the house*) the postposition में indicates the physical location of Sheila (the subject), while in "शीला घर की तरफ़ जा रही है ।" (*Sheila is going towards the house*) the postposition की तरफ़ indicates the direction in which Sheila is going. Although postpositions are often written and pronounced as independent words, they can never be used alone and must always follow a noun, pronoun, or noun phrase.

While simple and compound postpositions have already been covered in *Introduction to Hindi Grammar* (Chapter 7), this chapter provides some additional information on postpositions that will be useful for the advanced Hindi student.

Postpositions with Destinations

The postposition को can be used to express movement towards a physical destination. In such cases, however, को is generally understood and is not included.

Examples:

वह कल हमारे घर आया ।	*He came to our house yesterday.*
आप कब उसके दफ़्तर जाएँगे ?	*When will you go to her office?*

Though को has been dropped in the above sentences, the noun phrases हमारे घर and उसके दफ़्तर are still in the oblique form because को is implied.

The postposition तक is used to express movement towards a physical destination that is given as a boundary or limit.

Example:

चलो, चौराहे तक चलें ।	*Come, let's walk up to the intersection.*

When it is a person rather than a physical location that is one's destination, then Hindi uses the postposition के पास.

Examples:

आपको डाक्टर के पास जाना चाहिये ।	*You should go to the doctor.*
वह कल उसके पास जाएगी ।	*She will go to him tomorrow.*
वे मेरे पास सलाह लेने के लिये आये ।	*They came to me for advice.*

When the destination is a gathering of people, however, the postposition में is used in Hindi.

Examples:

वह कवि सम्मेलन में गया ।	*He went to the poetry reading.*
हम कल दावत में जाएँगे ।	*We will go to a party tomorrow.*

Postpositions in Sequence

In some instances, two postpositions can follow a noun phrase in sequence. The meaning conveyed by such sequences is generally self-explanatory.

Examples:

इनमें से दो साड़ियाँ चुन लो ।
Choose two saris from among these.
चुहिया दरवाज़े के नीचे से कमरे में घुस आई ।
The mouse came into the room from under the door.
पेड़ के ऊपर से चिड़िया उड़ी ।
The bird flew (from) over the top of the tree.

Omitting the Initial के/की of Certain Compound Postpositions

With the oblique pronouns इस, उस, किस, and जिस, the initial के/की of certain compound postpositions is dropped. Some of these compound postpositions include:

(की) ओर	*in the direction of, towards*
(के) बारे में	*about*
(की) तरह	*like, as, in the manner of*

(के) पार	*across, on the other side of*
(की) तरफ़	*in the direction of, towards*
(की) वजह से	*because of, on account of*
(के) कारण	*because of, on account of*
(के) सिलसिले में	*in connection with*

Thus Hindi speakers would say "इस ओर" instead of "इस की ओर" and "किस पार" instead of "किस के पार." The omission of के/की usually occurs when these postpositions govern inanimate objects. Thus, इस, उस, किस, and जिस must represent inanimate objects in order for the के / की to be dropped. Note, however, that when इस, उस, किस, and जिस are used as adjectives modifying a noun, के/की is retained.

Examples:

| उस तरफ़ चलो । | Walk in that direction. |
| उस इमारत की तरफ़ चलो । | Walk towards (in the direction of) that building. |

Inverted Postpositions

While most postpositions in Hindi follow the noun, pronoun, or noun phrase that they govern, a few compound postpositions may be inverted for the sake of variation or emphasis. In such cases a part of the compound postposition precedes the noun phrase it governs. For example, the postpositional phrase आप के बिना can be inverted to read बिना आप के. के बिना, के बग़ैर, के मारे, and के सिवाय/सिवा are among the few compound postpositions that are frequently inverted in Hindi. In rare cases, one finds के अलावा and के बजाय inverted as well.

Examples:

आपके बिना हम नहीं जाएँगे ।	बिना आपके हम नहीं जाएँगे ।
We won't go without you.	*We won't go without you.*
चीनी के बग़ैर चाय अच्छी नहीं लगती ।	बग़ैर चीनी के चाय अच्छी नहीं लगती ।
Tea without sugar doesn't taste good.	*Tea without sugar doesn't taste good.*

वह डर के मारे भाग गया ।

He ran away out of fear.

पपीते के सिवाय / सिवा मुझे सब फल पसन्द हैं ।

I like all fruits except for papaya(s).

सिवाय / सिवा पपीते के मुझे सब फल पसन्द हैं ।

I like all fruits except for papaya(s).

आप के अलावा वहाँ कौन कौन थे ?

Who all was there in addition to you?

अलावा आप के वहाँ कौन कौन थे ?

Who all was there in addition to you?

सोनिया के बजाय समीर ने हमें फ़ोन किया ।

Sameer phoned us instead of Sonia.

बजाय सोनिया के समीर ने हमें फ़ोन किया ।

Sameer phoned us instead of Sonia.

वह मारे डर के भाग गया ।

He ran away out of fear.

The Postposition पर with भी

The postposition पर generally means "on" or "at," but when it is used with भी and follows an oblique infinitive, it has a special meaning, "in spite of."

Examples:

बहुत मेहनत करने पर भी वह पास न हुआ ।

In spite of working very hard, he did not pass [the exam].

ग़रीब होने पर भी वह दूसरों की मदद करने की कोशिश करता है ।

In spite of being poor, he tries to help others.

Note that a list of common postpositions has been provided for reference in Appendix III.

Postpositions: Exercises

1. Substitution drill

Let's go to the park.
चलो, पार्क चलें ।

    to the teacher
    to the museum
    to Mother
    up to the market
    to Manish's party
    up to that hill
    to the tea shop
    to the meeting

2. Transformation drill

Tell us something about this country.
हमें इस देश के बारे में कुछ बताइये ।

उस इमारत की ओर चलिये ।

मैं उस नदी के पार जाना चाहता हूँ ।

उस पहाड़ की तरफ़ बहुत हवा चलती है ।

इस प्रोग्राम की वजह से मैं आजकल बहुत व्यस्त हूँ ।

इस बीमारी के कारण वह अस्पताल में है ।

इस मीटिंग के सिलसिले में वे अमरीका आएँगे ।

Tell us something about this.
हमें इस बारे में कुछ बताइये ।

3. Transformation drill

It is difficult to live without money.

पैसे के बिना / बग़ैर जीना मुश्किल है ।

तुम किताब के बग़ैर क्लास क्यों आए ?

छाते के बिना आज बाहर मत जाना ।

बच्चों के बिना घर सूना लगता है ।

मसालों के बिना भारतीय खाना अच्छा नहीं लगता ।

It is difficult to live without money.
बिना / बग़ैर पैसे के जीना मुश्किल है ।

मैं वीसा के बग़ैर भारत कैसे जाऊँ ?
मदद के बिना बच्चों को पालना मुश्किल है ।
मैं दोस्त के बिना पार्टी में नहीं जाऊँगी ।

4. Transformation drill

She began to dance with
(on account of) joy.

खुशी के मारे वह नाचने लगी ।

दर्द के मारे वह चीखने लगा ।

ठंट के गारे वह काँपने लगा ।

भूख के मारे उस के पेट में दर्द होने लगा ।

डर के मारे बच्चा रोने लगा ।

नींद के मारे मेरा बुरा हाल था ।

दुख के मारे उसकी आँखों में आँसू आ गये ।

She began to dance with
(on account of) joy.

मारे ख़ुशी के वह नाचने लगी ।

5. Transformation drill

She eats everything except for meat.

गोश्त के सिवा वह सब कुछ खाती है ।

आपके सिवाय वहाँ सब लोग थे ।

जलेबी के सिवा माँ को सब मिठाइयाँ पसन्द हैं ।

इस कविता के सिवाय उसने सब कविताएँ पढ़ीं ।

गणित के सिवाय मुझे सब विषय पसन्द हैं ।

खाना पकाने के सिवा मैं और सब काम कर सकती हूँ ।

वह आजकल पढ़ने के सिवाय कुछ और नहीं करता ।

फलों के सिवा उस दुकान में और कुछ नहीं मिलता ।

मैं कोट के सिवा सब कुछ सी सकती हूँ ।

She eats everything except for
meat.

सिवा गोश्त के वह सब कुछ खाती है ।

6. Transformation drill

I went to Delhi. I couldn't meet my friend.
मैं दिल्ली गई । मैं अपने दोस्त से न मिल सकी ।

In spite of going to Delhi, I couldn't meet my friend.
दिल्ली जाने पर भी मैं अपने दोस्त से न मिल सकी ।

वह वहाँ गया । उसका काम न हुआ ।

कल बहुत बारिश हुई । वे घूमने गये ।

उसको बुख़ार था । वह डाक्टर के पास नहीं गया ।

उसने रिश्वत दी । उसका काम नहीं हुआ ।

उसने बहुत कोशिश की । वह समय पर वहाँ नहीं पहुँच सकी ।

वह दुबला है । उसमें बहुत ताक़त है ।

उसने बहुत ढूँढ़ा । उसको सस्ता अपार्टमेंट नहीं मिला ।

उसको ठंड लग रही थी । उसने स्वेटर नहीं पहना ।

7. Translation exercise

1. Take my luggage out from the back of the car.
2. He came to me for help.
3. In spite of being tired, he didn't rest.
4. He couldn't sleep last night on account of the pain.
5. Without her morning tea, Mother gets a headache.
6. On seeing the police, the thief began to run out of fear.
7. In spite of trying hard, he didn't get a job.
8. He didn't buy anything except for a blue shirt.
9. The car can't move without gas.
10. Except for my grandmother, everyone in my family can speak English.

7. COMPOUND VERBAL FORMATIONS, PART 1
(WITH जाना, लेना, AND देना)

General Rules for Compound Verbs

Compound verbs are commonly used in both colloquial and literary Hindi (note that compound verbs do not occur in English). Compound verbs, though easy to understand conceptually, are difficult to master. Paying close attention to native speakers/writers and their use of compound verbs in various contexts will help improve command over the use of these constructions.

Two verbs are combined to form compound verbs in Hindi: the stem of a main verb followed by an auxiliary verb (compounder/intensifier). The main verb remains in its stem form while all changes due to number, gender, and tense agreement take place in the auxiliary verb. In compound verbal formations, the main verb retains its original meaning; the auxiliary verb, however, loses its meaning and serves only to intensify the meaning of the main verb or to subtly add shades of meaning (often untranslatable) to the original sense of the main verb.

Examples:

पैसे रखो ।	*Keep [Put] the money.* (simple verb)
पैसे अपनी जेब में रख लो ।	*Keep the money in your pocket.* (compound verb)
पैसे मेज़ पर रख दो ।	*Put the money on the table.* (compound verb)

In the above examples we see how an auxiliary verb modifies the meaning of the main verb. The first sentence has a simple verb, and there is no indication of the direction of the action. In the second sentence, the subject is asked to keep the money in his/her own pocket, indicating an action *towards* the subject. In the third sentence, the subject is directed to put the money on the table, indicating an action *away* from the subject.

In the above examples, auxiliary verbs are used to indicate the direction of an action. However, this is not their only use. In other cases, auxiliary verbs also add other shades of meaning to main verbs (e.g., emphasis, intensity, force, abruptness, or the completion of an activity).

Even though in a compound verb most verbs can be used as the main verb, only a few verbs can be used as auxiliary verbs. The three most commonly used auxiliary verbs are जाना, लेना, and देना. Other common auxiliary verbs -- including पड़ना, बैठना, उठना, डालना, and रखना -- will be discussed in Chapter 16.

There are two primary difficulties in learning the compound verbal system of Hindi. First, it is not easy to know which auxiliary verb can be used with a particular main verb. Second, even when the same auxiliary verb is used with several main verbs, it may lend a very different emphasis to each of the main verbs with which it is used, depending on the context. This will become clear when we discuss individual auxiliary verbs. There are also a few instances when an auxiliary verb does not add any special meaning to the main verb or, in other words, does not modify the meaning of the main verb. This is usually the case when a compound verb has become a fixed expression (Examples: अन्दर आ जाओ *come in,* has the same meaning as अन्दर आओ. वह मर गया *he died,* has the same meaning as वह मरा.)

Notes

1. Since the purpose of compound verbal formations is to intensify the meaning of the main verb, we find that they are commonly used in affirmative or interrogative sentences. They are not generally used in negative sentences.

Examples:

मैंने अपना काम ख़त्म कर लिया है ।	*I have completed my work.*
क्या बच्चा सो गया है ?	*Has the child gone to sleep?*

2. In long, complex sentences with a number of independent clauses, each of which has a verb, the compound verb is generally found only in the *final* clause.

Example:

मैं भारत में पैदा हुआ, वहाँ सब पढ़ाई ख़त्म की, माता-पिता की मर्ज़ी से शादी की, और काम करने के लिए अमरीका आ गया ।

I was born in India, finished my entire education there, married according to my parents' wishes, and came to America to work.

3. In perfect tenses a compound verb requires the postposition ने to mark its subject only if *both* the main verb and the auxiliary verb are transitive; if one or the other is intransitive, then the postposition ने cannot be used.

Examples:

मैंने यह फ़िल्म देख ली है ।	*I have [already] seen this film.*
वह सब खाना खा गया ।	*He ate up all the food.*

In the first sentence, both verbs are transitive. In this case the postposition ने is used with the subject, while in the second sentence खाना is transitive and जाना is intransitive. Hence, the postposition ने cannot be used with the subject.

4. Even though compound verbal formations are frequently used in Hindi, there are several instances where they are *never* used. Students are encouraged to memorize the following cases. Note, however, that these are not the only instances where compound verbs may not be used. One may come across other such situations.

(a) Compound verbs can be used in all tenses except the progressive tenses. Thus, वह पढ़ रहा है *He is studying,* and never वह पढ़ ले रहा है .

(b) Compound verbs are also not used with the verb stem + सकना construction. Therefore, मैं यह काम कर सकता हूँ *I can do this work,* and never मैं यह काम कर दे सकता हूँ .

(c) Compound verbs are never used in the verb stem + चुकना construction. Thus, वह अपना कमरा साफ़ कर चुका है *He has finished cleaning his room,* and never वह अपना कमरा साफ़ कर ले चुका है .

(d) Compound verbs are also not used in the verb stem + पाना construction. Therefore, शायद मैं अगले साल गाड़ी ख़रीद पाऊँ *Perhaps I will be able to buy a car next year,* and never शायद मैं अगले साल गाड़ी ख़रीद ले पाऊँ .

(e) Compound verbs should not be used in the oblique infinitive + लगना construction. Thus, वह गाना गाने लगा *He began to sing a song*, and never वह गाना गा देने लगा .

(f) The use of compound verbs is not possible with conjunctive participles (i.e., the verb stem + कर / के construction). Thus, वह खाना खाकर दफ़्तर गया *After eating [food], he went to the office,* and never वह खाना खा लेकर दफ़्तर गया .

5. It is unusual to find compound verbs used in negative sentences. On rare occasions when compound verbs are used in negative sentences, they convey that the subject/matter/issue under discussion is contrary to the expectations of the listener. In such usage, we often find the particle तो preceding नहीं, and both are placed between the main verb and the auxiliary verb.

Examples:
मैं आपको भूल तो नहीं जाऊँगी !
I won't forget you [although you seem to think I will]!

मैंने आपकी घड़ी खो तो नहीं दी !
I didn't lose your watch [although you seem to think I did]!

6. In addition to तो, भी and ही can also be used in compound verbs to add varying degrees of emphasis. Speakers can also convey other subtleties of meaning through a change in tone. While तो is generally used only in negative statements, this is not the case for भी and ही, which can be used for both negative and affirmative sentences.

Examples:

आख़िर उसने अपनी पी॰एच॰डी॰ ख़त्म कर ली ।	*He/she finally finished his/her Ph.D.*
आख़िर उसने अपनी पी॰एच॰डी॰ ख़त्म कर ही ली ।	*He/she finished his/her Ph.D. finally!*
मैंने सबको यह बता दिया है ।	*I have told everyone this.*
मैंने सबको यह बता भी दिया है ।	*I have <u>already</u> told everyone this[even though you don't think so].*

In the first pair of sentences above, ही is added to emphasize the word "finally." Although both these sentences can be translated in a similar manner, the second sentence clearly indicates that the speaker is commenting on the *length* of time the subject took to finish his/her Ph.D. The tone of the speaker would indicate to the listener whether he/she was trying to convey sarcasm or relief or some other emotion about the length of time taken. In the second pair, the addition of भी clearly distinguishes the meaning of these two statements. In contrast to the first sentence, in the second sentence the speaker is trying to reassure the listener, who doubts or is not aware of the fact that the speaker has "already told everyone this."

7. Sometimes it is difficult to distinguish between a compound verb and a conjunctive participle (see Chapter 11). This happens when the कर / के of the conjunctive participle is dropped. In the case of the conjunctive participle, the second verb continues to retain its original meaning even after कर / के is dropped. In contrast, in a compound verb, the second verb loses its original meaning.

Examples:

धोबी सब कपड़े दे (कर) गया ।	*The washerman delivered (gave) all the clothes and left.*
मैंने अपना सब काम कर लिया है ।	*I have finished all my work.*

In the first example, that of a conjunctive participle, both verbs retain their original meanings, so even when कर is dropped, there is no change in the meaning of the sentence. In the second example, that of a compound verb, the auxiliary verb लेना loses its original meaning and shows that the subject finished the work (for himself/herself).

Compound Verbs with जाना, लेना, and देना

Although Hindi uses many auxiliary verbs for compound verbal formations, जाना, लेना and देना are the most frequently used.

Compound Verbs with जाना

जाना *to go*: In compound verbs, जाना is the most commonly used auxiliary verb with intransitive verb stems. When used as an auxiliary verb in a compound verb, जाना is used to express the completeness and thoroughness of an action or a process. It is often used to show the completed transformation from one condition/situation/state to another. Examples of this include बैठ जाना (transition from standing to sitting), सो जाना (transition from being awake to falling asleep), and मर जाना (transition from being alive to being dead).

We cannot have a compound verb formation where जाना is used as an auxiliary with itself. In other words, जा जाना is not possible. In order to indicate the completeness of the action of going, चला जाना is used.

Examples:

पिताजी दूरदर्शन देखते हुए सो गए ।

Father fell asleep while watching television. (Here we see a transition from being awake to falling asleep.)

गंदा पानी न पियो । बिमार हो जाओगे ।

Don't drink dirty water. You will fall sick. (Here again the emphasis is on the transition from being healthy to falling sick.)

लम्बे सफ़र के बाद वह भारत पहुँच गया ।

After a long journey, he arrived in India. (The emphasis is on the completion of the journey.)

जाना can also be used with some transitive verbs such as समझना, पीना, and खाना. With such transitive verbs जाना emphasizes the completeness of understanding (समझ जाना) or the thoroughness of eating and drinking (खा जाना, पी जाना).

Examples:

दोहराने पर वह मेरी बात समझ गई ।

Upon [my] repetition, she understood my words thoroughly. (Here the emphasis is on the thoroughness of the action of understanding.)

वह सब शराब पी जाएगा ।

He will drink up all the liquor. (The emphasis is on the future completion of the action and the consumption of all the available liquor.)

मौक़ा पाकर बिल्ली सब खाना खा गई ।

Upon getting the opportunity, the cat ate up all the food. (Again the emphasis is on the consumption of all the food.)

Compound Verbs with लेना and देना

While जाना is generally compounded with intransitive verbs, लेना and देना form compound verbs with transitive verbs. लेना and देना are used to indicate a completed action. They further show the direction of that action towards or away from the subject. They can also indicate that either the subject or some other person is the beneficiary of a particular action. In contrast to जाना, लेना and देना can also occur as auxiliaries with themselves.

लेना *to take*: In compound verbs, लेना is commonly used as an auxiliary with transitive verbs. It is used to indicate the completion of a single action and it implies that the action is done for the benefit of the subject; moreover, the direction of the action is *towards* or upon the subject of the main verb. लेना may be used as an auxiliary verb with itself (e.g., ले लेना). Also, since लेना is a transitive verb and is generally used as an auxiliary with a transitive verb stem, the subject of such compound verbs is marked by ने in the perfect tenses.

Examples:

चोर ने उसका पर्स छीन लिया ।

The thief snatched her purse [from her]. (The action is performed for the benefit of the thief towards himself.)

बाहर बहुत ठंड है । गरम कपड़े पहन लो ।

It is very cold outside. Put on some warm clothes. (Here the direction of the action is towards the understood subject, as well as for his/her benefit.)

अपना काम ख़त्म कर लो फिर तुम बाहर खेल सकते हो ।

Finish your work; then you can play outside. (Here the subject addressed is being asked to finish his work for his own benefit.)

मैंने दर्ज़ी से अपने कपड़े ले लिये ।

I got my clothes from the tailor. (Here the emphasis is on the single completed action done for the benefit of the subject.)

देना *to give*: The verb देना is also used as an auxiliary with transitive verbs to indicate the completion of a single action. As is evident from its meaning (*to give*), देना implies that the action is done by the subject for the benefit of someone else, and/or the direction of the action is *away* from the subject of the main verb. देना can also be used as an auxiliary verb with itself (e.g., दे देना). As देना is a transitive verb and is generally used as an auxiliary with a transitive verb stem, the subject of such compound verbs is marked by ने in the perfect tenses.

Examples:

नौकर ने मेरा कमरा साफ़ कर दिया ।

The servant has cleaned my room. (The subject [the servant] performed the action for the benefit of someone else [the speaker].)

वापस आकर मैं आपकी कार की चाबी उस मेज़ पर रख दूँगा ।

When I return, I will put your car key on that table. (The action is away from the subject [the speaker]. Here the emphasis is on the future completion of the action.)

पिता जी ने मुझे अपनी गाड़ी दे दी ।

Father gave his car to me. (The emphasis is on the completed action of giving, done for the benefit of someone other than the subject.)

Contrast between लेना and देना

Despite the many similarities in their patterns, लेना and देना convey very clear differences.

(1) Since both these verbs indicate action in a particular direction, they cannot be combined with verb stems that indicate action in the opposite direction. For example, लेना implies action towards the subject. Therefore we cannot say मैं उसको यह बात बता लूँगा । Similarly देना cannot be used with

actions directed towards the subject. Hence मैं यह मिठाई खा दूँगा is not possible.

(2) With certain verb stems, both लेना and देना can be used to convey quite different meanings. This is clearly illustrated in the following pairs of sentences.

यह काम कर लो ।	*Do this work* (for yourself).
यह काम कर दो ।	*Do this work* (for someone else).
अख़बार पढ़ लो ।	*Read the newspaper* (to yourself).
अख़बार पढ़ दो ।	*Read the newspaper* (aloud to someone else).
पैसे मेज़ पर रख दो ।	*Put the money on the table.* (The implication is that the table is far away from the subject.)
पैसे मेज़ पर रख लो ।	*Put the money on the table.* (The implication is that the table is close to the subject.)

Intransitive Verb Stems + लेना and देना

There are a few instances where लेना and देना are used with some intransitive verb stems. In such cases, their meanings are often very specific. Therefore it is important to learn the meaning of each of these special combinations of compound verbs. Since both the stem of the main verb and the auxiliary verb are not transitive verbs, the subject is not marked by ने in the perfect tenses.

(a) Intransitive verb stem + लेना : There are very few examples of such compound verbs. They must be learned individually.

(1) चल लेना *to walk, to complete a walk*

Example:

मेरे पिताजी रोज़ पाँच मील चल लेते हैं ।	*My father completes (is able to complete) a five-mile walk every day.*

Here चल लेना subtly conveys that the father's ability to finish the walk is contrary to one's expectations. In contrast, मेरे पिताजी रोज़ पाँच मील चलते हैं would simply imply that father walks five miles every day and there is no doubt about his ability to do so.

(2) साथ हो लेना *to accompany; to join*

Example:
जब हम घर जा रहे थे तो वह भी हमारे साथ हो लिया ।
He also joined us when we were going home.

(3) काम हो लेना *for work to be completed/finished*

Example:
क्या रसोई में सब काम हो लिया ?
Is all the work in the kitchen done?

This construction can also be used with some other nouns to indicate that something must be completed or finished (e.g., with तैयारी in the following example):

सात बजे तक पूजा की सब तैयारी हो लेगी ।
Preparations for worship will be completed by seven o'clock.

(b) Intransitive verb stem + देना : देना may occur with a few intransitive verbs such as चलना, हँसना, मुस्कुराना, and रोना. Here देना often conveys a spontaneous or impulsive commencement of an action, except in the case of चल देना, which has become a fixed expression meaning "to start off."

(1) चल देना *to set off, to depart, to embark, to start off*

Example:
रिटायर होकर वे दुनिया की सैर के लिये चल दिये ।
After retiring, they embarked (started off) on a world tour.

(2) हँस देना *to burst out laughing*; *to not take someone seriously*

Examples:

उसके चुटकुले सुनकर बच्चे हँस दिये ।

Upon hearing his jokes, the children burst out laughing. (Here the laughter is impulsive/spontaneous.)

मेरी सलाह सुनकर तुम क्यों हँस देते हो ?

Why do you laugh when I give you advice? (Here the laughter is impulsive and also implies that the listener does not take the speaker's advice seriously.)

(3) मुस्कुरा देना *to smile*

Example:

उसको देखकर वह हमेशा मुस्कुरा देती है ।

When she sees him, she always smiles. (Here there is a sense of an impulsive action.)

(4) रो देना *to burst into tears*

Example:

वह अपने ग्रेड देखकर रो दिया ।

Upon seeing his grades, he burst into tears. (Here there is a sense of spontaneous action.)

Compound Verbal Formations, Part 1
(with जाना, लेना and देना): Exercises

1. Transform the following sentences to compound verbal formations with जाना, appropriately changing the verb in bold in each sentence.

The car will come at 5 o'clock.
गाड़ी पाँच बजे **आएगी** ।

आपका काम कब ख़त्म **होगा** ?

टिकट घर की खिड़की छह बजे **खुलेगी** ।

हर रोज़ क्लास नौ बजे **शुरू होती है** ।

हमारा दफ़्तर पाँच बजे **बन्द होता है** ।

बच्चा माँ की गोद में **सोया** ।

वे लोग ठीक समय पर वहाँ **पहुँचे** ।

वह थक कर पलंग पर **लेटा** ।

क्लास में आ कर सब छात्र चुपचाप **बैठे** ।

पुलिस को देख कर चोर **भागा** ।

मुझे कल अपना वेतन **मिला** ।

रेलगाड़ी स्टेशन पर **रुकी** ।

The car will come at 5 o'clock.
गाड़ी पाँच बजे आ जाएगी ।

2. Transform the following sentences to compound verbal formations with लेना, appropriately changing the verb in bold in each sentence.

Did you see this movie?
क्या आपने यह फ़िल्म **देखी** ?

अपने कपड़े **धोओ** ।

क्या बच्चे ने अपना स्कूल का **काम किया** ?

किसी ने मेरी साइकिल **चुराई** ।

मैंने आज दफ़्तर से छुट्टी **ली** ।

उसने मेरी बात **समझी** ।

हमने गरम चाय **पी** ।

क्या तुम ने आज का समाचारपत्र **पढ़ा** ?

उसने सुन्दर साड़ी **पहनी** ।

Did you see this movie?
क्या आपने यह फिल्म देख ली ?

58

आपके दोस्त ने सब मिठाइयाँ **खाईं** ।

क्या उसने अपना निबन्ध **लिखा** ?

3. Transform the following sentences to compound verbal formations with देना, appropriately changing the verb in bold in each sentence.

Please give that man some money.
उस ग़रीब आदमी को कुछ पैसा **दीजिये** ।

Please give that man some money.
उस ग़रीब आदमी को कुछ पैसा दे दीजिये ।

मैंने उसको कुछ पैसा **भेजा** ।

क्या मैं दरवाज़ा **बन्द करूँ** ?

मैंने उसको सब कुछ **समझाया** ।

उसने अपने सब फल **बेचे** ।

उसने मुझे सब कुछ **बताया** ।

वे सड़े फल **फेंको** ।

धोबी ने हमारे कपड़े **धोये** ।

नौकर ने मेरा कमरा **साफ़ किया** ।

उसने हमारे लिये चाय **बनाई** ।

क्या आपने मेरी कार की **मरम्मत की** ?

4. Transform the following sentences to (a) compound verbal formations with देना and (b) compound verbal formations with लेना by appropriately changing the verb in bold in each sentence.

I read Mother's letter.
मैंने माँ का पत्र **पढ़ा** ।

(a) I read Mother's letter (out loud).
मैंने माँ का पत्र पढ़ दिया ।

(b) I read Mother's letter (to myself).
मैंने माँ का पत्र पढ़ लिया ।

तुम यह काम **खत्म करो** ।

उसने दराज़ से पैसे **निकाले** ।

उसने खाना **बनाया** ।

लड़की ने खिड़की **खोली** ।

उसने सब काम **खत्म किया** ।

आदमी ने गाड़ी से सामान **उतारा** ।

59

उसने मेज़ पर किताबें **रखीं** ।

चीज़ों की फ़ेहरिस्त **लिखो** ।

इस बकस में सामान **रखो** ।

5. Transform the following sentences from affirmative to negative, replacing the compound verbal formations in bold with non-compounded forms.

I drank my tea.
मैंने अपनी चाय **पी ली** ।

I didn't drink my tea.
मैंने अपनी चाय नहीं पी ।

उसने मेरी किताब **दे दी** ।

धोबी ने हमारे कपड़े **धो दिये** ।

लड़की ने साड़ी **पहन ली** ।

दफ़्तर नौ बजे **खुल गया** ।

मैं उसका नाम **भूल गया** ।

उसने सब किताबें **बेच दीं** ।

हमने यह उपन्यास **पढ़ लिया** ।

मैं आपकी बात **समझ गया** ।

क्लास में वह खिड़की के पास **बैठ गया** ।

उसने मेरी गाड़ी की **मरम्मत कर दी** ।

6. In the following sentences underline the main verb and circle the auxiliary verb. Give the English translation and try to explain in parentheses what subtleties of meaning each individual auxiliary has added to the sentence.

१. भारत जाने से पहले उसने थोड़ी हिन्दी सीख ली ।

२. हम स्टेशन पर पहुँच गये ।

३. जल्दी चलो, दिल्ली की बस आ गई है ।

४. यह काम जल्दी कर दीजिये ।

५. छात्र कुरसी पर बैठ गया ।

६. मेरा सामान वहाँ रख दो ।

७. बच्चा बीमार हो गया ।

८. माँ से कहो कि भाई साहब आ गये हैं ।

९. जी हाँ, सब काम ख़त्म हो गया है ।

१०. मैं कल तक आपका सब काम कर दूँगा ।

११. बच्चे ने दूध पी लिया ।

१२. हम आपकी बात समझ गये ।

१३. तुमने ये चीज़ें क्यों फेंक दीं ?

१४. किसी ने मेरे पैसे चुरा लिये हैं ।

7. Translation exercises
(Use compound verbs.)

1. The weather is very hot today. Please drink some water before going out.
2. I'll return your book tomorrow.
3. The glass fell and broke.
4. Did you understand [completely] what I said?
5. He gave away all his money to the poor.
6. Every day my children go to sleep at 9 o'clock.
7. I'll finish my essay by tomorrow.
8. She sent a letter to her grandmother.
9. It's very hot here; please sit in front of the fan.
10. Have you taken (eaten) your medicine?
11. Please give these sweets to the children.
12. Don't worry. I'll get (arrive) there on time.

8. ADVERBS

Adverbs and adverbial phrases modify verbs, adjectives, or other adverbs. They generally indicate time, place, manner, or degree and answer questions such as when, where, how, how often, or to what extent.

Adverbs of time indicate when, for how long, or how often an action occurs.

मेरा भाई **परसों** आया ।	*My brother came the day before yesterday.*
वह **कल से** बीमार है ।	*She has been ill since yesterday.*
मैं **रोज़** कसरत करती हूँ ।	*I exercise every day.*

Adverbs of place indicate where an action occurs.

वे **यहाँ** काम करते हैं ।	*They work here.*
बच्चे **बाहर** खेल रहे हैं ।	*The children are playing outside.*
तुम्हें **घर में** पढ़ना चाहिये ।	*You should study at home.*

Adverbs of manner indicate how an action is performed.

चुपचाप बैठो ।	*Sit quietly.*
वह **तेज़ी से** भागा ।	*He ran quickly.*
तुरन्त वहाँ जाओ ।	*Go there immediately.*

Adverbs of degree indicate the extent or intensity of a quality or quantity when modifying an adjective or another adverb.

यह थैला **काफ़ी** भारी है ।	*This bag is quite heavy.*
हमारे शिक्षक **बहुत** ज़ोर से बोलते हैं ।	*Our teacher speaks very loudly.*
मैं आज **सिर्फ़** एक रोटी खाऊँगी ।	*Today I will eat only one roti.*

Word Order

The standard word order of a Hindi sentence is generally:

Subject + adverb + indirect object + direct object + verb.
OR
Adverb +subject + indirect object + direct object + verb.

Students should keep in mind that there is a great deal of flexibility in this word order. Some factors that contribute to changes in the standard word order of a sentence are emphasis, context, and poetic license; however, sometimes the word order can be changed without any special change in meaning or emphasis.

If there is more than one adverb in a sentence, the standard word order is adverbs of time, then adverbs of place, then adverbs of manner. Adverbs of degree generally precede the adjective or adverb they modify. Again, this word order is flexible and can be easily changed to give special emphasis.

Examples:

मैं अगले साल मराठी सीखूँगा ।	*I will learn Marathi next year.*
अगले साल मैं मराठी सीखूँगा ।	*Next year, I will learn Marathi.*
आपको अब वहाँ फ़ौरन जाना चाहिये ।	*Now you should go there immediately.*
मैं आपके दफ़्तर कल आऊँगा ।	*I will come to your office tomorrow.*

Notice that in the first sentence the adverb comes immediately after the subject, while in the second sentence, the adverb precedes the subject. Both uses are standard. The third sentence also demonstrates a standard word order, while the fourth sentence switches the order of the adverbs for emphasis.

Formation

There are two kinds of adverbs in Hindi: those that are adverbs in and of themselves and those that are formed from nouns, adjectives, or other adverbs. Thus, लगभग *approximately,* तुरन्त *immediately,* हमेशा *always*, and ज़रूर *certainly* are adverbs in and of themselves, while कठिनाई से *with difficulty* is an adverb formed from the noun कठिनाई *difficulty.* Seven of the common patterns of adverbial formation are given below.

(1) Various nouns when followed by postpositions function as adverbial phrases.

Noun + postposition

शाम *evening*	+	को	=	शाम को *in the evening*
शहर *city*	+	में	=	शहर में *in the city*

63

मेज़ *table*	+	पर	=	मेज़ पर *on the table*
घर	+	पर	=	घर पर *at home*

(2) One of the most common markers of an adverb in Hindi is the postposition से, which functions like the English "-ly." In such cases से usually follows an abstract noun.

Abstract noun + से

मुश्किल *difficulty*	+	से	=	मुश्किल से *with difficulty*
ख़ुशी *happiness*	+	से	=	ख़ुशी से *happily*
भाग्य *fortune*	+	से	=	भाग्य से *fortunately*
सावधानी *caution, care*	+	से	=	सावधानी से *cautiously; carefully*
आसानी *ease*	+	से	=	आसानी से *easily*
देर *delay*	+	से	=	देर से *with delay, late*
जल्दी *hurry, haste*	+	(से)	=	जल्दी (से) *quickly*
ठीक *correct*	+	से	=	ठीक से *correctly*
ज़ोर *force*	+	से	=	ज़ोर से *forcefully; loudly*
धैर्य *patience*	+	से	=	धैर्य से *patiently*
प्यार *love*	+	से	=	प्यार से *lovingly*
ध्यान *attention*	+	से	=	ध्यान से *attentively; carefully*
गर्व *pride*	+	से	=	गर्व से *proudly*

Note there are some adverbs, like जल्दी (से), where से can be dropped.

(3) In some cases the postpositions (को, में, से, पर, etc.) that help form adverbs from nouns are dropped. However, the adverbial phrase remains in the oblique.

Examples:
किस तरफ़ *in which direction*
इस तरह *in this manner*
अगले हफ़्ते *next week*
उस समय *at that time*

सारे साल *all year*

पिछले महीने *last month*

सवेरे *in the morning*

(4) Some adjectives and nouns function as adverbs in their masculine singular oblique form without having any implied postposition. Thus:

सीधा *straight*	becomes	सीधे *straight ahead*
नीचा *low*	becomes	नीचे *below, down*
पहला *first*	becomes	पहले *at first*
सामना *front (part)*	becomes	सामने *in front*
पीछा *rear, back (part)*	becomes	पीछे *behind, at the rear*

(5) Some adverbs are formed with भर (derived from the verb भरना *to fill*). In such cases, the preceding noun and all modifying adjectives take the oblique form.

Oblique noun + भर

महीना *month*	+	भर =	महीने भर *the whole month*
घंटा *hour*	+	भर =	घंटे भर *the whole hour*
साल *year*	+	भर =	साल भर *all year*
जीवन *life*	+	भर =	जीवन भर *entire life*
देश *country*	+	भर =	देश भर (में) *[in] the whole country*
पेट *stomach*	+	भर =	पेट भर (खाना) *[to eat] all that the stomach can hold*

(6) Some adverbs are formed by adding the suffix तौर से / पर to certain adjectives.

Adjective + तौर से / पर

ख़ास *special*	+ तौर से / पर =	ख़ास तौर से / पर *especially*
आम *usual, general*	+ तौर से / पर =	आम तौर से / पर *usually, generally*
विशेष *special*	+ तौर से / पर =	विशेष तौर से / पर *especially*

65

(7) In formal Hindi, some adverbs are also formed by the addition of Sanskrit suffixes such as –पूर्वक, रूप से, or –तः / –तया to certain nouns or adjectives.

(a) Abstract noun + –पूर्वक

शान्ति *peace*	+	–पूर्वक	=	शान्तिपूर्वक *peacefully*
ध्यान *attention*	+	–पूर्वक	=	ध्यानपूर्वक *attentively*
स्नेह *affection*	+	–पूर्वक	=	स्नेहपूर्वक *affectionately*
प्रेम *love*	+	–पूर्वक	=	प्रेमपूर्वक *lovingly*
आदर *respect*	+	–पूर्वक	=	आदरपूर्वक *respectfully*
आनन्द *happiness*	+	–पूर्वक	=	आनन्दपूर्वक *happily*

(b) Adjective + रूप से

सामान्य *general*	+	रूप से	=	सामान्य रूप से *generally*
पूर्ण *complete, full*	+	रूप से	=	पूर्ण रूप से *completely, fully*
विशेष *special*	+	रूप से	=	विशेष रूप से *especially*
मुख्य *chief, main*	+	रूप से	=	मुख्य रूप से *chiefly, mainly*

(c) Adjective + –तः (in some cases, –तया)

सामान्य *general*	+	–तः / –तया	=	सामान्यतः / सामान्यतया *generally*
पूर्ण *complete, full*	+	–तः / –तया	=	पूर्णतः / पूर्णतया *completely, fully*
मुख्य *chief, main*	+	–तः	=	मुख्यतः *chiefly, mainly*
सम्भव *possible*	+	–तः	=	सम्भवतः *possibly*

Indefinite Adverbs

Like the indefinite pronouns and adjectives कोई and कुछ (discussed in Chapter 37 of *Introduction to Hindi Grammar*), there are two indefinite adverbs in Hindi: कभी and कहीं .

The Adverb कभी

The basic meaning of the indefinite adverb कभी is *sometime, at any time, at one time*; in a question it means *ever*, and in a negative sentence, *never*.

Examples:

हम भी कभी भारत जाना चाहते हैं ।
We, too, want to go to India someday (sometime).

कभी हमारे घर आइये ।
Please come to our house sometime.

सास भी कभी बहू थी ।
A mother-in-law was also at one time a daughter-in-law.

क्या आप कभी राष्ट्रपति से मिले हैं ?
Have you ever met the President?

The adverb कभी also occurs in several common expressions in Hindi:

कभी कभी *sometimes, now and then, occasionally*
कभी भी *anytime at all*
कभी X कभी Y *sometimes X, sometimes Y*
कभी न कभी *sometime or other*
जब कभी *whenever*
कभी नहीं *never*

Examples:

कभी कभी मुझे भारतीय कपड़े पहनना अच्छा लगता है ।
Sometimes I like to wear Indian clothes.

आप कभी भी मुझे फ़ोन कर सकते हैं ।
You can call me anytime at all.

उसका कोई भरोसा नहीं । कभी हाँ कहता है कभी न ।
There's no relying on him. Sometimes he says yes, sometimes no.

कभी न कभी हम भी अलास्का घूमने जाएँगे ।
Sometime or another we will also go to Alaska for a trip.

जब कभी उसका फ़ोन आएगा मैं तुम्हें बताऊँगी ।
Whenever he calls, I will tell you.

वह ऐसा कभी नहीं कर सकता ।
He can never do such a thing.

मैं कभी तुमसे झूठ नहीं बोलूँगा ।
I will never tell you a lie.

As seen in the last two examples, कभी नहीं can occur in sequence or can be separated by other words in the sentence.

The Adverb कहीं

The basic meaning of the indefinite adverb कहीं is *somewhere, anywhere, some/any place* and in a negative sentence, *nowhere.*

Examples:

आपकी चाबी कमरे में कहीं होगी ।	*Your key(s) must be somewhere in the room.*
मैंने आपको कहीं देखा है ।	*I have seen you somewhere.*
हमें वह किताब कहीं नहीं मिली ?	*We didn't find that book anywhere.*

The adverb कहीं also occurs in several common expressions:

कहीं भी *anywhere [at all]*
कहीं और / और कहीं *somewhere else*
कहीं न कहीं *somewhere or other*
सब कहीं *everywhere*
कहीं कहीं *in some places, here and there*

कहीं X कहीं Y *somewhere X, somewhere Y*

जहाँ कहीं *wherever*

Examples:

आप ऐसी साड़ियाँ भारत में कहीं भी ख़रीद सकते हैं ।

You can buy such saris (saris like these) anywhere in India.

यहाँ तो बहुत भीड़ है । चलो, कहीं और चलें ।

It is very crowded here. Let's go somewhere else.

ऐसा लगता है कि मैंने आपको पहले कहीं न कहीं देखा है ।

It seems that I have seen you before somewhere or other.

नेता जी की मृत्यु का समाचार तुरन्त सब कहीं फैल गया ।

The news of the leader's death immediately spread everywhere.

उस रात को बस कहीं कहीं रोशनी थी ।

That night there was light only in some places.

इस देश में कहीं ग़रीबी है कहीं अमीरी ।

In this country, there is poverty in some places and wealth in other (some) places.

जहाँ कहीं मुझे अच्छी नौकरी मिलेगी वहीं मैं जाऊँगा ।

I will go wherever I get a good job.

The adverb कहीं has several other usages in addition to the ones given above. These will be discussed in Chapter 21. Note also that a list of common adverbs has been provided for reference in Appendix II.

Adverbs: Exercises

1. Substitution drill

He quickly finished his work.
उसने जल्दी से अपना काम ख़त्म किया ।

     easily
     with difficulty
     happily
     attentively
     correctly
     late (with delay)
     carefully
     patiently

2. Transformation drill

Yesterday there was a strike throughout the city.
कल सारे शहर में हड़ताल हुई ।

Yesterday there was a strike throughout the city.
कल शहर भर में हड़ताल हुई ।

सारे घर में दुख छा गया ।
वह सारी दुनिया में घूमा है ।
बच्चा सारा दिन क्यों रोया ?
वे सारी रात नाचेंगे ।
यह त्यौहार सारे देश में मनाया जाता है ।
सारे गाँव में यह अफ़वाह फैल गई है ।

3. Answer the following questions

I especially like the color blue. What color do you like?
मुझे ख़ास तौर से / पर नीला रंग पसन्द है । आपको कौन-सा रंग पसन्द है ?

70

I especially like the color red.
मुझे ख़ास तौर से / पर लाल रंग पसन्द है ।

में आम तौर से ग्यारह बजे सोती हूँ । आप कितने बजे सोते हैं ?

आम तौर पर में सुबह को सिर्फ़ कॉफ़ी पीती हूँ । आप सुबह को क्या पीते हैं ?

मुझे संगीत पसन्द है, विशेष तौर से शास्त्रीय संगीत । आपको कैसा संगीत पसन्द है ?

में यूरोप देखना चाहती हूँ, ख़ास तौर से पेरिस । आप क्या देखना चाहते हैं ?

फूलों में मुझे चमेली ख़ास तौर से पसन्द है । आपको कौन-सा फूल पसन्द है ?

आम तौर से में बस से घर जाती हूँ । आप कैसे घर जाते हैं ?

मुझे बंगाली मिठाइयाँ बहुत पसन्द हैं, ख़ास तौर से रसगुल्ले । आपको कौन-सी मिठाइयाँ पसन्द हैं ?

में आम तौर से रोज़ कसरत करती हूँ । आप कब कसरत करते हैं ?

4. <u>Answer the following questions</u>

Do you ever go to the temple?
क्या आप कभी मन्दिर जाते हैं ?

Yes, I go sometimes.
हाँ, में कभी कभी जाता हूँ ।

No, I never go to the temple.
नहीं, में कभी मन्दिर नहीं जाता ।

क्या आप कभी कैंपिंग करने जाते हैं ?

क्या तुम कभी भारतीय खाना पकाते हो ?

क्या आप कभी झूठ बोलते हैं ?

क्या तुम कभी बच्चों के साथ खेलते हो ?

क्या आप कभी रात को कॉफ़ी पीते हैं ?

क्या आप कभी हिन्दी की कहानियाँ पढ़ते हैं ?

क्या तुम कभी कविता लिखते हो ?

क्या तुम कभी पार्टी में अकेले जाते हो ?

5. Substitution drill

Sometime or another I want to see the Ajanta caves.
मैं कभी न कभी अजन्ता की गुफ़ाएँ देखना चाहता हूँ ।

        to go to Goa
        to learn French
        to see Australia
        to climb (up) Mt. Everest
        to learn to cook Chinese food
        to meet that famous writer

6. Answer the following questions

Where is my sweater?
मेरा स्वेटर कहाँ है ?

I don't know. It must be somewhere (or other) in your room.
मालूम नहीं । आपके कमरे में कहीं न कहीं होगा ।

मेरी साइकिल कहाँ है ?
मेरे जूते कहाँ हैं ?
मेरी अँगूठी कहाँ है ?
मेरा चश्मा कहाँ है ?
मेरे बैंक के कागज़ कहाँ हैं ?
मेरी डायरी कहाँ है ?
मेरा तौलिया कहाँ है ?
मेरा सेल फ़ोन कहाँ है ?

7. Translation exercise

1. Don't speak loudly in the museum.
2. Ordinarily I don't take milk in my tea.
3. He always does his work carefully (attentively).
4. Sometimes we all need a little rest.
5. Sometime or other I certainly want to meet your parents.
6. She especially wants to meet this writer.

7. He kept on watching TV the whole day.

8. Keep on trying. You wil! get a good job somewhere or other.

9. Sometimes we speak Hindi at home, sometimes English.

10. He never listens to what I say.

9. PARTICIPIAL CONSTRUCTIONS, PART 1

As discussed in Chapter 2, a participle represents a verbal form that has the qualities of both a verb and another part of speech (e.g., adjective, adverb, noun, or conjunction). In this book we will discuss five important participial constructions that use the invariable masculine singular oblique form of an imperfective or perfective participle:

(1) Imperfective participle + ही to denote "as soon as"

(2) Perfective participle with बिना / बग़ैर to express "without —ing"

(3) Imperfective participle + समय / वक़्त to convey "while —ing" or "at the time of —ing"

(4) Imperfective/perfective participle + a measure of time to indicate the passage of time since the beginning/completion of an activity or situation

(5) Reduplicated imperfective participle + बचना / रुकना / रहना to indicate an action that almost occurred

In this chapter, we will discuss the first two participial constructions, while the remaining three will be discussed in Chapter 12.

Imperfective Participle + ही

In order to convey that an action took place immediately before the action of the main verb, Hindi uses the imperfective participle in its invariable masculine singular oblique form followed by the emphatic particle ही. One of the most common ways to translate such constructions in English is with the phrase "as soon as."

Examples:

लड़की आई । लड़की बैठ गई ।	*The girl came. The girl sat down.*
आते ही लड़की बैठ गई ।	*As soon as the girl came, she sat down.*

Here we see that the action of "coming" (आते ही) immediately precedes the action of "sitting down" (बैठ गई).

Notes

1. In this construction, the imperfective participle always takes the invariable masculine singular oblique form (verb stem + ते) and does not agree with the subject.

2. In the example above, since the same subject performs two actions, this subject is mentioned only once (unlike in the English translation).

3. If the subject of the participle is different from the subject of the main verb, then this subject is always followed by the postposition के (possessive form).

Example:

संदीप आया । लड़की बैठ गई ।   *Sandeep came. The girl sat down.*

संदीप के आते ही लड़की बैठ गई ।   *As soon as Sandeep came, the girl sat down.*

4. If the subject of the participle is different from the subject of the main verb and it is inanimate, the use of the postposition के is optional.

Example:

अख़बार आया । लड़की उसको पढ़ने लगी ।

The newspaper came. The girl started to read it.

अख़बार (के) आते ही लड़की उसको पढ़ने लगी ।

As soon as the newspaper came, the girl started to read it.

Perfective Participle with बिना / बग़ैर

The perfective participle when used with बिना / बग़ैर denotes "without —ing." In this construction, बिना / बग़ैर may precede or follow the perfective participle, although it appears more commonly after the participle. The perfective participle is always in the invariable masculine singular oblique form.

Examples:

उसने पिताजी से नहीं पूछा । वह फ़िल्म देखने गया ।

He didn't ask his father. He went to see a film.

पिताजी से पूछे बिना / बग़ैर वह फ़िल्म देखने गया ।

OR

पिताजी से बिना / बग़ैर पूछे वह फ़िल्म देखने गया ।

He went to see a film without asking his father.

As with the imperfective participle + ही construction, in the example above, since the same subject performs two actions, this subject is mentioned only once. If the subject of the perfective participle is different from the subject of the main verb, then this subject is always followed by the postposition के (possessive form).

Example:

वह नहीं आएगा । दफ़्तर में कुछ काम नहीं होगा ।

He will not come. No work will be done in the office.

उसके आये बिना / बग़ैर दफ़्तर में कुछ काम नहीं होगा ।

No work will done in the office without his coming.

If the subject of the perfective participle is different from the subject of the main verb and it is inanimate, the use of the postposition के is optional.

Examples:

रेलगाड़ी नहीं आएगी । हम समय पर दिल्ली कैसे पहुँच सकेंगे ?

The train will not come. How will we be able to reach Delhi on time?

रेलगाड़ी (के) आये बिना / बग़ैर हम समय पर दिल्ली कैसे पहुँच सकेंगे ?

How will we be able to reach Delhi on time without the train's coming?

बारिश नहीं होगी । फ़सल अच्छी नहीं होगी ।

It won't rain. The crops will not be good.

बारिश (के) हुए बिना फ़सल अच्छी नहीं होगी ।

Without the rain [falling], the crops will not be good.

Note that the construction "without —ing" requires a perfective participle with बिना / बग़ैर; the imperfective participle is never used in such sentences (e.g., बारिश (के) होते बिना फ़सल अच्छी नहीं होगी is not possible in Hindi).

Participial Constructions, Part 1: Exercises

1. Substitution drill

As soon as I have eaten dinner, I will call you.

खाना खाते ही मैं आपको फ़ोन करूँगी ।

यह काम ख़त्म करते ही

उसके आते ही

भारत पहुँचते ही

माँ का पत्र मिलते ही

अपार्टमेंट लेते ही

पिता जी के दफ़्तर जाते ही

कल सबेरे उठते ही

नौकरी मिलते ही

2. Transformation drill

The mother went. The child cried.

As soon as the mother left (went), the child cried.

माँ के जाते ही बच्चा रोया ।

माँ गई । बच्चा रोया ।

बच्चे को दूध मिला । बच्चा चुप हो गया ।

बच्चा चुप हो गया । माँ काम करने लगी ।

शिक्षक क्लास में आये । सब छात्र चुप हो गये ।

छात्र चुप हो गये । शिक्षक ने लिखना शुरू किया ।

वह लड़का बोला । सब लोग हँसने लगे ।

सब लोग हँसने लगे । वह लड़का चुप हो गया ।

लड़की ने दोस्त को देखा । लड़की मुस्कुराने लगी ।

माता-पिता सो गये । वह दूरदर्शन देखने लगा ।

3. Transformation drill

The ticket booth opened. We bought tickets.

टिकट घर की खिड़की खुली । हमने टिकट ख़रीदे ।

As soon as the ticket booth opened, we bought tickets.
टिकट घर की खिड़की (के) खुलते ही हमने टिकट ख़रीदे ।

जाड़ों की छुट्टी होगी । हम भारत जाएँगे ।
शाम होगी । सब बच्चे अपने अपने घर जाएँगे ।
बारिश हुई । हम लोग अंदर गये ।
हवा चली । पत्ते बिखर गये ।
धूप निकलेगी । मैं घूमने जाऊँगी ।
संगीत शुरू होगा । सब लोग नाचने लगेंगे ।
फ़ायर एलार्म बजा । सब बाहर भागे ।

4. Substitution drill

He went somewhere without eating dinner.
खाना खाये बिना वह कहीं चला गया ।
काम ख़त्म किये बिना
माँ की मदद किये बिना
कुछ कहे बिना
अपने परिवार को बताये बिना
अपार्टमेंट का किराया दिये बिना
परीक्षा ख़त्म किये बिना
दरवाज़ा बन्द किये बिना
आराम किये बिना

5. Transformation drill

He didn't drink coffee. He went away.

He went away without drinking coffee.
वह कॉफ़ी पिये बिना चला गया ।

उसने कॉफ़ी नहीं पी । वह चला गया ।
उसने हिन्दी नहीं सीखी । वह भारत चला गया ।
वह मुझसे नहीं मिला । वह न्यू यॉर्क चला गया ।
उसने टिकट नहीं ख़रीदा । वह रेलगाड़ी में बैठ गया ।
उसने माँ को नहीं बताया । वह फ़िल्म देखने चली गयी ।

मैंने किताब नहीं पढ़ी । मैं सो गया ।

उसने नहीं सोचा । उसने शिक्षक को जवाब दिया ।

मैं कॉफ़ी नहीं पिऊँगी । मैं देर तक नहीं पढ़ सकूँगी ।

उसने हाथ नहीं धोये । वह खाना खाने लगा ।

6. Transformation drill

You will not come. We will not go to the party.
आप नहीं आएँगे । हम पार्टी में नहीं जाएँगे ।
We will not go to the party without your coming along.
आप के आये बिना हम पार्टी में नहीं जाएँगे ।

आप नहीं कहेंगे । वह यह काम नहीं करेगा ।

पिता जी घर नहीं लौटेंगे । माँ खाना नहीं खाएँगी ।

बच्चा नहीं सोएगा । मैं काम नहीं कर सकूँगी ।

नौकरानी नहीं आएगी । घर साफ़ नहीं होगा ।

नेता जी नहीं आएँगे । प्रोग्राम कैसे शुरू होगा ?

धूप नहीं निकलेगी । ये कपड़े नहीं सूखेंगे ।

हवा नहीं चलेगी । गर्मी कम नहीं होगी ।

छुट्टी नहीं मिलेगी । मैं बॉस्टन नहीं जा सकूँगी ।

7. Translation exercise
(Use participial constructions.)

1. He went to India without telling his parents.
2. As soon as the train stopped, we got off of it.
3. As soon as she read the letter, she began to cry.
4. As soon as he comes (will come), we'll start eating.
5. Don't go there without asking.
6. As soon as he got a job, he bought a new car.
7. The doctor went home without seeing his patient.
8. As soon as I left (exited from) home, it started raining.
9. Without trying, you will not get a good job.
10. You shouldn't go into the temple without taking off your shoes.

10. THE VERB STEM + पाना CONSTRUCTION

पाना as an independent verb is transitive and means "to get," "to find," "to obtain," or "to receive."

Examples:

वह हर महीने सिर्फ़ हज़ार डॉलर पाता है ।   *He gets (receives) only $1000 a month.*

मैंने यह बटुआ वहाँ पड़ा पाया ।   *I found this wallet lying over there.*

भारत ने सन्१९४७ में आज़ादी पाई ।   *India obtained (got) its freedom in 1947.*

उसने ज़िन्दगी में बहुत शोहरत पाई ।   *He earned (obtained) great fame in [his] life.*

When पाना is used as an auxiliary verb with the stem of another verb, it has the general meaning "to manage to," "to find it possible to," "to get a chance to," or "to be able to." Although it is found in both affirmative and negative statements, it is most often used in negative sentences, where it suggests that the subject of the sentence, despite his/her wishes, efforts, etc., is unable to perform the action of the main verb.

Examples:

कोहरे के कारण ड्राइवर देख नहीं पाया ।

Because of the fog the driver couldn't see (didn't find it possible to see).

मैं दफ़्तर में काम कर पाता हूँ, घर में नहीं कर पाता ।

I can [manage to] work in the office but not at home.

परीक्षा की वजह से मैं कल आपके साथ नहीं जा पाऊँगी ।

Because of the examination it will not be possible for me to go with you tomorrow.

मैं न्यू यॉर्क जाना चाहता था, लेकिन नहीं जा पाया ।

I wanted to go to New York but couldn't go (didn't get a chance to go).

क्या वह कल तक अपना निबंध लिख पाएगी ?

Will she be able to (manage to) write her essay by tomorrow?

वही इस पहाड़ पर चढ़ पाएगा ।
Only he will be able to climb this mountain.

Notes

1. The verb stem + पाना construction has approximately the same meaning as the verb stem + सकना construction (*Introduction to Hindi Grammar* Chapter 22), though there is a subtle difference between the two that is difficult to convey in English translation. While both the verb stem + सकना and the verb stem + पाना can refer to the ability of a subject to perform an action and can often be used interchangeably, the verb stem + पाना suggests that external factors or circumstances are also involved in the subject's ability or inability to perform an action. Note the following two examples:

Examples:

वह नहीं जा सका ।	*He couldn't go.*
वह नहीं जा पाया ।	*He couldn't manage to go.*
	OR
	He was unable to go.
	OR
	It was not possible for him to go.

2. As mentioned above, this construction is most often used in negative sentences, where the negative particle नहीं / न can come either before or after the verb stem.

Examples:

सिरदर्द के कारण मैं कल पढ़ नहीं पाई ।	*Because of a headache, I couldn't study yesterday.*
सिरदर्द के कारण मैं कल नहीं पढ़ पाई ।	*Because of a headache, I couldn't study yesterday.*

3. पाना as an independent verb is transitive, but in the verb stem + पाना construction, the subject is *not* marked by ने.

81

Example:

मैं कल यह काम ख़त्म नहीं कर पाया ।

I couldn't manage to finish this work yesterday.

4. Another less commonly used construction that is similar in meaning to the verb stem + पाना construction is the oblique infinitive of the main verb + पाना. There seems to be no real difference between these two forms; however, in affirmative sentences, the verb stem + पाना form is more common.

Examples:

कमज़ोरी की वजह से मरीज़ उठने नहीं पाया ।

It wasn't possible for the patient to get up due to [his] weakness.

बारिश के कारण मैं समय पर वहाँ पहुँचने न / नहीं पाई ।

It wasn't possible for me to arrive there on time because of the rain.

The Verb Stem + पाना Construction: Exercises

1. Substitution drill

He managed to do this work.
वह यह काम कर पाया ।

> managed to come on time
> managed to finish the work
> managed to sleep with (in) that noise
> managed to arrive at five o'clock
> managed to meet the President
> managed to sell all his vegetables
> managed to catch the bus
> managed to save some money for his trip

2. Transformation drill

We didn't arrive there on time.   We didn't manage to arrive there on time.

हम वहाँ समय पर नहीं पहुँचे ।   हम वहाँ समय पर नहीं पहुँच पाये ।

हमने उर्दू का अख़बार नहीं पढ़ा ।

उसने बहुत चीज़ें नहीं ख़रीदीं ।

मैंने आपकी बात नहीं समझी ।

वह स्कूल नहीं गया ।

उसने अपना काम नहीं किया ।

मैं अपने दोस्तों से नहीं मिला ।

उसने अपनी माँ को फ़ोन नहीं किया ।

मैंने आज खाना नहीं पकाया ।

3. Conversational response drill

Do you want to go to India next year?   Yes, but I won't manage to go.

क्या आप अगले साल भारत जाना चाहते हैं ?   जी हाँ, लेकिन जा नहीं पाऊँगा ।

क्या आप आज मेरे साथ फ़िल्म देखना चाहते हैं ?

83

क्या आप यह महँगा घर ख़रीदना चाहते हैं ?

क्या आप प्रेसीडेंट से मिलना चाहते हे ?

क्या आप भारत के गाँव देखना चाहते हैं ?

क्या आप माउँट ऐवरेस्ट पर चढ़ना चाहते हैं ?

क्या आप उन लोगों की मदद करना चाहते हैं ?

क्या आप अमीर होना चाहते हैं ?

क्या आप अगले साल अफ़्रीका जाना चाहते हैं ?

4. Substitution drill

Because of illness, she is unable to (can't manage to) work.
बीमारी के कारण वह काम नहीं कर पाती ।

> is unable to sleep
> is unable to go to class
> is unable to walk
> is unable to study
> is unable to play with her friends
> is unable to cook food
> is unable to dance
> is unable to exercise

5. Translation exercises

1. He couldn't (did not manage to) buy those expensive things.
2. We will manage to come on time.
3. Because of the noise, they couldn't (did not manage to) hear the speech.
4. He wanted to go to Pakistan, but he couldn't manage to go.
5. She will be able to (will manage to) finish her work by next week.
6. Who will be able to (will manage to) read this big book in one day?
7. Will your relatives be able to (manage to) come from India for (in) your wedding?
8. Because of her injury, she is unable to walk fast these days.
9. Without everyone's help, the government will not be able to (will not manage to) eliminate poverty.
10. We were not able to sleep last night because of the heat.

11. THE CONJUNCTIVE PARTICIPLE

Hindi frequently uses the conjunctive participle (कर construction) to link *two sequential actions* performed by the *same* subject. In such constructions, it is the first action that is transformed into a conjunctive participle, while the second action becomes the main verb.

Examples:

लड़की घर गई । लड़की सो गई ।	*The girl went home. The girl went to sleep.*
लड़की घर गई और सो गई ।	*The girl went home and went to sleep.*
लड़की घर जाकर सो गई ।	*The girl went home and went to sleep.* (lit., *Having gone home, the girl went to sleep.*)

Note that in the first example given above, the girl performs two sequential actions that are expressed in two separate sentences. These two sentences are joined in the second example with the conjunction और. In the third example, the verb stem + कर joins the two sentences, functioning much like the English conjunction "and"; hence it is called a *conjunctive* participle. Such conjunctive participles are extremely common in Hindi.

Formation

Conjunctive participles are formed by adding कर or के to the verb stem. Although कर and के can be used interchangeably, कर is used more in formal and written language, while के is frequently used in spoken language. If the verb stem is कर itself, then the conjunctive participle can be formed with only के (कर कर is not possible). In colloquial speech the verb stem may also be followed by करके.

Examples:

वह खाना खा कर जाएगा ।	*He will go after eating.*
वह खाना खा के जाएगा ।	*He will go after eating.*
वह खाना खा करके जाएगा ।	*He will go after eating.*

Occasionally, one finds that कर or के are dropped altogether and the verb stem itself becomes the conjunctive participle.

Example:

उसकी हालत देख माँ रोने लगी ।   *Seeing his condition, mother began to cry.*

When the कर construction is used, the verb conveying the first action becomes the conjunctive participle, while all changes due to number, gender, and tense agreement occur in the final verb. Thus, it is the final or the main verb of the sentence that determines if the postposition ने is to be used with the subject in the perfective tenses and *not* the verb that has become the conjunctive participle (e.g., verb stem + कर / के).

Examples:

उसने घर आकर पत्र लिखा ।   *He came home and wrote the letter.*

वह पत्र लिखकर मेरे घर आया ।   *He wrote the letter and [then] came to my house.*

In the first sentence above, the first action, आना, has become the conjunctive participle, and the second action, लिखना, becomes the main verb of the sentence. Since लिखना is a transitive verb, the subject is marked by ने. Note that the situation is reversed in the second example, where the second action, आना, an intransitive verb, becomes the main verb of the sentence.

Translating Conjunctive Participles

Conjunctive participles are used in Hindi to convey
(1) a sequence of two or more actions
(2) performed by the same subject.

While these two basic elements remain consistent throughout, conjunctive participles can be translated from Hindi into English in a number of ways.

(a) They can be literally translated into English as "having —ed" or "after —ing."

Example:

यह समाचार सुनकर वह हँसने लगी ।

Having heard this news, she began to laugh.

OR

After hearing this news, she began to laugh.

(b) Conjunctive participles can also be translated into English using a variety of other expressions, such as "when…then" or "and."

Examples:

वह भारत जाकर भारतीय शास्त्रीय संगीत सीखेगा ।

When he goes to India, [*then*] he will learn Indian classical music. (lit., *Having gone* to India, …)

वह बॉस्टन जाकर अपने भाई से मिली ।

She went to Boston and met her brother.

(c) Occasionally, these participles can be idiomatically translated into English -- e.g., with time expressions or using an infinitive.

Examples:

वह तीन बजकर बीस मिनट पर आएगा ।

He will come at twenty past three (lit., at twenty minutes after striking three).

आपसे मिलकर मुझे बड़ी प्रसन्नता हुई ।

I am very pleased to meet you. (lit., *Having met you*, …)

(d) Certain conjunctive participles may also be translated with adverbs/adverbial phrases in English. For example: कृपा करके / मेहरबानी करके *kindly*; छिपकर *secretly (while hiding)*; संभलकर *carefully*; जान-बूझकर *intentionally (knowingly)*; भूलकर *mistakenly*; मुस्कुराकर *while smiling*; सोचकर *thoughtfully*; जी भरकर / के *to one's heart's content*.

Examples:

कृपा करके / मेहरबानी करके अपनी अपनी सीट बेल्ट बाँध लीजिये ।

Kindly fasten your seat belts.

वह छिपकर सिगरेट पीता है ।

He _secretly_ smokes cigarettes.

संभलकर उतरना । ये सीढ़ियाँ बहुत ऊँची हैं ।

Come down _carefully_. These stairs are very steep.

नेता लोग जान-बूझकर जनता से सच छिपाते हैं ।

Politicians _intentionally_ (_knowingly_) hide the truth from the public.

वह भूलकर किसी और के कमरे में घुस गई ।

She entered someone else's room _by mistake_ (_mistakenly_).

उसने मुस्कुराकर कहा---।

While smiling, she said---. (lit., _She smiled and said---._)

सोचकर बोलो , नौकरी का सवाल है ।

Speak _thoughtfully_; it's a matter of your job.

आज मैंने जी भर कर खाना खाया ।

Today I ate _to my heart's content_.

(e) There are some fixed expressions with the conjunctive participle that are commonly used in Hindi:

X से होकर	_via X, through X, by way of X_
X से बढ़कर	_superior to X, more than X, better than X_
X को छोड़कर	_apart from X, besides X, with the exception of X_
एक-एक करके	_one by one_
विशेषकर / ख़ासकर	_especially_

88

Notes

1. Since a conjunctive participle is used only when the same subject performs two actions, the subject is mentioned only once. The subject can come either at the beginning of the sentence or after the conjunctive participle.

Example:

घर पहुँचकर मैं आपको फ़ोन करूँगी ।

          OR

मैं घर पहुँचकर आपको फ़ोन करूँगी ।

I will call you after I reach home.

2. कर / के in a conjunctive participle can either be joined to a verb stem as in "पढ़कर," or it can be written separately as "पढ़ कर."

3. To indicate the frequency or repetition of an action, the verb stem may be repeated before कर or के. Thus: सुन सुनकर *having heard [repeatedly]*; रो रोकर *having cried [continuously]*; सुबक सुबक कर *having sobbed [continuously]*; रुक रुक कर *having halted [repeatedly]*; (आँखें) मल मलकर *having rubbed [one's eyes] [repeatedly]*.

Example:

उसकी शिकायतें सुन सुनकर मैं थक गई ।

I got tired of [repeatedly] hearing his complaints.

4. The negative used with a conjunctive participle is always न.

Example:

वह लाइब्रेरी न जाकर अपने दोस्तों के साथ पार्टी में चली गई ।

She went to the party with her friends instead of going to the library.

5. Compound verbs are not used in conjunctive participles.

Example:

अपना निबंध लिखकर (not लिख लेकर) वह सो गया ।

He went to sleep after writing his essay.

6. In a sentence that already has a conjunction (e.g., और) or connectors such as जब...तब, the conjunctive participle cannot be used. (Thus, वह घर आकर और सो गया and जब वह घर आकर तब वह सो गया are not possible in Hindi.)

The Conjunctive Participle: Exercises

1. Substitution drill

He came home and drank tea.
उसने घर आकर चाय पी ।

दोस्त को फ़ोन किया

शाम का खाना पकाया

पार्टी का इंतज़ाम किया

अपनी पत्नी की मदद की

अपने कपडे इस्तरी किये

अपने पौधों को पानी दिया

नौकरी के लिये अर्ज़ी लिखी

सितार बजाने का अभ्यास किया

2. Substitution drill

I was very sad to see those poor people.
उन ग़रीब लोगों को देखकर मुझे बड़ा दुख हुआ ।

उसकी हालत देखकर

उसकी कहानी सुनकर

वह दुर्घटना देखकर

यह समाचार पढ़कर

उसकी शिकायतें सुनकर

अपने ग्रेड्स देखकर

उसकी समस्याओं के बारे में सुनकर

उसकी बीमारी के बारे में जानकर

3. Transformation drill

When I go to India, I will meet my friend's family.
जब मैं भारत जाऊँगा तब मैं अपने दोस्त के परिवार से मिलूँगा ।

I will go to India and meet my friend's family.
मैं भारत जाकर अपने दोस्त के परिवार से मिलूँगा ।

जब वह घर आएगा तब अपने बच्चों के साथ खेलेगा ।
जब मेरा भाई कॉलिज ख़त्म करेगा तब वह नौकरी ढूँढ़ेगा ।
जब वह पार्टी में गई तब उसने बहुत लोगों से बात की ।
जब उसने चोर को देखा तो उसने पुलिस को फ़ोन किया ।
जब छात्रों ने ये कविताएँ पढ़ीं तो उन्हें बहुत मज़ा आया ।
जब मैं तुम से मिलूँगी तब मैं तुम्हें सब कुछ बताऊँगी ।
जब मैं यह काम ख़त्म करूँगी तब मैं आपकी मदद करूँगी ।
जब माली आएगा तब सब पौधों को पानी देगा ।

4. Transformation drill

Wash [your] face and hands. Eat.
हाथ-मुँह धोओ । खाना खाओ ।
Wash [your] face and hands and eat.
हाथ-मुँह धोकर खाना खाओ ।

बाहर चलिये । खुली हवा में बैठिये ।
घर जाओ । माता-पिता की मदद करो ।
यहाँ बगीचे में बैठिये । गाने गाइये ।
कमरे में जाओ । एक कुरसी यहाँ लाओ ।
सामान उठाओ । टैक्सी में रखो ।
बाज़ार जाओ । कुछ फल और सब्ज़ियाँ ख़रीदो ।
ये मसाले पीसो । सब्ज़ी में मिलाओ ।
पार्टी में न जाओ । अपना काम करो ।
कृपा कीजिये । मैनेजर साहब को मेरी अर्ज़ी दे दीजिये ।

5. Transformation drill

He drank coffee. He began to do his work.
उसने कॉफ़ी पी । वह अपना काम करने लगा ।

He drank coffee and began to do his work.
वह कॉफ़ी पीकर अपना काम करने लगा ।

उसने पानी उबाला । उसने चाय बनाई ।

वह घर आया । उसने अपनी पत्नी की मदद की ।

उसने अपने को शीशे में देखा । वह मुस्कुराने लगी ।

छात्रों ने किताबें उठाईं । छात्र पढ़ने लगे ।

उसने इस ढाबे में खाना खाया । वह बीमार हो गया ।

उसने दफ़्तर में काम ख़त्म नहीं किया । वह घर चला गया ।

हम दावत में गये । हमने जी भरके खाना खाया ।

उसने मच्छरदानी लगाई । वह सो गया ।

वह अपनी पत्नी से नाराज़ हुआ । वह घर से चला गया ।

6. Substitution drill

He did this [work, thing] intentionally.
उसने जान-बूझकर यह काम किया ।

      बहुत सोचकर

      दोस्तों से छिपकर

      मुस्कुराकर

      हँसकर

      ध्यान देकर

      शिक्षक से पूछकर

      संभलकर

      माता-पिता से आज्ञा लेकर

      रुक रुक कर

      मजबूर होकर

7. Translation exercise
(Use the conjunctive participle.)

1. Go quickly and call an ambulance.
2. When I finish college, I will go to Europe with my friends.

3. When I drink coffee at night, I can't sleep.
4. He went to India and started his own company.
5. He intentionally (knowingly) lied to us about his age.
6. Kindly do not smoke in my room.
7. He jumped into the river and saved the little girl.
8. There is a lot of fog (कोहरा M, fog). Please drive the car carefully.
9. He secretly (hiddenly) taped their conversation.
10. The bride and groom danced to their heart's content at their wedding.

12. PARTICIPIAL CONSTRUCTIONS, PART 2

As mentioned earlier, a participle represents a verbal form that has the qualities of both a verb and another part of speech (e.g., adjective, adverb, noun, or conjunction). We have already discussed two important participial constructions in Chapter 9. This chapter focuses on three more participial contructions that use the invariable masculine singular oblique form of an imperfective or perfective participle:

(1) Imperfective participle + समय / वक़्त to convey "while —ing" or "at the time of —ing"

(2) Imperfective/perfective participle + a measure of time to indicate the passage of time since the beginning/completion of an activity or situation

(3) Reduplicated imperfective participle + बचना / रुकना / रहना to indicate an action that almost occurred

Imperfective Participle + समय / वक़्त

The imperfective participle in the invariable masculine singular oblique form immediately followed by समय / वक़्त expresses "while —ing" or "at the time of —ing."

Example:
आप घर आएँगे । आप बाज़ार से ये चीज़ें ले आइये ।
You will come home. Please bring these things from the market.
आप घर आते समय / वक़्त बाज़ार से ये चीज़ें ले आइये ।
While coming home, please bring these things from the market.

Note that if the same subject is performing two actions, this subject is mentioned only once. If the subject of the imperfective participle + समय / वक़्त is different from the subject of the main verb, then this subject is always followed by the postposition के (possessive form).

Example:

माँ भारत जा रही थीं । मैं जहुत उदास थी ।

Mother was going to India. I was very sad.

माँ के भारत जाते समय / वक़्त मैं बहुत उदास थी ।

At the time of Mother's departure for India, I was very sad.

If the subject of the imperfective participle + समय / वक़्त is different from the subject of the main verb and it is inanimate, the use of the postposition के is optional.

Example:

फ़ायर अलार्म बज रहा है । हमें इस इमारत में नहीं रहना चाहिये ।

The fire alarm is ringing. We should not stay in this building.

फ़ायर अलार्म (के) बजते समय / वक़्त हमें इस इमारत में नहीं रहना चाहिये ।

While the fire alarm is ringing, we should not stay in this building.

Imperfective/Perfective Participle + a Measure of Time

Imperfective participles in the invariable masculine singular oblique form + हुए can be used to indicate the passage of a certain amount of time since the *beginning* of an activity or situation that is still going on. Thus, "शीला को बर्कली में पढ़ते हुए तीन साल हो गये / चुके हैं " indicates that Sheila has been studying at Berkeley for three years now. Note that होना or चुकना is most often used as the main verb of such constructions.

Examples:

मुझे इस घर में रहते हुए सिर्फ़ दस महीने हुए हैं ।

It has been only ten months since I have been living in this house.

उसको सरकारी दफ़्तर में काम करते हुए बरसों हो गये हैं ।

It has been years since he began working in a government office.

Similarly, when perfective participles in the invariable masculine singular oblique form + हुए are used with a measure of time, the construction indicates the passage of time since the *completion* of an activity or situation.

Thus, "शीला को बर्कली आये हुए तीन साल हो गये / चुके हैं " indicates that it has been three years since Sheila came to Berkeley.

Examples:

उसको कॉलिज ख़त्म किये हुए कितने साल हो गये हैं ?

How many years has it been since he finished college?

हमें यह मकान खरीदे हुए बीस साल हो गये हैं ।

It has been twenty years since we bought this house.

Note the basic pattern for both these constructions is:

Noun/pronoun + को + imperfective/perfective participle (MSO) + हुए + measure of time + main verb (generally होना or चुकना).

Reduplicated Imperfective Participle + बचना / रुकना / रहना

Another less frequently encountered participial construction is when an imperfective participle (generally in masculine singular oblique form) is reduplicated and used in a sentence where the main verb is बचना, रुकना, or रहना. This construction implies that something *almost* occurred but was stopped in mid-act. Thus, "प्याला टूटते टूटते बचा" indicates that the cup almost broke (but was saved at the last minute).

Examples:

कार के एक्सीडेंट में वह मरते मरते बचा ।

He almost died in a car accident.

पिता जी का हाथ मुझ पर उठते उठते रुक गया ।

Father almost slapped me.

उसका दम घुटते घुटते रह गया ।

He almost choked.

Participial Constructions, Part 2: Exercises

1. Substitution drill

While studying in the library, we should remain quiet.
लाइब्रेरी में पढ़ते समय हमें चुप रहना चाहिये ।

संगीत सुनते समय

बच्चे के सोते समय

भाषण सुनते समय

फ़िल्म देखते समय

परीक्षा देते समय

दफ़्तर में काम करते समय

2. Transformation drill

When she was cooking [food], [then] she called the servant.
जब वह खाना पका रही थी, तो उसने नौकर को बुलाया ।

She called the servant while cooking.
खाना पकाते समय उसने नौकर को बुलाया ।

जब वह स्कूल जा रहा था, तो उसने हमें यह बात बताई ।

जब वह खाना खाता है, तो वह टी. वी. देखता है ।

जब वह दफ़्तर में काम करता है, तो वह सिर्फ़ कॉफ़ी पीता है ।

जब हम घर आ रहे थे, तो हमने आपको देखा ।

जब मैं पढ़ रही थी, तो मैंने टेलीफ़ोन नहीं सुना ।

जब हम कल स्कूल जाएँगे, तो हम आपके घर रुकेंगे ।

जब वह भारत जा रही थी, तो वह लंदन में रुकी ।

जब मैं हवाई जहाज़ में सफ़र करता हूँ, तो हमेशा सोता हूँ ।

3. Transformation drill

Rohit was going to India. His friend was very sad.
रोहित भारत जा रहा था । उसकी दोस्त बहुत उदास थी ।

His friend was very sad at the time Rohit went to India.
रोहित के भारत जाते समय उसकी दोस्त बहुत उदास थी ।

वह भाषण दे रहा था । आप बीच में क्यों बोले ?
वह लंदन जा रही थी । मैंने उसको एक उपहार दिया ।
बच्चा कमरे में सो रहा है । हमें वहाँ नहीं जाना चाहिये ।
वह दफ़्तर जा रहा था । मैंने उसको छाता दिया ।
वह गाना गा रहा था । लड़की मुस्कुरा रही थी ।
आप बग़ीचे में काम कर रहे थे । उसका फ़ोन आया ।
माँ पूजा कर रही हैं । हमें चुप रहना चाहिये ।
कल बारिश हो रही थी । बादल गरज रहे थे ।

4. Transformation drill

He has been learning Urdu for three years.
वह तीन साल से उर्दू सीख रहा है ।

It has been three years since [he began] to learn Urdu.
उसको उर्दू सीखते हुए तीन साल हो गये हैं ।

वह चार घंटे से सो रहा है ।
हम सात साल से अमरीका में रह रहे हैं ।
वह दो महीने से मेरी मदद कर रही है ।
बच्चा एक घंटे से टी॰वी॰ देख रहा है ।
मैं बहुत देर से बस का इन्तज़ार कर रही हूँ ।
वह चार साल से कथक सीख रही है ।
मेरी सहेली छह महीने से सितार सीख रही है ।
तुम कितने दिनों से इस दुकान में काम कर रही हो ?

5. Transformation drill

My sister-in-law went to India ten days ago.
मेरी भाभी दस दिन पहले भारत गईं ।

It has been ten days since my sister-in-law went to India.
मेरी भाभी को भारत गये हुए दस दिन हो गये हैं ।

मेरी बहन दो साल पहले न्यू यॉर्क आई ।
हमने एक हफ़्ते पहले यह नाटक देखा ।
मेरे मेहमान चार दिन पहले आये ।
वह सिर्फ़ दस मिनट पहले यहाँ पहुँची ।
तुमने कितने घंटे पहले कॉफ़ी पी ?
उसने दो दिन पहले अपना निबन्ध ख़त्म किया ।
मैं अपने परिवार से चार हफ़्ते पहले मिली ।
मैंने पाँच घंटे पहले अपनी दवाई खाई ।

6. <u>Answer the following questions according to the given pattern</u>

Did the child fall?   No, he almost fell.
क्या वह बच्चा गिरा ?   नहीं, वह गिरते गिरते बच गया ।

क्या उसको चोट लगी ? (use रह जाना)
क्या दुर्घटना हुई ? (use रह जाना)
क्या उसने कुछ कहा ? (use रुक जाना)
क्या वह छात्र फ़ेल हुआ ? (use रह जाना)
क्या उसने लड़के को थप्पड़ मारा ? (use रुक जाना)
क्या ग्लास टूट गया ? (use बच जाना)
क्या शहर में गड़बड़ हुई ? (use रह जाना)
क्या बिल्ली मर गई ? (use बच जाना)

7. <u>Translation exercise</u>
(Use participial constructions.)

1. When (while) going out, he wore his coat.
2. He almost died of (from) pneumonia.
3. While driving, we should not read the newspaper.
4. How many years have you been writing poetry?
5. When (while) going to sleep, I forgot to take (eat) my medicine.

6. It has been six months since I saw a Hindi play.
7. Yesterday while going home, we saw your brother.
8. It has been many years since I saw (met) my childhood friend.
9. He has been working on this project for two years.
10. There was almost an accident in front of my house yesterday (use रह जाना).

13. THE ITERATIVE CONSTRUCTION

In addition to the use of the habitual tenses to indicate the regular, frequent, or repeated occurrence of an action, Hindi speakers also use the iterative construction. While these constructions can be used interchangeably, the iterative construction places greater emphasis on the repetitive nature of an action.

The basic pattern for the iterative construction is:

Perfective participle of the main verb
(in invariable masculine singular form) + the inflected form of करना

Example:
वह रोज़ अपने माता-पिता को फ़ोन किया करती है ।
She phones her parents [regularly] every day.

As indicated by the example above, the perfective participle of the main verb is *always* in the masculine singular form, and all changes due to number, gender, and tense are made only to करना. Also, note that the translation of the example above would be the same if the verb were in the habitual tense (वह रोज़ अपने माता-पिता को फ़ोन करती है । *She phones her parents every day*). However, the use of the iterative construction indicates a greater emphasis on the regularity and/or recurrence of an action.

Examples:

यहाँ नवम्बर में बहुत बारिश हुआ करती है ।	*It rains a lot here in November.*
तुम क्यों हमेशा शिकायत किया करते हो ?	*Why do you always complain?*
हम इस दुकान में कॉफ़ी पिया करते थे ।	*We used to drink coffee in this shop.*
भारत में माँ रोज़ मंदिर जाया करेंगी ।	*Mother will go to the temple every day in India.*
वह मेरे लिये फूल लाया करता था ।	*He used to bring flowers for me.*
रोज़ हिन्दी बोलने का अभ्यास किया करो ।	*Practice speaking Hindi every day.*
मुझे देखकर वह हमेशा हँसा करती है ।	*When she sees me, she always laughs.*

Notes

1. When जाना is the main verb in an iterative construction, the special perfective participle जाया is used instead of the expected गया.

Example:
वह हर रोज़ बाज़ार जाया (not गया) करेगी ।
She will go to the market every day.

2. This is the only construction in Hindi by which the regularity of a future action can be expressed, since the habitual tenses can be used only in the present and the past (not in the future).

Example:
परीक्षा तक मैं रोज़ पुस्तकालय में पढ़ा करूँगा ।
I will study regularly in the library every day until the examination.

3. Since the iterative construction is used for indicating the regularity or frequency of an action, it is generally not found in the perfect tenses, which are used to describe a single, completed action. Thus, the postposition ने never occurs with the subject in an iterative construction.

4. This construction may also occur with compound verbs.

Example:
रोज़ अख़बार पढ़ लिया करो ।   *Read the newspaper every day [for your own benefit].*

5. In negative statements the particle नहीं comes directly before the entire verb.

Example:
अच्छे बच्चे गाली नहीं दिया करते ।   *Good children do not swear.*

The Iterative Construction: Exercises

1. Transformation drill

Every day he goes to the office at 9 o'clock in the morning.
वह रोज़ सवेरे नौ बजे दफ़्तर जाता है ।

Every day he goes to the office at 9 o'clock in the morning.
वह रोज़ सवेरे नौ बजे दफ़्तर जाया करता है ।

यह माली हमारे बाग़ में काम करता है ।

यहाँ जाड़ों में बारिश होती है ।

इस देश में लड़कियाँ साड़ी नहीं पहनतीं ।

पिता जी रोज़ सैर के लिये जाते हैं ।

मैं बस से कैम्पस आता हूँ ।

अमरीकन लोग फ़र्श पर नहीं बैठते ।

दादा जी हमें भारत के बारे में बताते हैं ।

तुम क्यों बच्चों पर नाराज़ होते हो ।

2. Transformation drill

You should come to class on time.
तुम्हें समय पर क्लास आना चाहिये ।

Come to class on time [regularly].
(तुम) समय पर क्लास आया करो ।

तुम्हें सिगरेट नहीं पीनी चाहिये ।

तुम्हें अपना काम स्वयं करना चाहिये ।

तुम्हें हमेशा सच बोलना चाहिये ।

तुम्हें हर हफ़्ते अपने कपड़े धोने चाहियें ।

तुम्हें शराब नहीं पीनी चाहिये ।

तुम्हें इस क्लास में हिन्दी बोलनी चाहिये ।

तुम्हें ध्यान से काम करना चाहिये ।

तुम्हें सोच कर बोलना चाहिये ।

3. Transformation drill

We will come here daily.
हम रोज़ यहाँ आएँगे ।

We will [regularly] come here daily.
हम रोज़ यहाँ आया करेंगे ।

मैं रोज़ बाँसुरी बजाऊँगा ।

हम रोज़ शाम को पुस्तकालय में पढ़ेंगे ।

मैं इस दफ़्तर में काम करूँगा ।

हम गर्मी में रोज़ तैरेंगे ।

भारत में मैं सिर्फ़ शाकाहारी खाना खाऊँगा ।

वह अपने भाई की मदद करेगा ।

मैं हर हफ़्ते अपने परिवार से मिलने जाऊँगा ।

हम रोज़ कसरत करेंगे ।

4. Transformation drill

वे छात्र कैम्पस पर मिलते थे ।

Those students used to meet on campus.
वे छात्र कैम्पस पर मिला करते थे ।

Those students used to meet [regularly] on campus.

माँ इस मंदिर में पूजा करती थीं ।

मेरे दादा जी इस गाँव में रहते थे ।

मैं परिवार से मिलने भारत जाता था ।

वह अपने बच्चों के बारे में चिंता करता था ।

वह हमें अपने देश के बारे में बताता था ।

बचपन में हम इस पार्क में खेलते थे ।

वे छात्र रात में देर तक पढ़ते थे ।

माँ हमारे लिये समोसे बनाती थीं ।

5. Transformation drill

You should take this medicine daily.
आप को रोज़ यह दवाई खानी चाहिये ।

Please take this medicine daily.
आप रोज़ यह दवाई खाया करें ।

आप को रोज़ तीन मील पैदल चलना चाहिये ।

आप को रोज़ सितार बजाना चाहिये ।

आप को अपना काम अच्छी तरह से करना चाहिये ।

आप को देर से दफ़्तर नहीं आना चाहिये ।

आप को दूरदर्शन ज़्यादा नहीं देखना चाहिये ।

आप को रोज़ अख़बार पढ़ना चाहिये ।

आप को अपनी पत्नी की मदद करनी चाहिये ।

आप को रोज़ आठ घंटे सोना चाहिये ।

6. <u>Translation exercises</u> (Use the iterative construction.)

1. She often used to come to our house to meet my sister.
2. Good children do not tell lies.
3. I always talk with my parents in Hindi.
4. I will [regularly] learn ten Hindi words every day.
5. Your brother will [regularly] study with me next year also.
6. Shall we meet in this coffee shop every day?
7. He often goes to Oakland to see (meet) his mother.
8. His brother will work [regularly] in this shop.
9. Every week we will go to see a Hindi film.
10. Should/shall we help those children every day?
11. He often used to bring flowers for his wife.
12. In childhood I used to sing Hindi film songs.

14. THE PASSIVE VOICE

The passive voice in Hindi and other languages indicates that the subject of a sentence is not actively engaged in an action but is being acted upon by some agent. The primary difference between a sentence in the passive voice and a sentence in the active voice is that the subject of a passive construction is the object in the corresponding active construction. For example, in English, "the food was cooked" is in the passive voice, while "I cooked the food" is in the active voice (note that "food" in the former construction is the grammatical subject, while in the latter construction it is the object of the sentence).

Generally, the passive voice is used in Hindi with actions and events for which we do not know the agent (actor), when we do not wish to reveal the identity of the agent, or when the identity of the agent is too obvious or unimportant to mention. If the agent is to be mentioned, such as in the English sentence "This picture was taken by me," then a Hindi speaker would rather use the active voice (e.g., "I took this picture").

Formation

The passive voice in Hindi is formed with the perfective participle of the main verb followed by the passive auxiliary जाना.

The verb in the passive voice agrees with the person or thing being acted upon (the grammatical subject), which is a direct object in the corresponding active voice.

Examples:

Active	Passive
मैंने अख़बार पढ़ा ।	अख़बार पढ़ा गया ।
I read the newspaper.	*The newspaper was read.*
मैंने खिड़कियाँ खोलीं ।	खिड़कियाँ खोली गईं ।
I opened the windows.	*The windows were opened.*
लड़की सेब खाएगी ।	सेब खाया जाएगा ।
The girl will eat the apple.	*The apple will be eaten.*

मैं सवाल पूछ रही हूँ ।   सवाल पूछा जा रहा है ।

I am asking a question.   *A question is being asked.*

Both the perfective participle of the main verb and the passive auxiliary जाना agree in number, gender, and person with the subject, but changes due to tense are seen only in the auxiliary verb जाना.

The passive voice in Hindi can be found in all tenses and mood forms.

Examples:
1. Present Habitual Tense

Active	मैं यह फल ख़रीदता हूँ ।	*I buy this fruit.*
Passive	यह फल ख़रीदा जाता है ।	*This fruit is bought.*

2. Past Habitual Tense

Active	मैं यह फल ख़रीदता था ।	*I used to buy this fruit.*
Passive	यह फल ख़रीदा जाता था ।	*This fruit used to be bought.*

3. Present Progressive Tense

Active	मैं यह फल ख़रीद रहा हूँ ।	*I am buying this fruit.*
Passive	यह फल ख़रीदा जा रहा है ।	*This fruit is being bought.*

4. Past Progressive Tense

Active	मैं यह फल ख़रीद रहा था ।	*I was buying this fruit.*
Passive	यह फल ख़रीदा जा रहा था ।	*This fruit was being bought.*

5. Future Tense

Active	मैं यह फल ख़रीदूँगा ।	*I will buy this fruit.*
Passive	यह फल ख़रीदा जाएगा ।	*This fruit will be bought.*

6. Perfect Tense

Active	मैंने यह फल ख़रीदा ।	*I bought this fruit.*
Passive	यह फल ख़रीदा गया ।	*This fruit was bought.*

7. Present Perfect Tense

Active	मैंने यह फल ख़रीदा है ।	*I have bought this fruit.*
Passive	यह फल ख़रीदा गया है ।	*This fruit has been bought.*

8. Past Perfect Tense

Active	मैंने यह फल ख़रीदा था ।	*I had bought this fruit.*
Passive	यह फल ख़रीदा गया था ।	*This fruit had been bought.*

9. Subjunctive Mood

Active	क्या मैं यह फल ख़रीदूँ ?	*Should/Shall I buy this fruit?*
Passive	क्या यह फल ख़रीदा जाए ?	*Should this fruit be bought?*

10. Presumptive Mood

Active	वह फल ख़रीद रहा होगा ।	*He must be (probably is) buying fruit.*
Passive	फल ख़रीदा जा रहा होगा ।	*Fruit is probably being bought.*

11. Compulsion Constructions

Active	मुझे यह फल ख़रीदना है ।	*I have to buy this fruit.*
Passive	यह फल ख़रीदा जाना है ।	*This fruit has to be bought.*
Active	मुझे यह फल ख़रीदना चाहिये ।	*I should buy this fruit.*
Passive	यह फल ख़रीदा जाना चाहिये ।	*This fruit should be bought.*

Note that the compulsion construction with पड़ना is not found in the Hindi passive.

Notes

1. In Hindi sentences in the active voice, objects, especially animate ones, are often marked by a postposition, generally को. In corresponding passive sentences this postposition को may be retained or dropped. If it is retained, it will block agreement, and the verb will take the neutral form (masculine singular form).

Examples:

Active	Passive
<u>Active</u>	<u>Passive</u>
हमने वहाँ आपकी बहन को देखा ।	आपकी बहन वहाँ देखी गई ।
We saw your sister there.	*Your sister was seen there.*
	OR
	आपकी बहन को वहाँ देखा गया ।
	Your sister was seen there.

As seen in the above example, the active form can be changed into two passive sentences. The first sentence is passive without को following the subject, while in the second sentence, which is also passive, the postposition को is retained.

2. Generally, the passive voice is formed with transitive verbs, but sometimes intransitive verbs are also used to form the passive. In such cases, there would be no subject in the passive voice construction and the verb will show neutral agreement (masculine singular form).

Examples:

Active	Passive
यहाँ लोग पलंग पर नहीं सोते हैं ।	यहाँ पलंग पर नहीं सोया जाता है ।
Here people don't sleep on a bed.	*Here people don't sleep on a bed.* (lit., *The bed is not slept on here.*)
यहाँ लोग ज़मीन पर बैठते हैं ।	यहाँ ज़मीन पर बैठा जाता है ।
Here people sit on the ground.	*Here people sit on the ground.* (lit., *The ground is sat upon here.*)
फ़्री वेज़ पर लोग पैदल नहीं चलते हैं ।	फ़्री वेज़ पर पैदल नहीं चला जाता है ।
People don't walk on freeways.	*People don't walk on freeways.* (lit., *Freeways are not walked upon.*)

3. When the verb जाना is used as the main verb in the passive voice, the special perfective forms जाया / जाये / जाई are used instead of its expected perfective forms गया / गये / गई .

Example:

ये सब्ज़ियाँ गाँव से शहर ले जाई जाएँगी ।

These vegetables will be taken from the village to the city.

4. The negative नहीं generally preceeds both parts of the verbs.

Example:

इस देश में हिन्दी नहीं बोली जाती है ।

Hindi is not spoken in this country.

5. When the agent (actor) is mentioned, it is not normal to use the passive voice in Hindi. "The book was written by me" is generally not said in Hindi. If the actor is to be mentioned, then the active voice must be used. However, in Hindi we occasionally find sentences in the passive voice where the agent is mentioned with the postposition के द्वारा *by, by the agency [of],* or in some limited instances with के हाथों , where it implies *by the hands of.*

Examples:

वह दुश्मन के द्वारा / के हाथों मारा गया ।
He was killed by the enemy.

यह लेख उस छात्र के द्वारा लिखा गया ।
This article was written by that student.

Such sentences in the passive voice, where the agent is mentioned with के द्वारा, are not very common in Hindi and are usually the result of a direct translation of English sentences.

Since no agent is mentioned in the passive voice, it is most commonly used in making official announcements.

Example:

यात्रियों से निवेदन किया जाता है कि... ।
The passengers are requested to...

The passive is also frequently used in impersonal sentences since no specific agent is mentioned in them.

Example:

(यह) कहा जाता है कि मेहनत का फल हमेशा मीठा होता है ।

It is said that hard work always pays off. (lit., *It is said that the fruit of hard work is always sweet.*)

6. Hindi uses the postposition से to express the instrument by which an action is performed.

Example:

यहाँ खेती मशीनों से की जाती है ।   *Here farming is done by machines.*

7. In the case of nominal conjunct verbs (e.g., इंतज़ार करना), the nominal element of the verb (e.g., इंतज़ार) acts as the subject of the passive construction and the verb agrees with it.

Examples:

Active	Passive
लड़की ने उसका इंतज़ार किया ।	उसका इंतज़ार किया गया ।
The girl waited for him.	*He was waited for.*
(lit., *The girl did his waiting.*)	(lit., *His waiting was done.*)
लड़की दोस्त की मदद करेगी ।	दोस्त की मदद की जाएगी ।
The girl will help her friend. (lit.,	*The friend will be helped.*
The girl will do her friend's help.)	(lit., *The friend's help will be done.*)
वह कार की मरम्मत कर रहा है ।	कार की मरम्मत की जा रही है ।
He is repairing the car. (lit.,	*The car is being repaired.*
He is doing the repair of the car.)	(lit., *The repair of the car is being done.*)

8. Hindi has many intransitive verbs, such as बनना *to be made* and धुलना *to be washed*, that are inherently passive in meaning and cannot occur in the passive construction (e.g., साड़ी धुली जाएगी is not possible). Therefore, there can be two types of constructions in Hindi that are passive in meaning:

112

(a) An intransitive verb with an inherent passive meaning in the active voice (e.g., पकना *to be cooked*)

Example:

यहाँ भारतीय खाना पकता है ।   *Indian food is cooked here.*

(b) The transitive counterpart in a passive construction (e.g., पकाया जाना *to be cooked*)

Example:

यहाँ भारतीय खाना पकाया जाता है ।   *Indian food is cooked here.*

Hindi has many such intransitive and transitive verb pairs, such as:

जलना *to be burned* - जलाना *to burn*

पकना *to be cooked* - पकाना *to cook*

रुकना *to be stopped* - रोकना *to stop (someone or something)*

बनना *to be made* - बनाना *to make*

बिकना *to be sold* - बेचना *to sell*

खुलना *to be opened* - खोलना *to open*

The existence of these pairs allows Hindi speakers to formulate two kinds of passive constructions that are quite similar in meaning.

Examples:

सड़कें बनाई जा रही हैं ।   सड़कें बन रही हैं ।
The roads are being built.   *The roads are being built.*

यहाँ किताबें बेची जाती हैं ।   यहाँ किताबें बिकती हैं ।
Books are sold here.   *Books are sold here.*

खिड़की खोली गई ।   खिड़की खुली / खुल गई ।
The window was opened.   *The window opened.*

Note that although the above examples have the same translations, subtle differences do exist between the pairs (sometimes these are difficult to convey in English translation):

First, while the construction with the intransitive verb (inherently passive) simply reports that an action has occurred (the actor is not important or is irrelevant), the passive construction we have discussed in this chapter alludes to, implies, and/or indirectly refers to the existence of an actor, giving him/her some degree of importance even though he/she is not present in the sentence.

Examples:

खाना पकाया गया ।

The food was cooked [by someone].

खाना पका / पक गया ।

The food was cooked.

Second, Hindi speakers can also differentiate between intentional and accidental actions by using two different constructions. When certain verbs are used in the passive voice, they imply that the action was intentional. However, when the action is accidental, natural, or occurs on its own, a Hindi speaker will use an intransitive verb (inherently passive). Hence, there may be two different ways of rendering an English sentence in Hindi. One translation will imply that the action was intentional, while the second translation will imply that the action was an accident or occurred on its own.

Examples:

Passive (intentional action)   Intransitive verb (natural/accidental)

साड़ी फाड़ी गई ।

The sari was torn.

साड़ी फटी / फट गई ।

The sari tore.

खिड़की तोड़ी गई ।

The window was broken.

खिड़की टूटी / टूट गई ।

The window broke.

दुकानें जलाई गईं ।

The shops were burned.

दुकानें जलीं / जल गईं ।

The shops burned.

The Use of the Passive to Express Inability

The passive voice is often used to express the inability (generally physical) or the incapacity of someone to perform an action. In such cases, the agent is *always* mentioned with the postposition से *with, by*. Since such sentences convey inability, they are always negative.

Examples:

बुख़ार के कारण, मुझसे बहुत देर तक नहीं बैठा जाएगा ।
Because of a fever, I won't be able to sit for a long time.

सिरदर्द की वजह से, उससे कल कुछ नहीं पढ़ा गया ।
Because of a headache, s/he could not read anything yesterday.

मेरी बूढ़ी दादी से जल्दी नहीं चला जाता ।
My old grandmother can't/is unable to walk fast.

One can also use an intransitive verb in such situations:

मुझसे यह काम नहीं होता ।   *I can't do this work.*
मुझसे यह काम नहीं किया जाता ।   *I can't/I am unable to do this work.*

Though both the above constructions are similarly translated in English, the former (with an intransitive verb) may indicate an unwillingness rather than an inability to perform an action. However, the difference between these two is very subtle.

115

The Passive Voice: Exercises

1. Substitution drill

Sanskrit is taught at this university.
इस यूनिवर्सिटी में संस्कृत पढ़ाई जाती है ।

बंगाली

हिन्दी

बहुत भाषाएँ

इतिहास

भारत का इतिहास

भारत के बारे में

दुनिया का इतिहास

विज्ञान

बहुत विषय

क्या

2. Substitution drill

Beautiful saris are being sold here.
यहाँ सुन्दर साड़ियाँ बेची जा रही हैं ।

हिन्दुस्तानी कपड़े

फूल

हिन्दी की किताबें

खिलौने

चप्पलें

हिन्दी और उर्दू के अख़बार

क्या

3. Transformation drill

I will read this book tomorrow.   This book will be read tomorrow.
मैं कल यह किताब पढ़ूँगा ।   कल यह किताब पढ़ी जाएगी ।

मैं कल एक फ़िल्म देखूँगा ।
मैं कल यह काम करूँगा ।
मैं कल कपड़े ख़रीदूँगा ।
मैं कल एक तसवीर बनाऊँगा ।
मैं कल कुछ कपड़े धोऊँगा ।
मैं कल पत्र लिखूँगा ।
मैं कल एक गीत सुनाऊँगा ।
मैं कल वे पुराने मन्दिर देखूँगा ।

4. Substitution drill

Beautiful things were seen there.
वहाँ सुन्दर चीज़ें देखी गईं ।

एक बड़ी मस्जिद

पुराने मन्दिर

एक बड़ा बाग़

एक सुन्दर पार्क

नये मकान

बहुत पुलिसवाले

बड़ी भीड़

हड़ताल करने वाले

हड़ताल करने वालों की भीड़

5. Substitution drill

Chairs are made here.
यहाँ कुरसियाँ बनाई जाती हैं ।

used to be made
are being made
were being made
were made
have been made
had been made
will be made

117

must have been made
may be made
should be made

6. Transformation drill

I help friends.   Friends are helped.
मैं दोस्तों की मदद करता हूँ ।   दोस्तों की मदद की जाती है ।

छात्र हिन्दी बोलने की कोशिश करते हैं ।

मैं कल काम शुरू करूँगी ।

नौकर घर साफ़ करेगा ।

लड़की खिड़की बन्द कर रही थी ।

हम शिक्षक का इन्तज़ार कर रहे थे ।

उसने कार की मरम्मत की ।

मैंने दोस्तों की मदद की ।

उन्होंने काम शुरू किया ।

7. Transformation drill

A taxi stopped.   A taxi was stopped.
टैक्सी रुकी ।   टैक्सी रोकी गई ।

खाना पका ।

सब कपड़े धुले ।

वह खिड़की खुली ।

मकान बन रहा है ।

ताज़ी सब्ज़ियाँ बिक रही हैं ।

काम शुरू हुआ ।

मकान की मरम्मत हुई ।

घर कल साफ़ होगा ।

दुकान कब बन्द होगी ।

8. Transformation drill

We study Hindi here.

हम यहाँ हिन्दी पढ़ते हैं ।

छात्र सवाल पूछते हैं ।

मैंने कुछ किताबें ख़रीदीं ।

उसने भारत के बारे में बताया ।

लड़की ने एक सुन्दर कविता लिखी ।

उसने एक कहानी सुनाई ।

वह लड़का अख़बार पढ़ रहा है ।

हम टैक्सी का इन्तज़ार कर रहे हैं ।

वह दोस्त की मदद कर रहा है ।

लड़का मोटर चला रहा है ।

मैं कल यह काम करूँगा ।

हम गाड़ी की मरम्मत करेंगे ।

हम कल वे मन्दिर देखेंगे ।

Hindi is studied here.

यहाँ हिन्दी पढ़ी जाती है ।

9. Substitution drill

Because of illness, he will not be able to do this work.

बीमारी की वजह से उससे यह काम किया नहीं जाएगा ।

इतना काम नहीं किया

क्लास नहीं आया

खाना नहीं पकाया

एक मील नहीं चला

बहुत देर तक नहीं बैठा

मसालेवाला खाना नहीं खाया

10. Oral questions

ये जूते कहाँ बनाये जाते हैं ?

ये साड़ियाँ कहाँ बेची जाती हैं ?

हिन्दी कहाँ बोली जाती है ?

हिन्दी कहाँ पढ़ाई जाती है ?

टेलीग्राफ़ ऐवन्यू पर क्या बेचा जाता है ?

यह पत्र कब लिखा गया ?

किसका इंतज़ार किया जा रहा है ?

उर्दू कहाँ बोली जाती है ?

उर्दू के अख़बार कहाँ बेचे जाते हैं ?

यह किताब कब पढ़ी जाएगी ?

अच्छा हिन्दुस्तानी कहाँ बेचा जाता है ?

मेरी कार की मरम्मत कब की जाएगी ?

साड़ी कहाँ पहनी जाती है ?

कल क्या किया जाएगा ?

कल कौन-सी फ़िल्म देखी जाएगी ?

कल किसकी मदद की गई ?

11. Translation exercise
(Use the passive voice.)

1. Today flowers are not being sold here.
2. Many books will be written on this subject.
3. These children were helped yesterday.
4. Because of her illness, she is unable to come to class.
5. The letter will be sent by mail.
6. This old man will not be able to do this much work.
7. Hindi films are generally shown in this theater.
8. These books were read yesterday.
9. A new house will be built.
10. My books were sent to Berkeley two months ago.
11. This work will be done tomorrow.
12. These days our house is being repaired.

15. REFLEXIVE FORMS

In addition to the reflexive possessive adjective अपना (discussed in Chapter 20, *Introduction to Hindi Grammar*), Hindi also has other reflexive forms that, like अपना, refer back to the subject of a sentence or clause and whose translation depends on the person or thing to which they refer (e.g., the subject of the sentence or clause). Thus, a reflexive form can be translated as "myself," "yourself," "himself," "herself," "itself," "themselves," "ourselves," and so forth, depending on the context and usage.

Reflexive Pronouns

Reflexive pronouns in Hindi include आप, or its expanded form अपने आप, ख़ुद, and स्वयं. While आप / अपने आप and ख़ुद are more common in colloquial speech, the reflexive pronoun स्वयं / स्वयम् occurs mostly in formal, written language. The following examples illustrate the difference between using a reflexive possessive adjective and a reflexive pronoun:

Examples:
छात्र अपना खाना पका रहा है ।
The student is cooking his [own] food.

छात्र आप / अपने आप / ख़ुद / स्वयं अपना खाना पका रहा है ।
The student is cooking his [own] food himself.

Reflexive pronouns in the direct case

When used in the direct case (e.g., when not followed by a postposition), all the above forms are often followed by ही. Adding ही is particularly useful in distinguishing the reflexive form आप from the second person pronoun आप (you).

Examples:

मैंने यह कविता आप / ख़ुद (ही) लिखी है ।
I have written this poem myself.

मैं ख़ुद / आप गोश्त नहीं खाती लेकिन अपने परिवार के लिये पकाती हूँ ।
I myself don't eat meat, but I cook it for my family.

मेरी दादी जी को अपना काम स्वयम् (ही) करना पसन्द है ।
My grandmother likes to do her work herself.

पिता जी अपने आप (ही) आपको इस के बारे में बताएँगे ।
Father will tell you about it himself.

Reflexive pronouns in the oblique case

The oblique form of the reflexive pronoun आप is अपने. अपने आप, ख़ुद, and स्वयं are invariable and do not change in the oblique case.

Examples:

वह छात्र अपने को बहुत होशियार समझता है ।
That student considers himself very intelligent.

लड़की ने अपने आप से पूछा कि मैं क्यों हमेशा उस लड़के के बारे में सोचती रहती हूँ ।
The girl asked herself, why do I always keep on thinking about that boy?

वह ख़ुद को ख़ुदा कहने लगा है ।
He has started calling himself God.

लड़की शीशे में स्वयं को देख कर मुस्कुरा रही थी ।
The girl, looking at herself in the mirror, was smiling.

Reflexive Forms Used Adverbially

In some instances, the Hindi reflexive form अपने आप may be used adverbially, conveying the sense "by oneself/itself," "of one's own accord," or "of one's own volition."

Examples:

ब्रेक लगाओ नहीं तो गाड़ी अपने आप चलने लगेगी ।

Put on the brake; otherwise the car will start moving by itself (of its own accord).

वह अपने आप संस्कृत सीखने लगा ।

He began to learn Sanskrit of his own volition [i.e., nobody else had to tell him to do it].

क्या तुम सोचते हो कि यह काम अपने आप ख़त्म हो जाएगा ?

Do you think that the work will be completed by itself (of its own accord)?

Note that it is sometimes ambiguous whether a reflexive form is being used pronominally or adverbially. Thus वह अपने आप घर साफ़ करेगा can be translated either as *"He will clean the house himself (alone, without any help)"* or as *"He will clean the house of his own volition [no one has to tell him to do it]."*

Another reflexive form used adverbially is आपस में. Like the reflexive adjectives and pronouns, it refers back to the subject of a sentence (which with this form is always plural). Depending on its context, आपस में can be translated as "among/between themselves," "among/between ourselves," "among/between yourselves," etc.

Examples:

ये लड़कियाँ आपस में बहुत हँसी-मज़ाक करती हैं ।

These girls laugh and joke a lot among themselves.

हमें आपस में बात करके ही इसके बारे में फ़ैसला करना चाहिये ।

We should make a decision about it only after discussing the matter among ourselves.

इन भाई-बहनों में आपस में बहुत प्यार है ।

There is a lot of love among these brothers and sisters.

Other Reflexive Forms

आपस का / आपसी is another reflexive form, related in meaning to the adverbial reflexive आपस में, though it is used adjectivally. आपस का / आपसी can be translated as "of/pertaining to ourselves/yourselves/themselves" (depending on the context).

Examples:
तुम क्यों बीच में बोलते हो ? यह हमारा आपस का / आपसी मामला है ।

Why are you interfering? This is a personal matter/This matter pertains only to us.

यह उनका आपस का / आपसी समझौता है । हमें इस के बारे में कुछ कहने का कोई हक़ नहीं है ।

This is their mutual agreement. We have no right to say anything about it.

Another reflexive form is आपा, used nominally (as a marked masculine noun) to indicate "oneself." Its occurrence, however, is infrequent. It refers back to the subject of the sentence, and thus its translation could be "myself," "himself," "herself," "ourselves," "yourselves," and so forth, based on the subject.

Examples:
अपने पति की मृत्यु का समाचार सुनकर उसने आपा पीट लिया ।

Upon hearing the news of her husband's death, she was devastated (lit., she beat herself).

जब मैं देर से आई तो वह ग़ुस्से में आपे से बाहर हो गया ।
He was beside himself with anger when I came late.

Reflexive Forms: Exercises

1. Transformation drill

I madc this painting mysclf.
मैंने ख़ुद यह तसवीर बनाई ।

I made this painting myself.
मैंने स्वयम् यह तसवीर बनाई ।

आपको ख़ुद वहाँ जाना चाहिये ।
पिता जी ख़ुद शिक्षक से मिलने गये ।
मैं ख़ुद अपनी गाड़ी चलाती हूँ ।
माँ को ख़ुद अपना काम करना पसन्द है ।
तुम ख़ुद उससे पूछो ।
वह ख़ुद अपना दुश्मन है ।
चोट के कारण वह ख़ुद नहा नहीं सकती ।
मैंने ख़ुद आपके लिए यह कविता लिखी ।

2. Transformation drill

He will go there himself.
वह आप ही वहाँ जाएगा ।

He will go there himself.
वह अपने आप (ही) वहाँ जाएगा ।

मैं आप ही अपनी मदद करूँगी ।
मैं आप ही अपने बच्चों को पढ़ाऊँगी ।
उसने आप ही सब खाना पकाया ।
तुम्हें आप ही शिक्षक को यह बताना चाहिये ।
मेरे भाई को आप ही बॉस्टन जाना पड़ेगा ।
मेरी माँ आप ही अपने कपड़े सीती हैं ।
वह आप ही बच्चों को पार्क ले गई ।
मेरी बहन ने आप ही पार्टी का सब इंतज़ाम किया ।

3. Transformation drill

She considers herself very
smart.
वह अपने आप को बहुत होशियार समझती है ।

She considers herself very
smart.
वह अपने को बहुत होशियार
समझती है ।

उसको अपने आप से बात करने की आदत है ।
उसने अपने आप को नया नाम दिया ।
मैंने अपने आप से पूछा, "अब मैं क्या करूँ ?"
उसने अपने आप को उसकी आँखों में देखा ।
अपने आप को धोखा देना भी ग़लत है ।
उसने अपने आप के लिए एक तोहफ़ा ख़रीदा ।
तुम्हें अपने आप के बारे में भी सोचना चाहिये ।
क्या तुम इसके लिए अपने आप को माफ़ कर सकते हो ?

4. Substitution drill

These students chitchat/gossip a lot among themselves.
ये छात्र आपस में बहुत गपशप करते हैं ।

       play
       laugh
       joke
       argue
       fight
       talk
       meet

5. Transformation drill

Their mutual friendship is ideal.
उनकी आपस की दोस्ती आदर्श है ।
यह हमारी आपस की बात है ।
वह उनका आपस का मामला है ।
क्या यह तुम्हारा आपस का फ़ैसला है ?

Their mutual friendship is ideal.
उनकी आपसी दोस्ती आदर्श है ।

यह इनका आपस का समझौता है ।

यह उनकी आपस की समस्या है ।

यह उनकी आपस की लड़ाई है ।

6. <u>Translation exercise</u>

1. She went to buy flowers for herself.
2. Will you be able to do this much work yourself?
3. He taught himself how to play the flute.
4. Why are they fighting among themselves?
5. Little children like to do their work themselves.
6. What did they decide among themselves?
7. Now my daughter can ride (drive) a bicycle herself.
8. I didn't say anything to her. She went there herself (of her own volition).
9. This is our personal (mutual) problem, but we want your advice.
10. He likes to talk about himself.

16. COMPOUND VERBAL FORMATIONS, PART 2
(WITH डालना, पड़ना, उठना, बैठना, AND रखना)

In Chapter 7, we discussed the general rules used in the formation of compound verbs and examined compound verbal formations with जाना, लेना, and देना. In this chapter we will cover the usage of several other commonly used auxiliaries in compound verbs. Students should keep in mind that these compound verbal formations are difficult to use and should be used with care and discretion.

डालना *to pour, to throw down, to put in/down, to drop*: डालना is a transitive verb, and it occurs as an auxiliary verb only with transitive verb stems. When used in such compound constructions, डालना as an auxiliary intensifies or adds force to an action, though it can add different meanings in different contexts. Thus, it can denote an action that is done violently, aggressively, forcefully, vigorously, thoughtlessly, decisively or with determination.

Examples:
हम दुश्मन को मार डालेंगे ।

We will kill the enemy. (Note that मारना literally means to "hit" or "strike," but when compounded with डालना, it always means "to kill.")

उसने ग़ुस्से में अपना गिलास तोड़ डाला ।

In anger he broke his glass. (The emphasis here is on the intensity of the action.)

चोर ने घर का दरवाज़ा खोल डाला ।

The thief opened the door of the house. (The implication is that he did so forcefully.)

फ़िल्म देखने के कारण उसने जल्दी से अपना सब काम ख़त्म कर डाला ।

In order to see the film, he finished all his work quickly. (i.e., he did his work intensively and with determination.)

तुमने यह क्या कर डाला ?

What [is this] you have done? (This is a comment on the thoughtlessness of the action in question.)

पड़ना *to fall, to lie idle or useless, to befall*: पड़ना is an intransitive verb and it occurs as an auxiliary verb generally with intransitive verbs. In compound verbal formations पड़ना is used to express sudden, abrupt, spontaneous, and possibly unanticipated actions. In short, it is used to convey a sudden change of state or circumstances. पड़ना, which means "to fall," is often combined with verb stems that also suggest a similar downward movement. This construction should not be confused with the infinitive + पड़ना construction, which means "have to," "must," "to be forced/obliged to," (i.e., the compulsion or obligation construction). Since पड़ना is an intransitive verb, the compound verb formed with the verb stem + पड़ना is always treated as a non- ने construction.

Examples:
दौड़ते-दौड़ते लड़की गिर पड़ी ।

The girl fell down while running. (The implication is of an abrupt change in circumstances--from running to falling--and the action is of downward movement.)

वह बात-बात पर हँस पड़ती है ।

She bursts into laughter on the smallest pretext. (In this sentence the emphasis is on the spontaneous action of "bursting" into laughter.)

हमारे परिवार पर यह क्या अजीब मुश्किल आ पड़ी ?

What strange, difficult situation has befallen our family? (The implication is that the difficulty was unanticipated. Note that the original meaning of the verb पड़ना, "to befall," is also retained.)

वह खिड़की से कूद पड़ा ।

He jumped out of the window. (The suggestion here is that the action is sudden and with a downward movement.)

शाम होते ही मज़दूर अपने-अपने घर की तरफ़ चल पड़े ।

With the onset of evening, the laborers started off for their homes. (Note that चल पड़ना is always used idiomatically to mean "to start off" and implies a spontaneity of action.)

उठना *to rise, to get up*: The auxiliary verb उठना is similar in meaning to पड़ना in that it implies the suddenness or spontaneity/impulsiveness of an action. Whereas पड़ना is combined with verb stems that indicate the downward direction of an action, उठना is combined with verb stems that suggest the upward direction of an action (compare to the horizontal directionality of देना and लेना). उठना is also used to indicate the commencement of an action or a feeling. It can also add intensity to an action. Since उठना is an intransitive verb, the compound verb formed with the verb stem + उठना is always treated as a non-ने construction.

Examples:

अपने देश की जीत का समाचार सुनकर, लोग ख़ुशी से नाच उठे ।

Upon hearing the news of their country's victory, the people danced with joy. (This sentence indicates a spontaneous action.)

शाम होते ही घरों में दीपक जल उठे ।

With the onset of evening, lamps began to be lit in homes. (Here the action is in the upward direction as the flames of numerous lamps rise when they are lit.)

चोर को देखकर, औरत डर से चीख़ उठी ।

Upon seeing the thief, the woman screamed with fear (an intense sudden action).

तुम क्यों हमेशा बड़ों के बीच बोल उठते हो ?

Why do you always speak (interrupt) when elders are conversing with each other (impulsive action).

A few verb stems can take either पड़ना or उठना to form compound verb constructions. Such compound verbs are often translated in the same manner. However, there are subtle differences between the two. While both indicate a sudden action, उठना, indicating an upward motion, also conveys a stronger degree of suddenness (i.e., a reflex action) than पड़ना. The difference, however, is very subtle and often untranslatable.

Examples:

पत्र पढ़कर माँ रो पड़ी ।	*Upon reading the letter, Mother burst into tears.*
पत्र पढ़कर माँ रो उठी ।	*Upon reading the letter, Mother burst into tears/cried loudly.*
दर्द से वह चीख़ पड़ा ।	*He screamed with pain.*
दर्द से वह चीख़ उठा ।	*He screamed out loud with pain.*
उसकी बात सुनकर हम हँस पड़े ।	*Upon hearing him, we burst into laughter.*
उसकी बात सुनकर हम हँस उठे ।	*Upon hearing him, we burst into laughter/ we laughed uproariously.*
मरीज़ की हालत देखकर मैं चौंक पड़ा ।	*Upon seeing the patient's condition, I was startled/taken aback.*
मरीज़ की हालत देखकर मैं चौंक उठा ।	*Upon seeing the patient's condition, I was visibly shaken (shocked).*

बैठना *to sit*: As an auxiliary in compound verbs, बैठना has several rather different meanings:

(a) It is used when an action is rash or foolish, and it implies that the subject was indifferent to or unaware of the ramifications of his/her action. The speaker in such cases is generally critical of the action and/or its consequences.

(b) It is used when force is used to obtain a desired object/goal. In this case, the speaker suggests that the subject is unworthy of this object/goal or has attained this goal through questionable means.

(c) It suggests something anticlimactic or a decline of some kind.

(d) It conveys the sense of an action completed thoroughly.

बैठना is an intransitive verb; therefore, the compound verb formed with verb stem + बैठना is always treated as a non-ने construction.

Examples:

वह समझ बैठा कि मैंने पिताजी से उसकी शिकायत की ।

He [mistakenly] thought that I complained about him to Father.

महाराज युधिष्ठिर जुए में अपना सब कुछ हार बैठे ।

Maharaj Yudhisthira [foolishly] lost everything in gambling. (This statement clearly indicates a decline in Yudhisthira's circumstances.)

माँ पूरी कोशिश कर बैठीं लेकिन बेटी को इस शादी के लिए राज़ी नहीं कर पाईं ।

Despite all of the mother's efforts, she was unable to persuade her daughter to accept this marriage proposal. (This is a completed action done thoroughly but with no result.)

पता नहीं ग़ुस्से में वह क्या कर बैठे ?

Who knows what he might do (what blunder he might make) in anger?

अगर जनता उसे अब नहीं रोकेगी तो वह एक दिन तानाशाह बन बैठेगा ।

Unless the public stops him now, one day he will become a dictator. (He will obtain absolute power using illegitimate methods.)

रखना *to put, to place, to keep*: When used as an auxiliary in a compound verb construction, रखना retains most of its original meaning, "to keep," but adds a sense of duration. In other words, it is often used in situations to describe a state resulting from a previous action (e.g., to be in a state of keeping a promise) and/or to describe something kept/retained over a period of time (e.g., food, memories, a promise, a debt).

Examples:

खाना पका रखा है । खा लो ।

The food has been cooked [and kept]. Eat it.

मैंने उसको पैसा दे रखा है ।

I have given him money. (The implication here is that he still has the money).

मैंने महाभारत की ये कहानियाँ सुन रखी हैं ।

I have heard these stories from the Mahabharat. (This statement suggests that the speaker still remembers these stories.)

मैंने माँ से वायदा कर रखा है कि मैं भारत वापस आकर भारतीय लड़की से ही शादी करूँगा ।

I have promised my mother that I will return to India and will marry only an Indian girl. (In this sentence, the promise to return to India and marry an Indian girl was made some time ago. The implication is that this promise will be kept.)

Additional Auxiliary Verbs

We have discussed the usage of eight of the most commonly used auxiliary verbs, both here and in Chapter 7. However, students of Hindi will encounter several other less commonly used auxiliary verbs in the course of conversation or while reading literature in Hindi. Their use is much more limited, specific, and/or idiomatic. For example, बसना *to dwell*, *to be settled* can be used in two ways: चल बसना, meaning "to die," and जा / आ बसना, meaning "to go/come and settle somewhere." Other auxiliary verbs include आना, मरना, मारना, चलना, निकलना, पहुँचना (among others).

Compound Verbal Formations, Part 2
(with डालना, पड़ना, उठना, बैठना and रखना): Exercises

1. Transformation drill
Transform the following sentences into compound verbal formations with डालना, appropriately changing the verb in bold in each sentence and omitting any other intensive auxiliary.

The girl tore up all [of] her lover's letters.
लड़की ने अपने प्रेमी के सब पत्र **फाड़े** ।

The girl tore up all [of] her lover's letters. (Intensity of action.)
लड़की ने अपने प्रेमी के सब पत्र फाड़ डाले ।

दुश्मन ने लोगों के घर **जला दिये** ।
पता नहीं, वह ग़ुस्से में क्या **करे** ।
हमें पार्टी में जाना है । जल्दी से काम **ख़त्म करो** ।
मैंने दो ही दिन में यह पूरा उपन्यास **पढ़ा** ।
बच्चों ने शैतानी में खिलौना **तोड़ा** ।
पागल आदमी ने अपने कपड़े **फाड़े** ।
उन्होंने कुछ सिपाहियों को **मारा** ।
किसी ने मेरी कार की खिड़की **तोड़ी** ।

2. Transformation drill
Transform the following sentences into compound verbal formations with पड़ना, appropriately changing the verb in bold in each sentence and omitting any other intensive auxiliary.

The child heard the noise and cried.   The child heard the noise and burst into tears.

शोर सुनकर बच्चा **रोया** ।   शोर सुनकर बच्चा रो पड़ा ।
हवा से काग़ज़ फ़र्श पर **गिरे** ।
तुम क्यों बात-बात पर **रोने लगती हो** ?
पिता जी आज सवेरे जल्दी ही घर से **निकले** ।
उसकी बात सुनकर मैं **हँसा** ।

135

खेलते खेलते बच्चे आपस में **लड़ने लगे** ।

चोर को देखकर वह डर से **चीख़ा** ।

काम ख़त्म करके वह अपने घर की तरफ़ **चला** ।

मेरी बात पूरी होने से पहले ही वह **हँसने लगा** ।

3. Transformation drill

Transform the following sentences into compound verbal formations with उठना, appropriately changing the verb in bold in each sentence and omitting any other intensive auxiliary.

Seeing the lion in front of him, he began to tremble with fear.
शेर को सामने देखकर वह डर से **कांपा** ।

Seeing the lion in front of him he [suddenly] began to tremble with fear.
शेर को सामने देखकर वह डर से कांप उठा ।

मेरे घर में घुसते ही टेलीफ़ोन की घंटी **बजी** ।

फ़िल्म ख़त्म होते ही कमरे में तालियों की आवाज़ **गूँजी** ।

वह भाषण के बीच में अचानक **बोला** ।

घाव पर दवाई लगते ही वह दर्द से **चीख़ा** ।

अचानक पुलिस को आते हुए देख कर वह **चौंका** ।

यह समाचार पढ़कर वह **रोने लगी** ।

अलार्म सुनते ही वह **जाग गया** ।

अपने अच्छे ग्रेड्स देखकर वह ख़ुशी से **नाचने लगी** ।

4. Transformation drill

Transform the following sentences into compound verbal formations with बैठना, appropriately changing the verb in bold in each sentence and omitting any other intensive auxiliary.

Do your work properly; otherwise you will lose [your] job.
ठीक से काम करो वरना नौकरी **खो दोगे** ।

Do your work properly; otherwise you will [foolishly] lose [your] job.
ठीक से काम करो वरना नौकरी खो बैठोगे ।

तुमने यह क्या **किया** ?

वह बात-बात पर अपने पति से **लड़ती है** ।

उसने पूरी **कोशिश की** लेकिन उसे कोई अच्छी नौकरी नहीं मिली ।

पूरी बात सुने बिना पिता जी ने बच्चे को **मारा** ।

इस भूकंप में बहुत लोगों ने अपने घर **खो दिये हैं** ।

इन लोगों ने अपनी भाषा और संस्कृति को **भुला दिया है** ।

सोच समझ कर फ़ैसला करो वरना **ग़लती करोगे** ।

इतने लोगों के बीच उसने यह बात **कह दी** ।

5. <u>Transformation drill</u>

Transform the following sentences into compound verbal formations with रखना, appropriately changing the verb in bold in each sentence and omitting any other intensive auxiliary.

Mother has made all of the arrangements for the party.

माँ ने पार्टी का सब **इंतज़ाम किया है** ।

Mother has made [and kept ready] all of the arrangements for the party.

माँ ने पार्टी का सब इंतज़ाम कर रखा है ।

उस लड़की ने आज सुन्दर साड़ी **पहनी है** ।

मैंने इन पुरानी इमारतों के बारे में बहुत **पढ़ा है** ।

उस अमीर आदमी ने बहुत पैसा **बचाया है** ।

मैंने उसको कुछ दिन के लिये अपनी साइकिल **दी है** ।

उसने अपनी कापी में भारत के बारे में **लिखा है** ।

पुलिसवाले ने चोर को जेल में **बन्द किया है** ।

हमने होटल में कमरा **रिज़र्व कराया है** ।

मैंने उससे **वायदा किया है** कि मैं उसकी मदद करूँगा ।

6. In the following sentences underline the main verb and circle the auxiliary verb. Give the English translation and try to explain in parentheses what subtleties of meaning each individual auxiliary has added to the sentence.

१. तुम क्यों उनको सब कुछ बता बैठी ।

२. मेरी माँ यह समाचार सुनते ही रो उठी ।

३. कार से टक्कर खाकर वह साइकिल से गिर पड़ा ।

४. आपके कुत्ते ने हमारा आज का अख़बार फाड़ डाला ।

५. मैंने अपने दोस्तों के लिये हिन्दुस्तानी खाना पका रखा है ।

६. उसने बहुत शराब पी रखी थी । इसलिये वह अपनी पत्नी से लड़ बैठा ।

७. दुर्घटना देखते ही वह ज़ोर से चीख़ उठा ।

८. हम लोग सुबह को चार बजे घर से चल पड़े ।

९. तुमने ये पेड़ क्यों काट डाले ?

१०. मेरे बच्चों ने रामायण की कहानी सुन रखी है ।

११. मैं सब जगह उस किताब की तलाश कर बैठा लेकिन मुझे वह कहीं नहीं मिली ।

१२. माँ के जाते ही बच्चा रो पड़ा ।

१३. टेलीफ़ोन की घंटी से वह चौंक उठा ।

१४. यह सुनकर सब लोग हँस पड़े ।

१५. पिता जी ने मुझे अपनी पुरानी गाड़ी दे रखी है ।

7. Translation exercise

1. The animals of the forest killed the clever jackal. (Use डालना.)
2. She burst into tears when she heard the news of her friend's death. (Use पड़ना.)
3. The little girl screamed with fear when she saw the big dog. (Use उठना.)
4. He became the owner of the company by cheating others. (Use बैठना.)
5. We have heard a lot about you. (Use रखना.)
6. Those students burned down some shops on Telegraph Avenue. (Use डालना.)
7. He [suddenly] jumped off the moving train. (Use पड़ना.)
8. Upon hearing the news of her brother's engagement, she danced with joy. (Use उठना.)
9. Without thinking, he [foolishly] asked a question at (in) the meeting. (Use बैठना.)
10. I have promised [to] my children to take them to Disneyland. (Use रखना.)

17. CONJUNCTIONS

Conjunctions are used to join words, phrases, or clauses. They can be divided into three general categories, depending on the relationship they establish between the words, phrases, or clauses they link: coordinate conjunctions, subordinate conjunctions, and correlative conjunctions.

A coordinate conjunction joins two or more words, phrases, or independent clauses. In the following examples, the first sentence uses the conjunction और to join two words, while the second sentence uses it to join two clauses, each of which can function independently as a complete sentence.

Examples:
भाई और बहन खेल रहे हैं ।
The brother and sister are playing.

घर जाओ और अपना काम करो ।
Go home and do your work.

A subordinate conjunction introduces a subordinate clause that depends on a main clause to convey a complete thought. In the following examples, the subordinate clauses are introduced by the conjunctions ताकि and क्योंकि.

Examples:
बच्चों को बाहर ले जाओ ताकि मैं आराम कर सकूँ ।
Take the children outside so that I can rest.

वह कल नहीं आ सकेगी क्योंकि उसकी माँ बीमार हैं ।
She won't be able to come tomorrow because her mother is sick.

Correlative conjunctions, like coordinate conjunctions, are also used to join two independent phrases or clauses; however, they always occur in pairs. In the following example या तो and या फिर function as a pair to link two alternatives (like the English "either...or").

Example:

या तो हमारी मदद करो या फिर चुप रहो ।

Either help us or keep quiet.

Coordinate Conjunctions

Coordinate conjunctions such as और, या, लेकिन, न कि, and इसलिये join two or more words, phrases, or independent clauses.

(1) और, तथा, व, and एवं / एवम् **connect** two or more independent words, phrases, or clauses, much like the English "and." While और and तथा can be used to join words, phrases, or clauses, व and एवं/एवम are generally used only to join words or phrases. In colloquial speech and writing, the use of और is most common.

Examples:

वह और उसके दोस्त रोज़ कसरत करते हैं ।

He and his friends exercise every day.

नेताओं तथा समाज सेवकों को मिलकर काम करना चाहिये ।

Politicians and social workers should work together.

पति व पत्नी दोनों ही सुशिक्षित तथा सुसंस्कृत हैं ।

Husband and wife, both are well-educated and cultured.

सूर्योदय हुआ और चिड़ियाँ चहकने लगीं ।

The sun rose and the birds began to chirp.

उसने भाषण दिया तथा हमारे प्रश्नों के उत्तर भी दिये ।

He gave a speech and also answered our questions.

सब शिक्षक एवं छात्र वहाँ उपस्थित थे ।

All teachers and students were present there.

राष्ट्रपति व प्रधान मंत्री दोनों सम्मेलन में आये ।

Both the President and the Prime Minister came to the assembly.

(2) The Hindi conjunctions या, अथवा, and sometimes कि are used to **separate and/or distinguish** two or more alternative words, phrases, or ideas, much like the English conjunction "or."

Examples:

आज हम हिन्दुस्तानी या अफ़गानी खाना खा सकते हैं ।

Today we can eat Indian or Afghani food.

आपने पहले प्रेमचंद की कहानियाँ पढ़ीं अथवा उनके उपन्यास ?

Did you read Premchand's stories first or his novels?

तुम अभी यह काम करोगी कि / या बाद में ?

Will you do this work right now or later?

वह छात्र आज क्लास आया कि / या नहीं ?

Did that student come to class today or not?

Of these conjunctions, या is the most frequently used, while अथवा is more formal. Note also that कि is generally used to introduce subordinate clauses and is translated as "that"; however, here it is used as a coordinate conjunction that means "or." This particular use of कि generally occurs in questions and is found only in colloquial speech.

(3) Conjunctions in Hindi that join two clauses containing **contrasting** ideas include पर, परन्तु, किन्तु, मगर, and लेकिन (much like the English "but").

Examples:

मैं आपके साथ जाना चाहती हूँ लेकिन आज मुझे फ़ुरसत नहीं है ।

I want to go with you, but I am not free today.

दादाजी को मिठाइयाँ बहुत पसन्द हैं मगर मधुमेह की बिमारी के कारण वे खा नहीं सकते ।

Dadaji likes sweets a lot, but because of [his] diabetes he cannot eat them.

मैं वे जूते ख़रीदना चाहती हूँ पर मेरे पास काफ़ी पैसे नहीं हैं ।
I want to buy those shoes, but I don't have enough money.

वह प्रतीक्षा करती रही परन्तु उसका प्रेमी नहीं आया ।
She kept waiting, but her beloved didn't come.

उसने बहुत प्रयत्न किया किन्तु सफलता न मिली ।
He tried very hard, but he didn't succeed.

Note that while all of these conjunctions are generally interchangeable, परन्तु and किन्तु are less common in colloquial speech.

(4) Another way to join two contrasting words or ideas in Hindi is by using the conjunction "न कि," which denotes "rather than" or "not."

Example:
मुझे चाय चाहिये न कि काॅफ़ी ।
I need tea, not (rather than) coffee.

(5) The Hindi conjunctions इसलिए, सो, अतएव, and अतः are used to connect two ideas where the second idea is the result of the first. These correspond to the English conjunctions "so" and "therefore" but can also be translated as "for this reason." Although these four conjunctions can be used interchangeably, इसलिए is the most common in colloquial speech.

Examples:
उसके पास पैसा नहीं था इसलिए उसको कालिज छोड़ना पड़ा ।
He didn't have money, so (for this reason) he had to leave college.

उसकी माँ बीमार थीं सो वह आज क्लास नहीं आ सका ।
His mother was ill, so he couldn't come to class today.

परीक्षाएँ निकट हैं अतएव / अतः हमें परिश्रम करना पड़ेगा ।
Exams are near; therefore we will have to work hard.

Subordinate Conjunctions

A subordinate conjunction introduces a subordinate clause, which, as its name indicates, is subordinate to or dependent on a main clause to convey a complete thought. क्योंकि *because*, कि *that*, ताकि *so that*, and वरना *otherwise* are a few examples of subordinate conjunctions in Hindi.

(1) क्योंकि / चूँकि / इसलिये कि are used to convey a cause or a reason and can be translated into English as "because."

Examples:
तुम ही उसे समझा सकते हो क्योंकि वह मेरी बात कभी नहीं मानता ।
Only you can explain it to him because he never listens to what I say.

प्रोफ़ेसर शर्मा कल पढ़ाने नहीं आयेंगे इसलिये कि उन्हें मुंबई कॉनफ़्रेन्स में जाना है ।
Professor Sharma won't come to teach tomorrow because he has to go to a conference in Mumbai.

चूँकि मैं जल्दी आई इसलिये मुझे काफ़ी देर इंतज़ार करना पड़ा ।
I had to wait for quite awhile because I came early (lit., *Because I came early, for this reason I had to wait for quite awhile.*)

क्योंकि, चूँकि, and इसलिये कि all introduce a subordinate clause that gives a reason or explanation for some action or event. When the subordinate clause follows the main clause of the sentence, as in the first two examples above, क्योंकि and इसलिये कि (rather than चूँकि) are used; however, when the subordinate clause precedes the main clause, चूँकि is used, and in such cases, the main clause should be introduced with one of the following phrases: इसलिये, इस कारण से, or इस वजह से (see the third example above).

(2) ताकि and जिससे (कि) introduce a subordinate clause that offers an explanation or reason for why the action of the main clause is, was, will be, or must be carried out. These subordinate conjunctions correspond to the English phrase "so that." Note that the subordinate clause that they introduce follows the main clause and must always be in the subjunctive mood. (Note that ताकि and जिससे (कि) are also covered in Chapter 19.)

Examples:

मुझे उसका फ़ोन नंबर दो ताकि मैं स्वयं उससे बात कर सकूँ।

Give me his phone number so that I can talk to him myself.

नानाजी ने उन ग़रीब बच्चों को कुछ पैसा दिया जिससे (कि) वे नये कपड़े ख़रीद सकें।

Grandfather gave those poor children some money so that they could buy new clothes.

(3) यानी and अर्थात् introduce a subordinate clause that further clarifies, explains, or paraphrases a word or an idea that has already been mentioned. They can be translated in English as "that is" or "in other words."

Examples:

मुझे छायावादी कवि यानी / अर्थात् जयशंकर प्रसाद, निराला, सुमित्रानन्दन पंत और महादेवी वर्मा बहुत पसन्द हैं।

I like Chayavadi poets a lot; that is, I like Jaishankar Prasad, Nirala, Sumitranandan Pant, and Mahadevi Varma [a lot].

बच्चों को आग के ख़तरों के बारे में बताना चाहिये यानी उन्हें समझाना चाहिये कि आग से घर भी जल सकता है।

Children should be told about the dangers of fire; in other words, it should be explained to them that fire can even burn the house down.

(4) मानो / मानों and जैसे *as if/as though* introduce a subordinate clause that uses a comparative word or phrase to refer back to the main clause. (Note that मानो/मानों and जैसे are also covered in Chapter 19.)

Examples:

वह खिड़की के पास ऐसे खड़ी थी मानो किसी का इंतज़ार कर रही हो।

She was standing by the window [in such a way] as if she was waiting for someone.

उनका घर इतना बड़ा है मानों महल हो।

Their house is as big as a palace (lit., *Their house is so big, as if it were a palace*).

वह इस तरह कुरसी पर बैठा था जैसे वही कम्पनी का मालिक हो ।

He was sitting on the chair [in such a way] as though he were the owner of the company.

Note that the verb in clauses introduced by मानो / मानों and जैसे is always in the subjunctive mood, and the main clause generally contains words like ऐसा, ऐसे, इतना, इतने, and इस तरह, which signal that some sort of comparative phrase will follow.

(5) नहीं तो, अन्यथा, and वरना *otherwise, or else* are used to introduce a subordinate clause that indicates the consequences of not carrying out the activity of the main clause. Often, such sentences are used as a warning.

Examples:
पुलिस को सच सच बता दो नहीं तो जेल जाओगे ।
Tell the truth to the police or else you will go to jail.

अपना व्यवहार सुधारो वरना मैं सदा के लिए चली जाऊँगी ।
Improve your behavior or else I'll leave you (go away) forever.

मेहरबानी करके मुझे यह नौकरी दे दीजिये वरना मेरे बच्चे भूखे मर जाएँगे ।
Kindly give me this job or else my children will die of hunger.

अच्छा हुआ कि आप वहाँ समय पर पहुँच गए अन्यथा मंत्री जी से भेंट न होती ।
It's a good thing that you arrived there on time; otherwise you wouldn't have met the minister.

(6) The conjunction कि, like the English "that," can introduce a wide variety of subordinate clauses expressing a thought, idea, feeling, opinion, possibility, etc. A subordinate clause introduced by कि serves as the object of a verb in the main clause. These verbs in the main clause range from verbs of saying, thinking, and knowing, like कहना, बताना, सोचना, मालूम होना, and जानना, to verbs expressing emotions, desires, hopes, opinions, and so forth, like ख़ुशी होना, दुख होना, चाहना, आशा / उम्मीद होना, राय होना, (X के लिये) ज़रूरी होना, and many more.

Examples:

गांधी जी ने कहा था कि अहिंसा सबसे शक्तिशाली शस्त्र है ।
Gandhiji said that non-violence is the most powerful weapon of all.

वह सोचता है कि उसे सब कुछ मालूम है ।
He thinks that he knows everything.

मैं जानती हूँ कि यह काम उसके लिए मुश्किल होगा ।
I know that this work will be difficult for him.

जनता चाहती है कि सरकार बच्चों की शिक्षा के लिए और पैसा दे ।
The public wants the government to give more money for children's education. (lit., *The public wants that the government give more money for children's education.*)

मुझे आशा / उम्मीद है कि सोनिया को जल्दी ही अमरीका आने का वीसा मिल जाएगा ।
I hope that Sonia will get her visa to come to America soon.

आप के लिए यह ज़रूरी है कि रोज़ सरोद बजाने का अभ्यास करें ।
It is necessary for you to practice playing the sarod every day.

सुनीता की राय है कि शाकाहारी खाना हमारी सेहत के लिए सबसे अच्छा है ।
It is Sunita's opinion that vegetarian food is the best for our health.

The above sentences represent just a few of the numerous instances where कि can function like the English "that." Additionally, कि can also be used to replace the Hindi जब *when* in a subordinate clause.

Example:

उनका भाषण शुरू होने ही वाला था कि (जब) बारिश होने लगी ।
His speech was just about to start when it began to rain.

Note, however, that while both कि and जब can be used to indicate sequential actions, कि conveys a greater sense of immediacy and usually introduces an action that is sudden or unexpected. Also, कि introduces a subordinate clause that must follow the main clause; thus, unlike जब, कि cannot occur at the beginning of a sentence. (जब will be further discussed as part of the correlative pair जब...तब in the following section.)

Examples:
मैं खाना खाने ही वाला था कि (जब) आपका फ़ोन आया ।
I was just about to eat when you called me.

जब आपका फ़ोन आया तब मैं खाना खाने ही वाला था ।
I was just about to eat when you called me.

Note also that कि, as previously mentioned, can also be used colloquially as a coordinate conjunction that means "or." Thus:

वह कल आयेगा कि परसों ?
Will he come tomorrow or the day after tomorrow?

Correlative Conjunctions

Like coordinate conjunctions, correlative conjunctions can be used to **link** two independent phrases or clauses. Correlative conjunctions, however, **must function as a pair** to convey a complete thought. For example, या (तो)...या (फिर) *either...or*; न...न *neither...nor*; चाहे...चाहे/या *whether...or*; X (ही) नहीं...बल्कि Y (भी) *not (only) X...but also/rather Y.*

(1) या (तो)...या (फिर) *either...or*

Examples:
मेरा बेटा या तो डॉक्टर बनेगा या इंजीनियर ।
My son will become either a doctor or an engineer.

या तो तुम मेरी दवाई लाओ या फिर अपने भैया को भेजो ।
Either you get my medicine or send your brother [to get it].

(2) न...न *neither...nor*

Examples:

न वह स्वयम् आया न उसने हमें अपना कोई समाचार भेजा ।
He neither came himself, nor did he send us any news about himself.

न उसने अपनी ग़लती मानी न माफ़ी माँगी ।
He neither accepted his mistake, nor did he ask for forgiveness.

(3) चाहे...चाहे / या *whether...or*

Examples:

मुझे मदद चाहिये चाहे आप मेरी मदद करें चाहे आपका भाई ।
I need help, whether you help me or your brother helps me.

मुझे ज़ेवर पसन्द नहीं हैं चाहे वे सोने के हों या चाँदी के ।
I don't like jewelry, whether it is made of gold or silver.

चाहे सुबह हो या शाम मैं उसके मुँह में हमेशा सिगरेट देखती हूँ ।
Whether it is morning or evening, I always see a cigarette in his mouth.

Notes
(a) The verb in the चाहे clause will always be in the subjunctive.
(b) Sometimes क्या... क्या can also be used colloquially to convey *whether...or.*

Example:

क्या देश क्या विदेश, सब जगह हमें मेहनत करनी पड़ती है ।
Whether [we are in] our own country or abroad, we have to work hard everywhere.

(4) चाहे...(लेकिन / पर / फिर भी / तो भी) *regardless...still (but, nonetheless); no matter how...still (but); even if...still (but)*

149

Examples:

चाहे आप कितनी ही कोशिश (क्यों न) करें (पर / फिर भी / तो भी) सच छिपा नहीं सकते ।

No matter (regardless of) how much you try, you still can't hide the truth.

चाहे उसने कुछ भी न किया हो (लेकिन / फिर भी) लोग उसी पर शक करते हैं ।

Even if he didn't do anything, (but/nonetheless/still) people suspect only him.

Note again that the verb in the चाहे clause will always be in the subjunctive.

(5) X (ही) नहीं...बल्कि Y (भी) *not (only) X…, but also/rather Y*

Examples:

मैंने मोहन राकेश का यह नाटक पढ़ा ही नहीं बल्कि उसको स्टेज पर भी देखा है ।

I have not only read this play by Mohan Rakesh, but I have also seen it on stage.

उसने अपना काम ख़त्म करने की कोशिश ही नहीं की बल्कि वह सीधे फ़िल्म देखने चला गया ।

He didn't even try to finish his work, but rather he went straight to see a movie.

आपको बच्चों को ज़्यादा डाँटना नहीं चाहिये बल्कि उनको समझाना चाहिये ।

You should not scold children too much; rather you should explain [things] to them.

Note: As seen in the above examples, बल्कि is generally used after a clause that contains a negative statement.

(6) हालाँकि...फिर भी / तो भी / लेकिन or यद्यपि...तथापि *although/even though…still/nonetheless/but*

Examples:

हालाँकि वह विदेशी है फिर भी उसे हमारे देश की राजनीति में दिलचस्पी है ।

Although he is a foreigner, he (nonetheless) is interested in the politics of our country.

हालाँकि उसने सब कुछ देखा था तो भी उसने पुलिस को कुछ नहीं बताया ।
Even though he saw everything, he still told the police nothing.

हालाँकि लोग उसे कंजूस कहते हैं लेकिन मैं जानती हूँ कि वह बहुत उदार है ।
Although people call him a miser, (nonetheless) I know that he is very generous.

यद्यपि उनके पास बहुत धन है तथापि / फिर भी वे सुखी नहीं हैं ।
Even though they have a lot of money, they are still not happy.

यद्यपि मुझे ये नेता बहुत पसन्द हैं तथापि मैं इनकी इस नीति से सहमत नहीं हूँ ।
Although I like this leader a lot, I still don't agree with this policy of his.

(7) यदि / अगर...तो *if...then*

Examples:
अगर आप को जल्दी न हो तो मेरे घर चलिये ।
If you are not in a hurry, (then) please come to my house.

यदि मैं आज न आ सकूँ तो क्या हम कल मिल सकते हैं ?
If I can't come today, (then) can we meet tomorrow?

अगर वह मेरी बात मानता तो वह आज सफल आदमी होता ।
If he had listened to me, (then) he would be a successful man today.

Note: The correlative conjunctions यदि...तो and अगर...तो are discussed in detail in Chapter 20 of this book, as well as in *Introduction to Hindi Grammar*.

(8) The relative-correlative pairs discussed in detail in *Introduction to Hindi Grammar* (Chapter 42) can also be categorized as correlative conjunctions since they also work in pairs to link two clauses. Relative-correlative pairs consist of two elements: the first element is generally a relative pronoun, adjective, or adverb that is used only in conjunction with a second element, which in such sentences functions as a correlative pronoun, adjective, or adverb. Note that this second element can also function independently

outside of the pair. Examples of such pairs include जो...वह *who/what/which...he/she/they/that*; जहाँ...वहाँ *where...there*; जिधर...उधर *in which direction...in that direction*; जैसा...वैसा *of which kind...of that kind*; जैसे...वैसे *in which manner...in that manner*; जितना...उतना *as much...that much*; and जब...तब *when...then*.

Examples:

जो आपने कहा, वह वाक़ई सच है ।
What you said (that) is really true.

जब उसने मुझे देखा, तो वह मुस्कुराई ।
When she saw me, (then) she smiled.

There are a few other such relative-correlative pairs in addition to the ones covered in *Introduction to Hindi Grammar*, including ज्यों ज्यों...त्यों त्यों or जैसे जैसे...वैसे वैसे *as (gradually)...so*; जिस प्रकार का...उस प्रकार का or जिस तरह का...उस तरह का *of which kind...of that kind*; जिस प्रकार से...उस प्रकार से or जिस तरह से...उस तरह से *in which manner...in that manner*; and जैसे ही...(वैसे ही) or ज्यों ही...(त्यों ही) *as soon as...(then)*.

Examples:

ज्यों ज्यों आकाश में बादल घिरने लगे, (त्यों त्यों) अंधेरा होने लगा ।
As the clouds [gradually] gathered in the sky, (so) it began to grow dark.

जैसे जैसे उसकी आमदनी बढ़ती गई (वैसे वैसे) उसका घमंड बढ़ने लगा ।
As his income [gradually] grew, (so) his arrogance began to increase.

जिस प्रकार की कसीदाकारी लखनऊ में होती है, उस प्रकार की और कहीं नहीं होती ।
The kind of embroidery done in Lucknow (that kind) is not done anywhere else.

जिस तरह (से) वह नाचती है, उस तरह (से) मैं भी नाचना चाहती हूँ ।
I also want to dance the way she dances.

जैसे ही मैं खाने बैठी, (वैसे ही) उसका फ़ोन आ गया ।

As soon as I sat down to eat, (then) I got his phone call.

ज्यों ही नाटक शुरू हुआ, (त्यों ही) बच्चा रोने लगा ।

As soon as the play began, the child began to cry.

Note that a list of common conjunctions has been provided for reference in Appendix IV.

Conjunctions: Exercises

1. Transformation drill

I should work hard because exams are near.
मुझे मेहनत करनी चाहिये क्योंकि परीक्षाएँ पास हैं ।

Because exams are near, [therefore] I should work hard.
चूँकि परीक्षाएँ पास हैं इसलिये मुझे मेहनत करनी चाहिये ।

वह घर देर से आया क्योंकि उसको दफ़्तर में बहुत काम था ।
उसने बहुत संतरे ख़रीदे क्योंकि वे काफ़ी सस्ते थे ।
वह डॉक्टर के पास जायेगा क्योंकि उसका बच्चा बीमार है ।
मैं आज खाना नहीं पका सकती क्योंकि मैं बहुत थकी हूँ ।
हमें जल्दी चलना चाहिये क्योंकि बारिश होनेवाली है ।
माँ ने बहुत मिठाइयाँ बनाईं क्योंकि कल मेरा जन्म-दिन था ।
मैं अपना कमरा साफ़ करूँगी क्योंकि मेहमान आनेवाले हैं ।

2. Complete the following sentences

I miss my country -- that is, _____ -- a lot.
मुझे अपना देश यानी _____ बहुत याद आता है ।

I miss my country -- that is, India -- a lot.
मुझे अपना देश यानी भारत बहुत याद आता है ।

मैं पुस्तकालय में यानी _____ पढ़ूँगी ।
क्या आप इस कविता का अर्थ यानी _____ समझे ?
क्या उसका व्यवसाय यानी _____ अच्छा चल रहा है ?
आप का कल का कार्यक्रम यानी _____ क्या है ?
उसको यह फल यानी _____ बहुत पसन्द है ।
वह परीक्षा यानी _____ की तैयारी कर रहा है ।

यह विश्वविद्यालय यानी _____ बहुत मशहूर है ।
मुझे यह भाषा यानी _____ बहुत आसान लगती है ।

3. Transformation drill

Come on, let's go home quickly; otherwise Mother will be angry.
चलो, जल्दी घर चलो नहीं तो माँ नाराज़ होंगी ।

Come on, let's go home quickly; otherwise Mother will be angry.
चलो, जल्दी घर चलो वरना माँ नाराज़ होंगी ।

मेरी बात मानो नहीं तो बाद में पछताओगे ।

यह कागज़ संभाल कर रखो नहीं तो खो जाएगा ।

खाना अन्दर रखो नहीं तो ख़राब हो जाएगा ।

पौधों को पानी दो नहीं तो सूख जाएँगे ।

भागो नहीं तो तुम्हारी बस छूट जाएगी ।

मुझे सच सच बताओ नहीं तो हमारा रिश्ता टूट जाएगा ।

अच्छा हुआ कि आप खुद वहाँ गये नहीं तो आपका काम न होता ।

छाता ले जाओ नहीं तो बारिश में भीग जाओगे ।

4. Complete the following sentences

It's my opinion that...
मेरी राय है कि ...

It's my opinion that you all should see India.
मेरी राय है कि आप सब को भारत देखना चाहिये ।

शिक्षक कहते हैं कि...

उसने हमें बताया कि...

माँ को ख़ुशी है कि...

हमें मालूम है कि...

तुम जानते हो कि...

उनको दुख है कि...
जनता चाहती है कि...
मुझे आशा / उम्मीद है कि...
छात्रों के लिये यह ज़रूरी है कि...
मेरा ख़याल है कि...

5. Complete the following sentences

Either you cook the food or...
या तो तुम खाना पकाओ या (फिर)...

Either you cook the food or wash the dishes.
या तो तुम खाना पकाओ या (फिर) बर्तन साफ़ करो ।

या तो वह स्वयम् आएगा या...
या तो कॉलिज जाओ या...
हम आज या तो फ़िल्म देखेंगे या...
या तो आराम करो या...
या तो हम दोपहर को आएँगे या...
या तो मैं जापान पढ़ने जाऊँगी या...
या तो मैं कहानी सुनाऊँगी या...
या तो ख़ुद मंत्री जी से मिलने जाओ या...

6. Complete the following sentences

He neither cleaned the house himself nor...
न उसने स्वयम् घर साफ़ किया न...

He neither cleaned the house himself nor did he let his wife clean it.
न उसने स्वयम् घर साफ़ किया न अपनी पत्नी को करने दिया ।

न मुझे चाय पसंद है न...

न मुझे सितार बजाना आता है न...

न उसने स्वयम् फ़ोन किया न...

न उसने अपने भाई की मदद की न...

न वह पार्टी में नाची न...

उसका कुरता न लाल था न...

भारत जाने से पहले न उसने हिन्दी सीखी न...

क्लास के बाद न वह घर गया न...

7. Complete the following sentences

I need some money, whether you give [it to me] or…
मुझे कुछ पैसा चाहिये चाहे आप दें चाहे/या...

I need some money, whether you give [it to me] or Nita [does].
मुझे कुछ पैसा चाहिये चाहे आप दें चाहे नीता ।

सब बच्चों को स्कूल जाना चाहिये चाहे लड़के हों चाहे...

तुम्हें माँ को फ़ोन करना चाहिये चाहे आज करो चाहे...

वह हर वक़्त पढ़ता रहता है चाहे सुबह हो चाहे...

वह सबको एक-सा समझता है चाहे अमीर हो चाहे...

मैं वह घर ख़रीदना चाहती हूँ चाहे महँगा हो चाहे...

हमें समाज सेवा करनी चाहिये चाहे हम देश में हों चाहे...

वह हर त्यौहार पर घर जाती है चाहे होली हो चाहे...

उसको जानवर रखना पसन्द है चाहे बिल्ली हो चाहे...

8. Transformation drill

You are rich. You cannot buy everything.
आप अमीर हैं । आप सब कुछ नहीं ख़रीद सकते ।

No matter (regardless of) how rich you may be, you cannot buy everything.
चाहे आप कितने ही अमीर (क्यों न) हों (फिर भी/ तो भी) आप सब कुछ नहीं ख़रीद सकते ।

वह थका है । वह दिन में आराम नहीं करता ।

आप अच्छी सलाह देंगे । वह नहीं मानेगा ।

वह कोशिश करेगा । वह समय पर वहाँ नहीं पहुँच पाएगा ।

खाना अच्छा है । मैं आज नहीं खाऊँगी ।

वह तेज़ दौड़ेगा । वह यह बस नहीं पकड़ सकेगा ।

काम आसान है । उसको मन लगाकर करना चाहिये ।

वह मोटी हो गई है । वह मिठाई खाना नहीं छोड़ेगी ।

9. Transformation drill

He is fond of eating food. He is fond of cooking.
उसको खाने का शौक़ है । उसको पकाने का शौक़ है ।

He is not only fond of eating food, but he is also fond of cooking.
उसको खाने का ही शौक़ नहीं है बल्कि (उसको) पकाने का भी शौक़ है ।

वह अमीर है । वह उदार है ।

वह झूठ बोलता है । वह चोरी करता है ।

वह सितार बजाता है । वह गाता है ।

वह होशियार है । वह मेहनती है ।

मैं क्रिकेट खेलता हूँ । मैं बास्केटबॉल खेलता हूँ ।

वह हिन्दी पढ़ सकता है । वह उर्दू पढ़ सकता है ।

उसने अपना काम ख़त्म किया । उसने मेरी मदद की ।

उसने विदेश में धन कमाया । उसने नाम कमाया ।

10. Transformation drill

He is Indian. He doesn't like spicy food.
वह भारतीय है । उसको मसालेवाला खाना नहीं पसन्द है ।

Although he is Indian, (nonetheless) he doesn't like spicy food.
हालाँकि वह भारतीय है फिर भी उसको मसालेवाला खाना नहीं पसन्द है ।

वह बी॰ ए॰ पास है । उसको नौकरी नहीं मिली ।

वह बीमार है । वह आराम नहीं करती ।

बाहर बारिश होने लगी थी । पिताजी घूमने गये ।

वह अमरीकन है । उसको हिन्दुस्तानी फ़िल्में पसन्द हैं ।

मौसम बहुत ख़राब था । वह दोस्त से मिलने गया ।

पहाड़ बहुत ऊँचा था । वे उस पर चढ़े ।

वह बहुत अमीर है । वह किसी ग़रीब की मदद नहीं करता ।

डॉक्टर ने उसे मना किया । वह सिगरेट पीता रहता है ।

11. Transformation drill

The demand for petrol kept on increasing. The price of petrol kept on rising.
पैट्रोल की माँग बढ़ती गई । पैट्रोल का दाम बढ़ता गया ।

As the demand for petrol [gradually] kept on increasing, (so) its price kept on rising.
जैसे जैसे पैट्रोल की माँग बढ़ती गई (वैसे वैसे) उसका दाम बढ़ता गया ।

बच्चे बड़े होते जाते हैं । वे समझदार होते जाते हैं ।

मंज़िल नज़दीक आती गई । हमारी हिम्मत बढ़ती गई ।

सूरज डूबता गया । अन्धेरा होता गया ।

वह बड़ी होती गई । उसकी सुन्दरता बढ़ती गई ।

शिक्षा फैलती गई । देश की उन्नति होती गई ।

उसकी उम्र बढ़ती गई । उसकी याददाश्त कम होती गई ।

12. Transformation drill

The rain kept on falling. The water in the river kept on rising.
बारिश होती गई । नदी में पानी बढ़ता गया ।

As the rain [gradually] kept on falling, (so) the water in the river kept on rising.
ज्यों ज्यों बारिश होती गई (त्यों त्यों) नदी में पानी बढ़ता गया ।

समय बीतता जाता है । ज़माना बदलता जाता है ।

उसकी आयु बढ़ती गई । उसकी आँखें कमज़ोर होती गईं ।

हवा चलने लगी । पत्तियाँ बिखरने लगीं ।

शादी में मेहमान आने लगे । घर में रौनक बढ़ने लगी ।

देश में प्रगति होती गई । देश में ग़रीबी घटती गई ।

उसकी शोहरत फैलती गई । उसकी किताबों की माँग बढ़ने लगी ।

13. <u>Transformation drill</u>

She came home. She called her friend.
वह घर आई । उसने दोस्त को फ़ोन किया ।

As soon as she came home, she called her friend.
जैसे ही / ज्यों ही वह घर आई (वैसे ही / त्यों ही) उसने दोस्त को फ़ोन किया ।

वह दफ़्तर से निकली । बारिश होने लगी ।

पिताजी ने यह बात सुनी । वे ग़ुस्सा करने लगे ।

ट्रेन आई । लोग उसकी तरफ़ दौड़े ।

मैं पढ़ने बैठी । मेरा बच्चा रोने लगा ।

मुझे उसका समाचार मिलेगा । मैं तुम्हें बताऊँगी ।

उसको नौकरी मिली । उसने महँगी गाड़ी ख़रीदी ।

तुम्हारी शादी हुई । तुम हम सब दोस्तों को भूल गये ।

वह सोलह साल की हुई । उसने कार चलानी शुरू की ।

14. <u>Translation exercise</u>

1. I know he is very busy (in) writing his book these days.
2. He neither slept himself, nor did he let anyone else sleep.
3. Either play quietly or play outside.
4. My best friend -- that is, Sheila -- will definitely come to my graduation.
5. No matter how much it rains, I'll definitely go to the party tonight.
6. Although she was sick, she still kept on working.
7. You people must finish this work by tomorrow, whether it takes five hours or six [hours].

8. We will not only go to London, but we will also go to Paris.
9. You tell the manager about it; otherwise I will have to (will be forced to) tell him.
10. As the wedding day [gradually] came closer, her nervousness [gradually] increased.
11. As soon as he came towards me, I got up and walked away.
12. Send the application for this job soon, because you won't get an opportunity like this again.

18. CAUSATIVE VERBS

Hindi verbs can often be divided into three phonetically and semantically related categories: intransitive verbs, transitive verbs, and causative verbs. We have thus far distinguished between intransitive and transitive verbs. As we have learned, intransitive verbs are those that cannot take a direct object (e.g., "The window opened"). Transitive verbs, on the other hand, can take a direct object or both a direct and an indirect object (e.g., "I opened the window" or "I gave the book to him"). The third category is causative verbs. Unlike intransitive and transitive verbs, where the subject of the sentence is directly involved in the activity of the verb, causative verbs express an action that is not carried out by the subject of the sentence himself/herself, but he/she "causes" it to be carried out by a third party (an external agent). For example, "I had him (caused him to) open the window."

Examples:

Intransitive verbs
(subject + intransitive verb)

यह घर पिछले साल बना ।   *This house was built last year.*

Transitive verbs
(subject + direct and/or indirect object + transitive verb)

मैंने पिछले साल अपना घर बनाया ।   *I built my house last year.*

                                     (i.e., I built my house myself.)

Causative verbs
(subject + external agent + direct and/or indirect object + causative verb)

मैंने पिछले साल उनसे अपना घर बनवाया ।

Last year I had them build my house. (i.e., I caused someone else to build my house.)

Note that all causative verbs are transitive (though not all transitive verbs are causative), and their verb stems generally have the –वा ending. As seen in the third example, when the external agent is mentioned, he/she is always marked by the postposition से.

Often the external agent is not mentioned, and the very fact that the verb is in a causative form (–वा) indicates that the subject does not carry out the action himself/herself but causes it to be carried out by a third party.

Thus:

मैंने पिछले साल अपना घर बनवाया ।   *Last year I had my house built.*

Formation

Phonetically and semantically related verbs, which are divided into three categories (intransitive, transitive, and causative), follow several general patterns of formation.

(1) In Hindi, transitive verbs are often formed by adding आ to an intransitive verb stem, while causative verbs are formed by adding वा to an intransitive verb stem.

Examples:

Intransitive	Transitive	Causative
बनना to be made	बनाना to make	बनवाना to cause to make/ to have an external agent make
बचना to be saved	बचाना to save	बचवाना to cause to save/to have an external agent save
उठना to rise, to get up	उठाना to raise, to lift	उठवाना to cause to raise/lift, to have an external agent raise/lift
उगना to sprout, to grow	उगाना to sprout or grow something (e.g., crops)	उगवाना to cause to sprout or grow (crops)/ to have an external agent sprout or grow (crops)
जलना to burn/be burned	जलाना to burn something	जलवाना to cause to burn/to have an external agent burn something
पकना to be cooked	पकाना to cook	पकवाना to cause to cook/ to have an external agent cook
चलना to move, to go	चलाना to drive, to move someone or something	चलवाना to cause to drive or move/to have an external agent drive/move someone or something

बजना to be played (music)	बजाना to play (a musical instrument)	बजवाना to cause to play/to have an external agent play (a musical instrument)
लगना to be applied	लगाना to apply	लगवाना to cause to apply/to have an external agent apply

(2) In some cases, in addition to adding आ (for transitive verbs) and वा (for causative verbs) to an intransitive verb stem, if there is a long vowel in the preceding syllable of the intransitive verb stem, it is shortened or changed according to the following rules:

आ	becomes	अ
ई, ए or ऐ	becomes	इ
ऊ or ओ	becomes	उ

Examples:

Intransitive	Transitive	Causative
जागना to wake up	जगाना to wake (someone) up	जगवाना to have an external agent wake someone up
भीगना to get wet	भिगाना to make someone or something wet	भिगवाना to have an external agent make someone or something wet
लेटना to lie down	लिटाना to lay someone or something down	लिटवाना to have an external agent lay someone or something down
बैठना to sit down	बिठाना to seat someone	बिठवाना to have someone seated
घूमना to wander around	घुमाना to show someone around	घुमवाना to have someone shown around
रोना to weep, to cry	रुलाना to make someone weep or cry	रुलवाना to have an external agent make someone weep or cry

Note that in the last example (रोना), the consonant ल is also inserted before adding आ (for transitive verbs) and वा (for causative verbs).

(3) In contrast to the previous pattern, some transitive verbs are formed by changing the initial or medial short vowels of the intransitive verb stems. However, the causative verbs are still formed by simply adding वा to the intransitive verb stem. Thus, for transitive verbs, the changes are as follows:

अ	becomes	आ
इ	becomes	ई or ए
उ	becomes	ऊ or ओ

Examples:

Intransitive	Transitive	Causative
संभलना to be careful	संभालना to take care of someone or something	संभलवाना to have an external agent take care of someone or something
निकलना to get out	निकालना to take someone or something out	निकलवाना to have an external agent take someone or something out
उतरना to get down	उतारना to take someone or something down	उतरवाना to have an external agent take someone or something down
कटना to be cut	काटना to cut	कटाना / कटवाना to have an external agent cut
पिटना to be beaten	पीटना to beat	पिटवाना to have an external agent beat
घिरना to be surrounded	घेरना to surround	घिरवाना to have an external agent surround
लुटना to be robbed	लूटना to rob	लुटवाना to have an external agent rob
रुकना to be stopped	रोकना to stop someone or something	रुकवाना to have an external agent stop someone or something
खुलना to be opened	खोलना to open	खुलवाना to have an external agent open
धुलना to be washed	धोना to wash	धुलाना / धुलवाना to have an external agent wash

165

(4) Some sets also show consonantal changes. If the verb stem is only one syllable, ending in a long vowel, then in addition to the vowel changes discussed above, ल is also inserted before adding आ (for transitive verbs) and वा (for causative verbs).

Examples:

Intransitive	Transitive	Causative
सोना to sleep	सुलाना to put someone to sleep	सुलवाना to have an external agent put someone to sleep
रोना to weep, to cry	रुलाना to make someone weep or cry	रुलवाना to have an external agent make someone weep or cry

(5) Other consonantal changes that occur often take place when an intransitive verb stem ends with ट (and sometimes क). Note that such consonantal changes occur in addition to the vowel changes discussed above.

Example:

Intransitive	Transitive	Causative
टूटना to break	तोड़ना to break something	तुड़वाना / तुड़ाना to have an external agent break something
छूटना to be free, to be released	छोड़ना to let go, to set someone or something free	छुड़वाना / छुड़ाना to have an external agent set someone or something free
फूटना to burst, to break, to crack	फोड़ना to burst, break, or crack something	फुड़वाना to have an external agent burst, break, or crack something
फटना to be torn	फाड़ना to tear, to rip	फड़वाना / फटवाना to have an external agent tear something
बिकना to be sold	बेचना to sell	बिकवाना to have an external agent sell

Note that in the first three examples above a vowel change from "ऊ" to "ओ" occurs in addition to the consonantal changes being made.

(6) Some verbs in Hindi do not have an intransitive verb form. Such verbs may still have three separate forms: transitive, first causative, and second causative. In such sets, the first causative is used when the subject of the sentence (the "causer") is directly involved in the action of the verb, while in the second causative the subject of the sentence (the "causer") is *not* directly involved in the action but gets some external agent to perform the action. Thus, a transitive verb such as "to study/learn" will have as its first causative "to teach" (to cause to learn) and as its second causative "to have someone taught (by an external agent)." Thus:

हम हिन्दी पढ़ते हैं ।	*We study Hindi.*
शर्मा जी हमें हिन्दी पढ़ाते हैं ।	*Mr. Sharma teaches us Hindi.*
पिताजी हमें शर्मा जी से हिन्दी पढ़वाते हैं ।	*Father has Mr. Sharma teach us Hindi.*

Transitive	First Causative	Second Causative
सुनना to listen	सुनाना to tell, to relate, to recite (to cause to listen)	सुनवाना to have an external agent tell, relate, or recite
देखना to see	दिखाना to show (to cause to see)	दिखवाना to have an external agent show
सीखना to learn	सिखाना to teach (to cause to learn)	सिखवाना to have an external agent teach
पढ़ना to study	पढ़ाना to teach (to cause to learn)	पढ़वाना to have an external agent teach
समझना to understand	समझाना to explain (to cause to understand)	समझवाना to have an external agent explain

Note: All the phonetic changes discussed in sections (1) through (4) above also apply to transitive, first causative, and second causative verb sets. Thus:

Transitive	First Causative	Second Causative
खाना to eat	खिलाना to feed (to cause to eat)	खिलवाना to have an external agent feed
पीना to drink	पिलाना to give someone something to drink (to cause to drink)	पिलवाना to have an external agent give someone something to drink

(7) Some transitive verbs have only a transitive form and a single causative form.

Examples:

Transitive	Causative
देना to give	दिलवाना / दिलाना to have an external agent give
करना to do	करवाना / कराना to have an external agent do
भेजना to send	भिजवाना to have an external agent send
ख़रीदना to buy	ख़रीदवाना to have an external agent buy
सीना to sew	सिलवाना / सिलाना to have an external agent sew
लिखना to write	लिखवाना / लिखाना to have an external agent write
पूछना to ask	पूछवाना to have an external agent ask

Note that some of the causative verbs above have two possible forms that are synonymous.

Notes

1. All causative verbs are transitive and will require the postposition ने with the subject in the perfect tenses.

Example:
मैंने मोहन से अपने लिए टैक्सी रुकवाई ।
I had Mohan stop a taxi for me.

2. When mentioned, the external agent (marked by the postposition से) generally comes after the subject. However, if a sentence has both a direct and an indirect object, the external agent can come either before or after the indirect object.

Example:
मैंने उनको अपने दोस्त से अमरीका के बारे में सुनवाया ।
मैंने अपने दोस्त से उनको अमरीका के बारे में सुनवाया ।
I had my friend tell them about America.

3. All the conjunct verbs that are formed with adjective/noun + करना (transitive) have as their intransitive counterpart an adjective/noun + होना and will have their causative form as adjective/noun + करवाना or कराना.

Examples:

दफ़्तर पाँच बजे बन्द हुआ ।
The office was closed at 5 o'clock.

उसने पाँच बजे दफ़्तर बन्द किया ।
He closed the office at 5 o'clock.

उसने नौकर से पाँच बजे दफ़्तर बन्द करवाया / कराया। ।
He had the office closed by the servant at 5 o'clock.

4. The rules of causative verb formation discussed above are those that are the most commonly used in Hindi. Though a number of exceptions and further additions do exist, a general knowledge of these rules will help students to understand and recognize changes that may occur to verbs not explicitly discussed in this chapter.

5. Not all Hindi verbs have forms for the categories discussed above (either intransitive/transitive/causative or transitive/first causative/second causative). For example, the intransitive verbs आना, जाना, होना, and रहना do not have any transitive or causative forms, and the transitive verbs जानना, पाना, and बताना / बतलाना do not have any causative forms. Some verbs like ख़रीदना have only two forms, as discussed in section (7) above.

6. Causative verbs are not listed independently in dictionaries.

Causative Verbs: Exercises

1. Transformation drill

Transform the following sentences using वह as the agent in all these sentences.

I cook food.	I have him cook the food.
मैं खाना पकाती हूँ ।	मैं उससे खाना पकवाती हूँ ।

पिता जी दादा जी को पत्र लिखते हैं ।

मेरा दोस्त कार की मरम्मत करता है ।

मैं अपने कपड़े धोता हूँ ।

वह अपनी कार चलाता है ।

मैं बच्चे को दूध पिलाती हूँ ।

वह अपने भाई की मदद करता है ।

माँ बच्चे को खाना खिलाती है ।

मैं गाड़ी चलाती हूँ ।

2. Transformation drill

Transform the following sentences using the agent given in parentheses.

He will make a big table.	He will have the carpenter make a big table.
वह एक बड़ी मेज़ बनाएगा । (बढ़ई)	वह बढ़ई से एक बड़ी मेज़ बनवाएगा ।

वह दरवाज़ा खोलेगा । (नौकर)

हम अपने कपड़े धोएँगे । (धोबी)

मैं माँ को फ़ोन करूँगी । (भाई)

डाक्टर मरीज़ की चोट पर दवाई लगाएँगे । (नर्स)

मेरी बहन कुछ कपड़े सिएगी । (दर्ज़ी)

वह खाना पकाएगी । (अपना पति)

वह फ़ायरप्लेस में आग जलाएगी । (नौकरानी)

मैं बच्चों को कहानी सुनाऊँगी । (दादा जी)

3. Transformation drill

Transform the following sentences using the agent given in parentheses.

The mother put the child to sleep.	The mother had the nanny put the child to sleep.
माँ ने बच्चे को सुलाया । (आया)	माँ ने आया से बच्चे को सुलवाया ।

उसने ये पेड़ काटे । (मज़दूर)

हमने कूड़ा बाहर निकाला । (नौकर)

पिता जी ने माँ की मदद की । (हम)

मैंने नौकरी की अर्ज़ी भेजी । (अपना भाई)

माँ ने यह कमरा साफ़ किया । (मैं)

उसने बच्चों को मिठाइयाँ दीं । (हम)

मैंने अपने बच्चों को अँग्रेज़ी पढ़ाई । (शिक्षक)

यात्री ने अपना सामान उतारा । (कुली)

4. Substitution drill

Write your essay yourself. Don't have your friend write it.
तुम स्वयं अपना निबन्ध लिखो । दोस्त से न लिखवाओ ।

अपना काम करो

अपना सामान उठाओ

अपनी किताबें बेचो

अपने बच्चों को पढ़ाओ

अपनी कार की मरम्मत करो

अपना कमरा साफ़ करो

अपने लिए टैक्सी रोको

अपनी चाय बनाओ

5. Individual conversation response drill

अमीर लोग किससे अपनी कार चलवाते हैं ?

वह किससे अपने बच्चों को उर्दू सिखवाता है ?

वह किससे अपना खाना पकवाता है ?

171

भारत में स्टेशन पर लोग किससे अपना सामान उठवाते हैं ?

आप किससे अपने लिए टैक्सी रुकवाएँगे ?

वह किससे अपना मकान बिकवाएगा ?

आप किससे अपना घर साफ़ करवाएँगे ?

आपने किससे अपनी कार की मरम्मत करवाई ?

भारत में आप किससे अपने कपड़े सिलवाएँगे ?

राष्ट्रपति किससे अपना भाषण लिखवाएँगे ?

उसने किससे छात्रों को कविताएँ सुनवाईं ?

आपने किससे यह किताब ख़रीदवाई ?

उसने किससे कुत्ते को खाना खिलवाया ?

दादाजी ने किससे अपनी चिट्ठी लिखवाई ?

शाहजहाँ ने किनसे ताजमहल बनवाया ?

6. Translation exercises

1. He had the taxi driver stop the taxi in front of his house.
2. I always get my husband to drive the car.
3. He had his friend tell his students this story.
4. I will have my mother buy a sari for me.
5. We will have the servant lift that heavy table.
6. Why do you get your wife to do all your work?
7. In India, I will have the washerman wash all [of] my clothes.
8. She got her servant to open the door for us.
9. In India, I had a tailor sew some clothes for me.
10. Yesterday my father had his car repaired by a mechanic.
11. Mother had me clean my room.
12. My grandfather had me give some money to that poor man.

19. SUBJUNCTIVES

The subjunctive mood was introduced in *Introduction to Hindi Grammar*. In this chapter we will review the basic characteristics of subjunctives before moving on to explore the wide range of their usage. The basic precepts of the subjunctive are easy to understand, though they may take a little time to master because subjunctives are used in a variety of situations and can convey different meanings in different contexts.

Examples:

हम आपके साथ चलें ?	*Shall we go with you?*
चलो, बाहर चलें ।	*Come on, let's go out.*
आप हमारे साथ पार्टी में चलें ।	*Please come with us to the party.*

In the above three examples, the verb चलें is used in three different contexts, and its meaning changes accordingly. In the first sentence it is used to ask *permission*. In the second sentence, the speaker is *persuading* someone to join him/her in going out, while the third sentence is a *polite invitation* asking someone to accompany the speaker (and his/her group) to a party.

Subjunctive verb forms are generally used to convey desirability, possibility, probability, uncertainty, or a wish about some future action or event.

Formation

Subjunctive forms in Hindi are identical to those of the future tense except that the suffix गा, गे, or गी is omitted.

Examples:

Future	Subjunctive
मैं जाऊँगा ।	मैं जाऊँ ?
I will go.	*Shall I go ?*

आप पढ़ेंगे ।   आप पढ़ें ।

You will study.   *Please study.*

शायद मेरी बहन यहाँ काम करेगी ।   शायद मेरी बहन यहाँ काम करे ।

Perhaps my sister will work here.   *Perhaps my sister may work here.*

Notes

1. Three verbs that have irregular future forms (होना, लेना, देना) also have irregular subjunctive forms. Also note that मैं has two future forms: मैं हूँगा and मैं होऊँगा. Thus the subjunctive could be either मैं हूँ or मैं होऊँ. Since the former is also the present tense form of "I am," the latter is more commonly used to indicate the subjunctive.

2. The subjunctive form of a verb remains the same regardless of whether it refers to a masculine or a feminine subject.

Examples:

Future

शायद वह कल नहीं आएगा / आएगी ।

Perhaps he/she will not come tomorrow.

Subjunctive

शायद वह कल न आए ।

Perhaps he/she may not come tomorrow.

3. The negative particle used with the subjunctive is always न, as seen in the above example.

The subjunctive is used in two kinds of sentences: simple sentences and conditional sentences. In this chapter we will cover simple sentences. Conditional sentences will be discussed in Chapter 20.

Subjunctives in Simple Sentences

Subjunctive forms convey a variety of meanings in simple sentences. Generally, it is only the context that can clarify the precise meaning of the particular subjunctive form in a simple sentence. The following list summarizes the most common uses of subjunctive forms. Numbers (1) through (6) are extensively covered in the *Introduction to Hindi Grammar* but are briefly reviewed here.

(1) The subjunctive is commonly used to ask for advice or permission. In short, it is found in "should," "shall," or "may" questions.

Examples:

मैं अब क्या करूँ ?	*What shall I do now?*
हम शाम को मिलें ?	*Shall/should we meet in the evening?*

(2) The subjunctive is often used to persuade someone to do something with the subject (i.e., in "let's" constructions). In such sentences the subject हम is generally understood and the verb is in the plural. Very often such sentences are introduced with the imperative forms of आना or चलना (e.g., आओ , चलो , चलिये) to signal this particular usage of the subjunctive.

Examples:

चलिये, कुछ कॉफ़ी पिएँ ।	*Please come; let's drink some coffee.*
आओ, अंदर चलें ।	*Come on, let's go inside.*

(3) Hindi speakers employ subjunctive forms to be extremely polite when asking someone to do something. In other words, it is the most polite form of making a request. It is almost like suggesting that someone do something rather than asking the person to do it. The subject आप is generally understood and the verb is always in the plural.

Examples:

(आप) भारत पहुँचकर पत्र ज़रूर लिखें ।	*Please definitely write [to us] when you reach India.*

(आप) अपना नाम और पता यहाँ लिखें ।   *Please write your name and address here.*

(आप) उसको यह न बताएँ ।   *Please don't tell him this.*

कृपया अपनी-अपनी सीट बेल्ट बाँध लें ।   *Kindly buckle your own seat belt.*

(4) In phrases used in congratulating someone or in expressing good wishes or blessings the verb is always in the subjunctive.

Examples:

भगवान करें कि तुम जल्दी वापस आओ ।   *May God bring you back soon.*

जन्म-दिन मुबारक हो ।   *Happy birthday.* (lit., *May [your] birthday be auspicious.*)

भगवान तुम्हें सफलता दें ।   *May God grant you success.*

हमेशा ख़ुश रहो ।   *May you always be (remain) happy.*

(5) The subjunctive, when used with adverbs such as शायद *perhaps*, conveys maximum uncertainty in the mind of the speaker. शायद can also be used in other moods (e.g., the indicative or the presumptive moods); however, with different moods, it conveys different degrees of certainty.

Examples:

शायद वह अपने दफ़्तर में हो ।

Perhaps/Maybe he is in his office [but I really don't know].

शायद वह अपने दफ़्तर में होगा ।

Perhaps/Maybe he is (will be) in his office [at least I suppose he is].

शायद वह अपने दफ़्तर में है ।

Perhaps/Probably he is in his office [as a matter of fact, I am fairly sure he is].

(6) All of the examples of the subjunctive in (1) – (5) above refer to the future. This "future subjunctive" always occurs as a single word because it is the main verb itself that takes the subjunctive form. However, the subjunctive can also be used in other tenses. In such situations, a subjunctive

form of होना is added as an auxiliary to the habitual, progressive, or perfective form of the main verb. Note that when used in other tenses, the subjunctive consists of two or more parts (main verb + होना). While the future subjunctive can have multiple meanings, the subjunctive used in other tenses indicates only doubt or uncertainty. The adverb शायद is generally used in such sentences.

Examples:

<u>Subjunctive habitual</u>

शायद वह वहाँ काम करता हो ।

Perhaps he works/used to work there.

<u>Subjunctive progressive</u>

शायद वह वहाँ काम कर रहा हो ।

Perhaps he is/was working there.

<u>Subjunctive perfective</u>

शायद उसने वहाँ काम किया हो ।

Perhaps he worked/has worked/had worked there.

Note: In the above sentences there is no indication of the actual tense of the action, which could be in either the past or present. This can be clarified only by the context.

(7) The subjunctive form is also used in third-person commands ("Let him/her..."; "Let them..."; "He/she/they should…"; etc.).

Examples:

बच्चे पार्क में खेलें ।

Let the children play in the park

OR

The children should play in the park.

देखो, इस कमरे में कोई न आए ।

Look, let no one come into this room

OR

Look, no one should come into this room.

177

(8) When one is expressing doubt or supposition about some future action, the verb will be in the subjunctive (generally conveying the sense "No one knows…" or "Who knows…").

Examples:
शहर में बड़ी गड़बड़ हो रही है । न जाने कल क्या हो ।
There is a lot of unrest in the city. No one knows what will (may) happen tomorrow.

कौन जाने कल बारिश हो या न हो ।
Who knows (whether) it will rain tomorrow or not.

(9) Subjunctives are also found in subordinate clauses, following verbs that express orders (these are often indirect commands).

Examples:
बच्चों से कहो कि सड़क पर न खेलें ।
Tell the children not to play on the street.

नौकर से कहो कि बाज़ार से कुछ मिठाइयाँ लाए ।
Ask (lit., tell) the servant to bring some sweets from the market.

उनसे कहो कि बाहर मेरा इंतज़ार करें ।
Ask (lit., tell) them to wait for me outside.

(10) In sentences with जब तक …न the subjunctive form is generally used (if the reference is to a future action).

Examples:
जब तक पिताजी न आएँ , (तब तक) कहीं न जाना ।
Don't go anywhere until father returns.
(lit., *As long as father doesn't come, till then don't go anywhere.*)

जब तक काम ख़त्म न हो, (तब तक) वह घर नहीं जा सकता ।
He can't go home until the work is finished.
(lit., *As long as the work is not finished, till then he can't go home.*)

जब तक मैं न बुलाऊँ , (तब तक) अंदर न आना ।

Don't come in until I call you.

(lit., *As long as I don't call, till then do not come in.*)

(11) The subjunctive is used in "as if/as though" clauses that indicate supposition or imagined actions or situations, particularly after expressions such as "it seems as if/as though..." or "it appears as if/as though..."

Examples:
(a) जैसे *as if/as though*

हमें ऐसा लगा जैसे हम वहाँ अजनबी हों ।

It seemed to us/ We felt as if we were strangers there.

(b) मानो / मानों *as though*

वह इतनी सुन्दर है मानो गुलाब हो ।

She is as pretty [that you would think of her] as though she were a rose.

(12) Various words or phrases are used in Hindi to express a wish, necessity, possibility, appropriateness, or apprehension. The subjunctive form of the verb is *always* used in the subordinate clause after these words or phrases.

Expressing a wish

(a) X चाहता है कि...   *X wants/wishes that...*

मैं चाहती हूँ कि आप हिन्दी बोलें ।

I wish that you would speak Hindi.

(b) X की इच्छा है कि...   *It is X's wish/desire that...*

माँ की इच्छा है कि मैं सितार बजाना सीखूँ ।

It is Mother's wish/desire that I learn how to play the sitar.

(c) कितना अच्छा हो कि...   *How nice it would be if...*

कितना अच्छा हो कि हम साथ-साथ ताज महल देखें ।
How nice it would be if we [could] see the Taj Mahal together.

(d) काश (कि)...   *If only...*

काश कि वह वापस आ जाए ।
If only he would come back.

काश कि उसे लड़ाई में न जाना पड़े ।
If only he didn't have to go to war.

Expressing necessity

(a) X को चाहिये कि...   *It is needed/expected of X that...*

आपको चाहिये कि अपने दोस्त की मदद करें ।
You should help your friend. (lit., It is needed/expected of you that you help your friend.)

(b) (यह) ज़रूरी / आवश्यक है कि... *It is necessary that...*

(यह) ज़रूरी / आवश्यक है कि हम सब कल मिलें ।
It is necessary that we all meet tomorrow.

(c) X का कर्त्तव्य / फ़र्ज़ है कि...   *It is X's duty to...*

आपका कर्त्तव्य / फ़र्ज़ है कि अपने माता-पिता की देखभाल करें ।
It is your duty to take care of your parents.

Expressing possibility

(a) (यह) मुमकिन / संभव है कि...   *It is possible that...*

(यह) मुमकिन / संभव है कि आज वह यह काम ख़त्म करे ।
It is possible that he/she may finish this work today.

(यह) मुमकिन / संभव नहीं है कि बच्चे दिन भर चुप रहें ।
It is not possible for children to remain quiet all day long.

(b) (यह) हो सकता है कि...   *It is possible that...*

(यह) हो सकता है कि हम अगले साल भारत में मिलें ।
It is possible that next year we may meet in India.

Expressing appropriateness

(a) (यह) उचित / मुनासिब है कि...   *It is appropriate that...*

(यह) उचित / मुनासिब है कि आप स्वयं ही उसे यह बताएँ ।
It is appropriate that you tell her/him this yourself.

(यह) उचित / मुनासिब है कि आप घर जाकर अपनी पत्नी की मदद करें ।
It is appropriate that you should go home and help your wife.

(b) (यह) अच्छा / बेहतर है / होगा कि...   *It is/will be better if...*

(यह) अच्छा / बेहतर होगा कि आप भविष्य के लिए कुछ पैसा बचाएँ ।
It would be better if you saved some money for the future.

Expressing apprehension
(This use of the subjunctive will be discussed further in Chapter 21.)

(कहीं) ऐसा न हो कि...   *Let it not be that... / May [it] not ...*

(कहीं) ऐसा न हो कि वह इस परीक्षा में फ़ेल हो जाए ।
May he not fail in the examination. (Let it not be that he should...)

Expressing "in order that"/"so that"

ताकि / जिससे (कि)...   *so that...*

पुस्तकालय जाइये ताकि आप वहाँ शान्ति से पढ़ सकें ।
Please go to the library so that you are (may be) able to study there in peace and quiet.

जल्दी चलो जिससे (कि) हम रात होने से पहले घर पहुँच सकें ।
Walk fast so that we can (may be able to) reach home before nightfall.

(13) Whereas the above-mentioned words and phrases require the use of subjunctives in the subordinate clause, the following words and phrases may be followed by the subjunctive. However, they may also occur with other forms of verbs.

(a) शायद   *perhaps*

शायद मैं अगले साल लंदन में पढ़ूँ ।
Perhaps I will study in London next year.

(b) X का इरादा है कि...   *It is the intention of X that...*

मेरा इरादा है कि आज फ़िल्म देखूँ ।
I intend to see a film today.

182

(c) X का ख़याल / विचार है कि...   *X thinks that...*

मेरी माँ का ख़याल / विचार है कि मैं भारत न जाऊँ।
My mother thinks that I should not go to India.

(14) When adverbs are used to express "wherever," "whenever," "however," "however much," etc., the verb in these clauses generally takes the subjunctive form.

Examples:
जितनी भी मिठाइयाँ आप चाहें, (उतनी) ले लीजिये।
Please take as many sweets as you would like (wish).

जब भी वह वापस आए, उसे यह पत्र दे दीजिये।
Whenever he comes back, please give him this letter.

जब भी तुम मेरी मदद चाहो, मुझे फ़ोन करना।
Whenever you want my help, call (phone) me.

Subjunctives: Exercises

1. Transformation drill

I can bring some tea for you.

मैं आपके लिये कुछ चाय ला सकता हूँ ।

मैं आपके लिये भारतीय खाना पका सकती हूँ ।

मैं आपको इस किताब के बारे में बता सकता हूँ ।

हम पाँच मिनट और उसका इन्तज़ार कर सकते हैं ।

हम आपके साथ उसका भाषण सुनने चल सकते हैं ।

हम शाम को आपके घर आ सकते हैं ।

मैं आपको अपनी कविता सुना सकती हूँ ।

Shall/ Should I bring some tea for you?

मैं आपके लिये कुछ चाय लाऊँ ?

2. Substitution drill

Come on, let's go to see a movie.
आओ/चलो, फ़िल्म देखने चलें ।

        play outside
        finish our work
        read some Urdu stories
        go to Lake Tahoe next week
        go to drink some coffee
        go to Sproul Plaza and see the spectacle

3. Transformation drill

Please sit on this big chair.
इस बड़ी कुरसी पर बैठिये ।

आप कुछ और चावल लीजिये ।

आप मुझे वह किताब दीजिये ।

यहाँ से पढ़ना शुरू कीजिये ।

कृपया खिड़की न खोलिये ।

धीरे बोलिये ।

वहाँ धूप में न बैठिये ।

Would you please sit on this big chair?
इस बड़ी कुरसी पर बैठें ।

4. Substitution drill

Happy New Year!
नया साल मुबारक हो / नये साल की बधाई हो !

Merry Christmas!
Happy birthday!
Happy Diwali!
Happy Eid!
Happy Hanukkah!
Congratulations on your wedding!

5. Individual conversational response drill
(Use the same tense in the response.)

Where will this bus go?

यह बस कहाँ जाएगी ?

वे लोग कौन-सी भाषा बोल रहे हैं ?

आपका दोस्त कब भारत जाएगा ?

आपकी पत्नी अभी क्या कर रही है ?

भारत के प्रधान मंत्री कब अमरीका आएँगे ?

उस कमरे में कौन सो रहा है ?

वह कहाँ गया है ?

उसने कल कितनी कहानियाँ पढ़ीं ?

कपड़ेवाले ने कल कितनी साड़ियाँ बेचीं ?

लड़का कितने बजे स्कूल गया ?

आपका भाई कल किससे मिला ?

I don't know; perhaps it will (may) go to Delhi.
(मुझे) मालूम नहीं, शायद दिल्ली जाए ।

6. Substitution drill

Ask/tell him not to go there.
उससे कहो कि वहाँ न जाए ।

       those children not to play on the street
       that student to return my books
       those students to come to class on time

185

your servant to bring some tea for me
your servant to stop a taxi for me
them to wait for me outside the library

7. <u>Substitution drill</u>

She will stay home until her children come from school.
जब तक उसके बच्चे स्कूल से न आएँ, तब तक वह घर में रहेगी ।

उसका काम ख़त्म न हो जाए

उसको नौकरी न मिले

डाकिया न आए

उसका पति वापस न आए

बारिश न रुके

उसकी माँ की तबियत ठीक न हो

8. <u>Substitution drill</u>

We felt (It seemed to us) as if we were strangers there.
हमें लगा जैसे / मानों हम वहाँ अजनबी हों ।

we were Indians also
our lives were useless
we were very famous
we were also rich
he was waiting for someone
she knew everything

9. <u>Substitution drill</u>

He wanted us to learn English.
वह चाहता था कि हम अँग्रेज़ी सीखें ।

her to make some tea
us to go there
you to talk to them
me to finish my work
the children not to play on the street
his wife to go to college

10. Transformation drill

It is Mother's wish that I learn Hindi.

Mother wishes for me to study Hindi.

माँ की इच्छा है कि मैं हिन्दी सीखूँ ।

माँ चाहती है कि मैं हिन्दी सीखूँ ।

सरकार की इच्छा है कि लोग अपना टैक्स दें ।

मेरी इच्छा है कि तुम मेहनत से काम करो ।

हमारे शिक्षक की इच्छा है कि हम अच्छी हिन्दी बोलें ।

पिता जी की इच्छा है कि मैं आज रात को पार्टी में न जाऊँ ।

मेरी इच्छा है कि आप शाम को मेरे साथ खाना खाएँ ।

मेरी माँ की इच्छा है कि मैं एक हिन्दुस्तानी लड़की से शादी करूँ ।

11. Transformation drill

It would be great if she came back!
(How great would it be if she came back!)

If only she would come back!

कितना अच्छा हो कि वह वापस आ जाए ।

काश कि वह वापस आ जाए ।

कितना अच्छा हो कि ट्रेन आज लेट न हो ।

कितना अच्छा हो कि लोग धर्म के नाम पर न लड़ें ।

कितना अच्छा हो कि वह शराब पीना छोड़ दे ।

कितना अच्छा हो कि दुनिया में कोई ग़रीब न हो ।

कितना अच्छा हो कि मेरे भाई को नौकरी मिल जाए ।

कितना अच्छा हो कि आप मेरी बात समझने की कोशिश करें ।

12. Transformation drill

You should exercise every day.

It is necessary for you to exercise every day.

आपको चाहिये कि आप रोज़ कसरत करें ।

यह ज़रूरी है कि आप रोज़ कसरत करें ।

आपको चाहिये कि आप ज़्यादा मिठाई न खाएँ ।

उनको चाहिये कि वे रोज़ घूमने जाएँ ।

छात्रों को चाहिये कि वे रोज़ पढ़ें ।

उसको चाहिये कि वह जल्दी (से) अपनी रिसर्च ख़त्म करे ।

उसको चाहिये कि वह अपनी पत्नी की मदद करे ।

उसको चाहिये कि वह अपना कमरा ख़ुद साफ़ करे ।

13. Individual conversational response drill

Will he come tomorrow?

Yes, it is possible that he will come tomorrow.

क्या वह कल आएगा ?

हाँ, मुमकिन / संभव है/ हो सकता है कि वह कल आए ।

क्या बस समय पर नहीं पहुँचेगी ?

क्या आपका भाई मेरी मदद करेगा ?

क्या आप को अगले साल नौकरी करनी पड़ेगी ?

क्या ये नेता जी इस बार भी चुनाव में जीतेंगे ?

क्या उसको यह नौकरी नहीं मिलेगी ?

क्या इस साल आप भारत नहीं जाएँगे ?

14. Substitution drill

It would be better if you went to the market yourself.
बेहतर होगा कि आप ख़ुद बाज़ार जाएँ ।

        spoke only Hindi in this class
        told your parents about this
        exercised daily
        found some other job
        helped your friend
        did your work by yourself

15. Substitution drill

She is working hard so that she can save some money.
वह मेहनत कर रही है ताकि / जिससे (कि) वह कुछ पैसा बचा सके ।

        can complete her degree quickly
        can go to the party tonight
        can go home soon
        can get a good job

can get good grades
can go on vacation

16. <u>Complete the following sentences with an appropriate clause</u>

Whenever he comes, please let me know.
जब भी वह आए, (तब / तो) मुझे बताएँ / बताइये ।

जब भी आप को उसकी ख़बर मिले...

जो भी आप करना चाहें...

जहाँ भी आप जाना चाहें...

जब भी तुम्हें उसकी ई-मेल मिले...

जहाँ भी अच्छा अपार्टमेंट मिले...

जितना भी काम तुम आज कर सको...

17. <u>Translation exercise</u>

1. He is not in his office. May be he has gone home.
2. Kindly speak loudly.
3. I am very tired. Come on, let's drink some coffee.
4. Tell/ask your brother to come tomorrow to my office.
5. Shall/should we go with you to the airport?
6. I will stay right here till my son comes back. (Use जब तक...न.)
7. My parents want me to go to medical school, but I want to be a teacher.
8. We should try to finish our work on time. (Use X को चाहिये कि ...)
9. If only my parents would try to understand me.
10. You should do whatever he tells you.
11. I felt as if I were a foreigner in my very own country.
12. He is learning Hindi so that he can do his research in India.
13. It is possible that students will have to (must) pay more fees next year.
14. It would be better if you yourself went there.

20. CONDITIONAL SENTENCES

General Rules for Conditional Sentences

As in English, conditional sentences are commonly used in both spoken and written Hindi. They consist of two clauses: the conditional clause (the "if" clause) and the main clause (the "then" clause). The conditional clause in Hindi normally precedes the main clause. The conditional clause is usually introduced by अगर / यदि (the conjunction "if") and the main clause is always introduced by तो (the conjunction "then"). Thus the basic structure of these sentences is "if…then…."

Example:

अगर आप कॉफ़ी पीना चाहें तो हम भी आप के साथ कैफ़े चलेंगे ।

If you want to drink coffee, (then) we will also accompany you to a café.

Notes

1. In Hindi, the "if" clause always comes first, though this is not always the case in English.

Example:

अगर आप मेरी मदद न करें तो मैं क्या करूँगी ।

What will I do if you don't help me?

2. In spoken Hindi, अगर / यदि may be dropped even though they are implied by the presence of तो in the second clause. On the other hand, तो is never dropped from the main clause.

Example:

आप कॉफ़ी पीना चाहें तो हम भी आप के साथ कैफ़े चलेंगे ।

If you want to drink coffee, we will also accompany you to a café.

Students should note that the reverse is true in English, where "if" is never dropped while "then" is frequently omitted, as can be seen in the English translation of the above sentence.

3. The relative pronoun जो is sometimes used in colloquial Hindi instead of अगर / यदि.

Example:
जो वह यहाँ आए तो मैं उससे ज़रूर मिलूँगी ।
If he comes here, (then) I will certainly meet him.

We can broadly divide conditional sentences into two main categories: (1) conditional sentences used for present and future conditions, and (2) conditional sentences used for past conditions (the contrary-to-fact construction).

Conditional Sentences for the Present and the Future

These are used for conditions that can be fulfilled in the present or future. Note that when we use the present tense in conditional sentences, it may imply the immediate future. In such sentences, the verbs of the two clauses can be in different tenses. For example, the "if" clause may be in the present tense, while the "then" clause could be in the future.

Such sentences are further divided into two main categories, depending on the degree of certainty of the condition and its fulfillment:

Sentences with the subjunctive: The use of the subjunctive mood implies that the speaker is expressing a wish, supposition, or possibility and realizes that its fulfillment is uncertain.

Sentences with the indicative: Even though conditional sentences have an "if" clause, the use of the indicative mood expresses certainty in the mind of the speaker that the condition(s) will be met.

The basic nature of conditional sentences is that unless certain conditions are met, the result or outcome is uncertain. The difference between conditional sentences with the subjunctive and conditional sentences with the indicative is that the former imply a higher degree of uncertainty, whereas the latter convey a higher degree of certainty that both the condition and the outcome will be met.

191

Conditional Sentences with the Subjunctives

In sentences that convey doubt about the fulfillment of a condition, the subjunctive form of a verb is employed in the conditional clause. Depending on the degree of certainty in the mind of the speaker concerning the outcome, the verb of the main clause can be in the subjunctive, the present, the future, or the imperative.

(1) Conditional clause is in the subjunctive and main clause is in the present:

अगर आप चाहें तो हम अब काम शुरू कर सकते हैं ।

If you like (wish), (then) we can start work now.

Since the first clause is in the subjunctive, it indicates uncertainty about the wishes of the listener, but the main clause (in the present tense) indicates certainty of the action if the listener's wishes are met.

(2) Conditional clause is in the subjunctive and main clause is in the future:

अगर मैं भारत जाऊँ तो ज़रूर ताज महल देखूँगी ।

If I go to India, (then) I will certainly see the Taj Mahal.

Here again the first clause is in the subjunctive and expresses uncertainty about the speaker's going to India. The main clause (in the future tense) indicates certainty of seeing the Taj Mahal if the speaker goes to India.

(3) Conditional clause is in the subjunctive and main clause is in the subjunctive:

अगर वह आए तो काम शुरू हो ।

If he comes, (then) perhaps work will start.

Since his arrival is uncertain, both parts of the sentence are presented as if describing a situation that is unlikely to happen (though still possible).

Similarly:

अगर लोग लड़ना बंद करें तो दुनिया में शान्ति हो ।
If people would stop fighting, (then) there would be peace in the world.

(4) Conditional clause is in the subjunctive and main clause is in the imperative:

अगर आप हिन्दुस्तानी खाना खाना चाहें तो मेरे घर आइये ।
If you wish to eat Indian food, (then) please come to my house.

In this sentence the speaker is unsure whether the listener likes Indian food. However, if the listener does wish to eat Indian food, then the invitation to eat a meal is certain.

Conditional Sentences with the Indicative

Indicative verbs are used in *both* clauses in sentences that indicate certainty in the mind of the speaker about the fulfillment of a condition and its result. Note that in contrast to conditional sentences with subjunctives, which may have indicative verbs in the main clause, both clauses in this case have indicative verbs.

Conditional sentences with indicative verbs can be categorized as:

(1) Using the present and/or future tenses in both clauses
(2) Using the perfect tense in the conditional clause and the future tense in the main clause.

(1) Using the present and/or future tenses in both clauses:

The following examples will illustrate the use of various combinations of indicative verbs in both clauses.

(a) Conditional clause is in the present and main clause is in the present.

अगर उसको संगीत में दिलचस्पी है तो वह भी मेरे गुरु जी से सीख सकता है ।
If he is interested in music, (then) he can also learn from my guruji.

193

(b) Conditional clause is in the present and main clause is in the future.

अगर आप फ़्रैंच जानते हैं तो आप यह फ़िल्म समझ सकेंगे ।
If you know French, (then) you will be able to understand this film.

(c) Conditional clause is in the future and main clause is in the future.

अगर मेरा भाई अमरीका आएगा तो मैं उसको बॉस्टन दिखाऊँगी ।
If my brother visits America, (then) I will show him Boston.

(d) Conditional clause is in the present and main clause is in the imperative.

अगर आप भारत जाना चाहते हैं तो हिंदी सीखिये ।
If you want to go to India, (then) please learn Hindi.

(2) Conditional clause in perfect, main clause in the future tense:

A special case of the use of indicative verbs occurs in conditional sentences where the conditional clause is in the perfect tense and the main clause is in the future. This is a very common pattern used in Hindi for a future condition. By using the perfect tense in the conditional clause, the speaker places an emphasis on the completion of a condition in the future before the stated outcome can occur or the results can be fulfilled.

Examples:
अगर उसने मेहनत की तो उसकी तरक़्क़ी होगी ।
If she/he works hard, (then) she/he will be promoted.

अगर तुमने यह काम नहीं / न किया तो माँ नाराज़ होंगी ।
If you don't do this work, (then) Mother will be angry.

Note that the first clause in both of these sentences can also be translated into English in the perfect tense. Thus, the first sentence can also be translated as *"If she/he worked hard, then she/he would be promoted."*

Similarly, the second sentence can be rendered as *"If you didn't do this work, then Mother would be angry."*

Conditional Sentences for the Past (Contrary-to-Fact Construction)

Conditional sentences for the past are also called contrary to fact because they are used in specific situations where they indicate that the condition was not met and hence there could be no result. A typical sentence construction of this type is, "If Sarita had come, then you would have met her" (but she did not come, so you could not meet her). This construction can also have hypothetical implications in the present.

Examples:
अगर बारिश ठीक समय पर होती तो हमारी फ़सल अच्छी होती ।

If it had rained at the right time, (then) our crops would have been good (but it did not).

अगर मैं करोड़पति होती तो यह नौकरी क्यों करती ?

If I were a millionaire, (then) why would I be doing this job?

These sentences are formed with imperfective participles (without an auxiliary verb) in both clauses (i.e., conditional clause and main clause). Thus such sentences are signaled by the use of the suffixes –ता/–ते/–ती/–तीं with the verb stem in both clauses. We will discuss contrary-to-fact statements in a variety of tenses (which range from the simple past to progressive forms of the past tense), as well as in other constructions (such as the verb stem + सकना and the oblique infinitive + लगना). The negative particle used with contrary-to-fact constructions is always न.

Simple Past Conditional

In order to express that a condition was not carried out in the past, one can use the imperfective participle of the main verbs in both clauses.

Examples:
अगर तुम मेरे साथ आते तो मैं बहुत ख़ुश होती ।

If you had come with me, (then) I would have been very happy (but you didn't come and I was not happy).

अगर मैं अमरीका में पैदा होता तो अच्छी अँग्रेज़ी बोलता ।

If I were born in America, (then) I would speak good English (but I was not).

Past Perfect Conditional

Sometimes Hindi speakers use the perfective participle of the main verb + the imperfective participle of the auxiliary verb होना in one or both of the clauses to emphasize a reference to the past. Although the meaning of the simple past conditional constructions discussed above is identical to the meaning of past perfect conditional constructions, in the case of the latter, the speaker is emphasizing the completion of a past action/condition (which, of course, did not occur).

Examples:
अगर मैं अमरीका में पैदा हुआ होता तो अच्छी अँग्रेज़ी बोलता ।

If I had been born in America, (then) I would speak good English (but I was not).

अगर उन लोगों ने एक दूसरे से बात की होती तो उनमें लड़ाई न हुई होती ।

If those people had talked to each other, (then) they would not have fought with each other (but they didn't talk).

Other Forms of Past Conditional

Like conditional sentences for present and future, past conditional sentences can occur with various verb forms and tenses. The use of the suffixes –ता / –ते / –ती / –तीं with the verb stem in both clauses still signals that these sentences are contrary-to-fact constructions.

Examples:
अगर मैं बगीचे में काम कर रही होती तो आपको जाते हुए ज़रूर देखती ।

If I had been working in the garden, (then) I certainly would have seen you passing by (but I wasn't).

अगर मैं गाना गा सकता तो कल आपकी पार्टी में ज़रूर गाता ।

If I could sing, (then) I would certainly have sung at your party yesterday (but I can't).

अगर वह न्यू यॉर्क में न रहती होती तो आपके परिवार से कैसे मिलती ?

If she didn't live in New York, (then) how would she have met your family? (But she does live in New York, so she did meet them.)

अगर उस ज़माने में लोग लड़कियों को पढ़ने देते तो माँ डॉक्टर बन जातीं ।

If people in those times had allowed girls to study, (then) Mother would have become a doctor (but they didn't allow it).

Contrary-to-Fact Expressions That Do Not Follow the "If…then…" Format of Conditional Sentences

Some contrary-to-fact expressions do not follow the "if…then…" format of conditional sentences. These include various phrases and expressions in Hindi denoting doubt, desire, necessity, suggestion, obligation, etc. When used in the past tense, these phrases will convey that the statement of the subordinate clause was not realized. These sentences consist of two parts: the first part will have a phrase/expression in the past, and the second part will be a subordinate clause introduced with कि. In such cases, the verb in the subordinate clause will take the contrary-to-fact form (i.e., verb stem + –ता / –ते / –ती / –तीं).

Example:

आपको चाहिये था कि आप समय पर वहाँ पहुचते ।

You should have reached there on time (but you did not).

Notes

1. Although the suffixes (–ता / –ते / –ती / –तीं) indicate that the statement of the subordinate clause is contrary to fact, these sentences are not conditional sentences and do not follow the "if…then…" format.

2. If the phrases or expressions in the main clause indicate (or suggest) a present or future tense, then they require the subjunctive form of the verb in the subordinate clause. (See Chapter 19 on subjunctives.) The following examples illustrate the difference between two types of constructions: one requires the use of the contrary-to-fact form of the verb in the subordinate clause, while the other requires the verb in the subordinate clause to be in the subjunctive.

Examples:

बेहतर होता / था कि वह भारत जाने से पहले हिन्दी सीखता ।

It would have been better if he had learned Hindi before going to India (but he did not).

बेहतर है / होगा कि वह भारत जाने से पहले हिन्दी सीखे ।

It is/will be better if he learns Hindi before going to India.

The following examples further illustrate this difference:

(a) कितना अच्छा होता कि... *How nice it would have been...*

कितना अच्छा होता कि मैं आपसे पहले मिली होती ।

How nice it would have been if only I had met you earlier (but I did not).

कितना अच्छा होगा / हो कि मैं आपसे कल फिर मिल सकूँ ।

How nice it will be/would be if only I can/could meet you again tomorrow.

(b) काश कि... *If only...*

काश कि मेरे भाई को अच्छी नौकरी मिलती ।

If only my brother had found/got a good job (but he did not).

काश कि मेरे भाई को अच्छी नौकरी मिले ।

If only my brother would find/get a good job.

(c) X को चाहिये था कि... *X should have...*

आपको चाहिये था कि आप अपने माता-पिता की सलाह मानते ।

You should have followed your parents' advice (but you did not).

आपको चाहिये कि आप अपने माता-पिता की सलाह मानें ।

You should follow your parents' advice.

(d) X के लिए जरूरी / आवश्यक था कि... *It was necessary for X to ...*

उसके लिए यह ज़रूरी / आवश्यक था कि वह समय पर दफ़्तर पहुँचता ।

It was necessary for him to reach the office on time (but he did not).

उसके लिए यह ज़रूरी / आवश्यक है कि वह समय पर दफ़्तर पहुँचे ।

It is necessary for him to reach the office on time.

(e) X का कर्त्तव्य (फ़र्ज़) था कि...   *It was X's duty to...*

आपका कर्त्तव्य (फ़र्ज़) था कि आप ग़रीब लोगों की मदद करते ।

It was your duty to have helped poor people (but you did not).

आपका कर्त्तव्य (फ़र्ज़) है कि आप ग़रीब लोगों की मदद करें ।

It is your duty to help poor people.

(f) X के लिए उचित / मुनासिब था कि... *It would have been appropriate for X ...*

(आप के लिये) उचित / मुनासिब था कि आप स्वयं मंत्री जी से मिलने वहाँ जाते ।

It would have been appropriate for you to go there yourself to meet the minister (but you did not).

(आप के लिये) उचित / मुनासिब होगा कि आप स्वयं मंत्री जी से मिलने वहाँ जाएँ ।

It will be appropriate for you to go there yourself to meet the minister.

(g) बेहतर होता / था कि...   *It would have been better that...*

बेहतर होता / था कि वह हमें सच बताता ।

It would have been better if he had told us the truth (but he did not).

बेहतर होगा कि वह हमें सच बताए ।

It will be better if he tells us the truth.

(h) भला कैसे / क्या / कहाँ...   *Say, how/what/where (in the world) ...*

भला मैं कैसे वहाँ जाता ?

Say, how (in the world) could I have gone there? (So I did not.)

भला मैं कैसे वहाँ जाऊँ ?

Say, how (in the world) am I to go there?

Conditional Sentences: Exercises

1. Substitution drill

If you say so, (then) I will go with you.
अगर आप कहें तो मैं आप के साथ चलूँगा ।

> I will phone her
> I will write a letter to the Prime Minister
> I will tell Father about this
> I will tell you my opinion about this
> I will help you
> I will also invite (call) your friend to the party
> I will come to your home in the evening
> I will take your picture

2. Individual conversational response drill

Can you come to my home this evening?
क्या तुम आज शाम को मेरे घर आ सकते हो ?

Yes; if you wish, I will certainly come.
हाँ, अगर तुम चाहो तो मैं ज़रूर आऊँगा ।

क्या तुम मेरी कार की मरम्मत कर सकते हो?

क्या तुम इन बच्चों को कुछ मिठाइयाँ दे सकते हो ?

क्या तुम हमें भारत के बारे में कुछ बता सकते हो?

क्या तुम मेरे लिये पुस्तकालय से कुछ किताबें ला सकते हो?

क्या तुम मुझे हिन्दुस्तानी खाना पकाना सिखा सकते हो?

क्या तुम हमें कुछ चाय पिला सकते हो?

क्या तुम कल मेरी मदद कर सकते हो?

क्या तुम आज हमारे साथ फ़िल्म देखने चल सकते हो?

3. Complete the sentence with an appropriate clause

If the child cries, (then)…
अगर बच्चा रोए तो ...

If the child cries, (then) feed her milk.
अगर बच्चा रोए तो उसको दूध पिलाना ।

अगर ऐक्सीडेंट हो जाए तो
अगर वह सो रहा हो तो
अगर तुम अच्छी नौकरी चाहते हो तो
अगर आपको कल कुछ फुरसत हो तो
अगर तुम्हें मेरी मदद चाहिये तो
अगर तुम अच्छे ग्रेड्स चाहते हो तो
अगर तुम अपना वज़न कम करना चाहते हो तो
अगर तुम उस लड़की से मिलना चाहते हो तो

4. Transformation drill

He will go to India. He will see the Taj Mahal.
वह भारत जाएगा । वह ताज महल देखेगा ।
If he goes to India, (then) he will see the Taj Mahal.
अगर वह भारत जाएगा तो ताज महल देखेगा ।

मैं बॉस्टन जाऊँगी । मैं दोस्त से मिलूँगी ।
बारिश होगी । हम घर पर रुकेंगे ।
वह परीक्षा की तैयारी करेगा । वह परीक्षा में उत्तीर्ण होगा ।
मैं उसको अपना पता भेजूँगा । वह मुझे पत्र लिखेगा ।
हम भारत जाएँगे । हम वहाँ रेलगाड़ी से सफ़र करेंगे ।
आप हिन्दी सीखेंगे । आप भारत में अपने सब रिश्तेदारों से बात कर सकेंगे ।
आप कोशिश करेंगे । आपको अच्छी नौकरी मिलेगी ।
मुझे फुरसत होगी । मैं आपकी मदद करूँगा ।

5. Transformation drill

I will receive his letter. I will call you.
मुझे उसका पत्र मिलेगा । मैं आपको फ़ोन करूँगा ।

If I receive his letter, I will call you.
अगर मुझे उसका पत्र मिला तो मैं आपको फ़ोन करूँगा ।

माँ जल्दी नहीं लौटेंगी । बच्चा रोने लगेगा ।
आप मेहनत नहीं करेंगे । आप परीक्षा में उत्तीर्ण नहीं होंगे ।
वह भारत जाएगी । वह बालीवुड के अभिनेताओं से मिलने की कोशिश करेगी ।
मुझे पैसा मिलेगा । मैं नई कार ख़रीदूँगा ।
आपको यह नई नौकरी मिलेगी । क्या आप हमें पार्टी देंगे ?
वह सच बताएगा । पुलिस उसको छोड़ देगी ।
वह कोशिश करेगा । वह ज़रूर सफल होगा ।
कोहरा होगा । ड्राइवर रास्ता नहीं देख सकेगा ।

6. Transformation drill

I didn't go there. I didn't meet him.
मैं वहाँ नहीं गया । मैं उससे नहीं मिला ।
If I had gone there, I would have met him (but I didn't).
अगर मैं वहाँ जाता तो मैं उससे मिलता ।

उसने मेहनत नहीं की । वह परीक्षा में पास नहीं हुआ ।
मेरे पास पैसा नहीं था । मैं कालिज नहीं जा सका ।
आपने मुझे पार्टी में नहीं बुलाया । मैं नहीं आया ।
वह वहाँ समय पर नहीं पहुँचा । वह सब लोगों से नहीं मिल सका ।
उसने अपने जूते नहीं उतारे । वह मंदिर के अंदर नहीं जा सका ।
उसने माँ की सलाह नहीं मानी । उसने यह ग़लती की ।
तुमने मुझे फ़ोन नहीं किया । मैं तुम्हें लेने एयरपोर्ट नहीं आया ।
उसने दवाई नहीं खाई । उसकी बीमारी बढ़ गई ।

7. Complete the sentence with an appropriate clause

If I had not been sleeping at that time, (then)…
अगर मैं उस समय सो न रहा होता तो ...

If I had not been sleeping at that time, (then) I would have heard your voice (but I didn't).

अगर मैं उस समय सो न रहा होता तो आपकी आवाज़ सुनता ।

अगर मैं अमीर होता तो

अगर आपने कोशिश की होती तो

अगर आपने मुझे इसके बारे में बताया होता तो

अगर उस समय बारिश न हो रही होती तो

अगर डाक्टर समय पर आ जाता तो

अगर वह पुलिस को सच बताता तो

अगर हम भारत में पैदा होते तो

अगर वह ध्यान से गाड़ी चलाता तो

8. Transformation drill

He should work hard.   He should have worked hard.

उसको चाहिये कि वह मेहनत करे ।   उसको चाहिये था कि मेहनत करता ।

उसको चाहिये कि वह सच बताए ।

हमें चाहिये कि हम हिन्दी बोलने का अभ्यास करें ।

आपको चाहिये कि आप अपना काम समय पर ख़त्म करें ।

उसको चाहिये कि वह नौकरी के लिये अर्ज़ी भेजे ।

9. Transformation drill

It is necessary that you tell the truth.

यह ज़रूरी / आवश्यक है कि आप सच बताए ।

It was necessary for you to tell the truth (but you didn't).

यह ज़रूरी / आवश्यक था कि आप सच बताते ।

यह ज़रूरी / आवश्यक है कि आप समय पर आएँ ।

यह ज़रूरी / आवश्यक है कि मरीज़ समय पर दवाई खाए ।

यह ज़रूरी / आवश्यक है कि तुम अपना काम स्वयं करो ।

यह ज़रूरी / आवश्यक है कि आप शराब पीकर गाड़ी न चलाएँ ।

10. Transformation drill

If only I had (have/will have) more time.
काश कि मेरे पास ज़्यादा समय हो ।

If only I had had more time (but I didn't).
काश कि मेरे पास ज़्यादा समय होता ।

काश कि एक औरत हमारी राष्ट्रपति हो ।

काश कि दुनिया में ग़रीबी न हो ।

काश कि वह जल्दी वापस आए ।

काश कि तुम भी मेरे साथ भारत आओ ।

11. Transformation drill

How nice it would be if we all could meet in India.
कितना अच्छा हो कि हम सब भारत में मिल सकें ।

How nice it would have been if we all could have met in India (but we didn't).
कितना अच्छा होता कि हम सब भारत में मिल सकते ।

कितना अच्छा हो कि हमारे पास बहुत पैसा हो ।

कितना अच्छा हो कि मेरे माता-पिता मुझे समझने की कोशिश करें ।

कितना अच्छा हो कि कल बारिश न हो ।

कितना अच्छा हो कि वह भी हमारे साथ आए ।

12. Transformation drill

It would be better if you helped him.
बेहतर होगा कि आप उसकी मदद करें ।

It would have been better if you had helped him (but you didn't).
बेहतर होता / था कि आप उसकी मदद करते ।

बेहतर होगा कि आप स्वयं उससे मिलने जाएँ ।

बेहतर होगा कि वह अपनी माँ की मदद करे।

बेहतर होगा कि आप यह नौकरी न छोड़ें ।

बेहतर होगा कि आप हमें पूरी बात बताएँ ।

13. Transformation drill

It would be appropriate if you helped her.

उचित / मुनासिब होगा कि आप उसकी मदद करें ।

It would have been appropriate if you had helped her (but you didn't).

उचित / मुनासिब होता / था कि आप उसकी मदद करते ।

उचित / मुनासिब होगा कि वह अपनी डिग्री जल्दी ख़त्म करे ।

उचित / मुनासिब होगा कि वह अपने माता-पिता की सलाह माने ।

उचित / मुनासिब होगा कि आप शादी के मामले में सोच-समझ कर फ़ैसला करें ।

उचित / मुनासिब होगा कि आप उससे इस के बारे में कुछ न कहें ।

14. Transformation drill

It is your duty to properly care for the patient.

आपका फ़र्ज़ / कर्त्तव्य है कि आप मरीज़ की अच्छी तरह देखभाल करें ।

It was your duty to properly care for the patient (but you didn't).

आपका फ़र्ज़ / कर्त्तव्य था कि आप मरीज़ की अच्छी तरह देखभाल करते ।

आपका फ़र्ज़ है कि आप पर्यावरण को दूषित न करें ।

आपका फ़र्ज़ है कि आप अपना काम ध्यान से करें ।

आपका फ़र्ज़ है कि आप समाज के नियमों का पालन करें ।

आपका फ़र्ज़ है कि आप अपने माता-पिता की मदद करें ।

15. Transformation drill

Say, how (in the world) will I do this much work?

भला मैं कैसे इतना काम करूँ ?

Say, how (in the world) would I have done this much work?

भला मैं कैसे इतना काम करता ?

भला मैं क्यों वहाँ जाऊँ ?

भला मैं कैसे उनकी मदद करूँ ?

भला मैं कहाँ से इतना पैसा लाऊँ ?

भला मैं किस से पैसा माँगूँ ?

भला मैं क्यों उसको सब कुछ बताऊँ ?

भला मैं कैसे इस गाड़ी की मरम्मत करूँ ?

16. Translation exercise

1. If he had given up smoking cigarettes, he would not have gotten sick.
2. If I go (went) to India, I will bring (would bring) an Urdu dictionary for you.
3. We should have come to class on time. (Use…चाहिये था कि… .)
4. If he hadn't quit his job, he would have been able to buy a new car.
5. It was necessary for him to go to India to do his research (but he did not go).
6. If she comes home late, her mother will be angry.
7. If only he had told me the truth.
8. If you had been driving carefully, you wouldn't have gotten hurt.
9. How nice it would have been if we all had gone to Hawaii together.
10. If you learn Hindi, you will be able to talk with everyone in Delhi.
11. It would have been better if you had written your essay yourself.
12. If you had telephoned me, I certainly would have come to help you.
13. It would have been appropriate for you to give her a gift on her birthday.
14. If you had been listening in class, you would have known the answer to this question.
15. How (in the world) would she have reached the hospital in ten minutes?
16. It was your duty to vote in the election.

21. THE ADVERB कहीं

The adverb कहीं, which was discussed in Chapter 8, ordinarily means "somewhere" or "anywhere" and, in negative sentences, "nowhere." In this chapter, we will cover several of its other uses.

(1) कहीं can sometimes be used in rhetorical questions, where it denotes "ever" or "at all." In such questions, the speaker assumes a negative response.

Examples:

ऐसा भी कहीं हो सकता है ?   *Can such (a thing) ever happen ?* (Never.)

वह भी कहीं समय पर आ सकती है ?   *Can she ever come on time ?* (Never.)

(2) कहीं also occurs in sentences where it conveys such general meanings as "should it happen that...," "somehow/by chance"; "rather/considerably."

Examples:

अगर कहीं पिता जी को इसके बारे में पता चल जाए, तो वे बहुत नाराज़ होंगे ।

Father will be very angry if he somehow (by chance) finds out about it.

अगर कहीं अभिनेता न आया, तो लोग बहुत निराश होंगे ।

People will be very disappointed if the actor doesn't (by chance) turn up.

दूसरी किताब इस किताब से कहीं ज़्यादा महँगी है ।

The other book is rather/considerably more expensive than this book.

(3) The idiomatic use of कहीं in the phrase "X कहीं का" means "an X of some sort" (lit., an X of some place). This exclamatory phrase can be used in both an affectionate manner (as with children) or, more commonly, in a derogatory or disapproving manner.

Examples:

चल चल, पागल कहीं की !   *Come on, you silly (girl)!*

जा जा, आया बड़ा नेता कहीं का ! *Come on, as if you were some sort of big leader!*

बुद्धू कहीं का !   *You idiot [of some sort]!*

(4) The adverb कहीं, when used with न and the verb in the subjunctive, conveys a general meaning of apprehension or unpleasant possibility. It conveys the sense "lest" or "let it not be the case that." It may follow a phrase expressing fear or apprehension. In some cases, it is also used as a warning.

Examples:
कहीं वह बीमार न हो ।
I hope he is not ill.
मुझे डर है कि कहीं वह बीमार न हो ।
I am afraid that he may be ill.
(कहीं) ऐसा न हो कि उसका एक्सीडेंट हो जाए ।
Let it not be that he have an accident. (As in English: "Heaven forbid he has an accident.")

Note that in this construction, न serves to identify the element about which apprehension is expressed by immediatelty following it.

Examples:

देखिये, कहीं वह गिर न जाए ।	*Watch out, lest he **fall**.*
देखिये, कहीं वह न गिर जाए ।	*Watch out, lest **he** fall.*

This construction shows a marked preference for compound verbs. When the apprehension is expressed about the action of the main verb, न occurs after the stem of the main verb.

Examples:

कहीं वह जानवरों को मार न डाले।	*I hope he doesn't kill the animals.*
कहीं वह गन्दा पानी पी न ले ।	*I hope she doesn't drink the dirty water.*

The Adverb कहीं: Exercises

1. Substitution drill

Can he ever help me? (Never.)
वह भी कहीं मेरी मदद कर सकता है ?

> come on time
> give up telling lies
> exercise every day
> give up eating sweets
> give up smoking
> clean his room
> listen to me
> try to understand me

2. Substitution drill

If by chance the lights go out, then what will we do?
अगर कहीं बिजली चली जाए तो हम क्या करेंगे ?

> वह किताब न मिली
>
> वह समय पर न आया
>
> दूध ख़त्म हो गया
>
> बटुआ खो जाए
>
> बारिश होने लगे
>
> ट्रेन छूट जाए
>
> गाड़ी रास्ते में टूट जाए
>
> सुबह को अलार्म न बजे

3. Substitution drill

I was afraid that he might go away.
मुझे डर था कि कहीं वह चला न जाए ।

> बीमार न हो जाए ।
>
> गिर न जाए ।
>
> आना न भूल जाए ।

रोने न लगे ।

क्लास में सोने न लगे ।

सब से लड़ने न लगे ।

बस चली न जाए ।

दुकान बंद न हो जाए ।

4. <u>Complete the following sentences</u>

The thief was afraid that …
चोर को डर था कि कहीं …

The thief was afraid that the police might see him.
चोर को डर था कि कहीं पुलिस उसे देख न ले ।

माँ को डर था कि कहीं …
दादा जी को डर था कि कहीं …
राष्ट्रपति को डर था कि कहीं …
जनता को डर था कि कहीं …
छात्रों को डर था कि कहीं …
हमें को डर था कि कहीं …
मेरी पत्नी को डर था कि कहीं …

5. <u>Transformation drill</u>

He will get angry.   I hope that he doesn't get angry.
वह नाराज़ हो जाएगा ।   कहीं वह नाराज़ न हो जाए ।

तूफ़ान आ जाएगा ।
वह ट्रैफ़िक में फंस जाएगा ।
कैंपस पर हड़ताल हो जाएगी ।
उसकी नौकरी छूट जाएगी ।
यूनिवर्सिटी फ़ीस बढ़ा देगी ।
वह रास्ता भूल जाएगा ।

210

वह अपना पासपोर्ट खो देगी ।
देश में गड़बड़ हो जाएगी ।

6. Translation exercise

1. Watch out, lest the food burn.
2. I am afraid that my rent may increase this year.
3. If by chance you meet him, please give him my phone number.
4. Can my parents ever try to understand me? (Never.)
5. Drive carefully, lest there be an accident.
6. If by chance it starts raining, many people will not come to see our play.
7. I was afraid that I might fail in the examination.
8. Can he ever reach his office on time? (Never.)
9. The weather is very bad. I am afraid that my grandfather may get sick.
10. His wife is afraid that he may lose his job.

22. THE VERB लगना

The intransitive verb लगना was introduced in two different chapters in *Introduction to Hindi Grammar*. Chapter 34 covered some basic usages of the verb लगना where it means "to be attached/adhered to," "to feel (to be felt by)," "to seem" or "to appear," and "to require." In Chapter 40 we discussed the construction where लगना is preceded by the oblique infinitive of the main verb to mean "to begin (to do something)." In this chapter we will review the basic concepts previously covered and discuss further usages of the verb लगना.

Even though लगना has a few basic meanings, it occurs in a variety of expressions and has different connotations in different contexts. For the sake of clarity, its usage can be divided into the following five broad categories:

(1) लगना literally means "to be attached/adhered to." This use of लगना is usually found in a direct construction.

(2) A more frequent connotation of लगना is "to be felt." In such cases, it is used in an indirect verb construction and conveys:

(a) Physical sensations/feelings, such as heat, cold, hunger, thirst, fear, sunshine, wind, and injury

(b) Judgment or the expression of one's feelings about someone or something. This includes judgments about liking/disliking someone or something, finding an object (e.g., a book) or activity (e.g., watching a movie) interesting or boring, easy or difficult, etc.

(c) A perception about someone or something ("it appears that," "it seems like"). Examples of this usage would be "It appears to me that she will not return tomorrow" or "It appears/seems that he is from Japan."

(3) लगना in an indirect verb construction is also used to express the amount of something (time, money) required to perform some activity.

(4) लगना can be used to express "to be arranged" or "to be set up," as with flowers, furniture, booths, stalls, etc.

(5) लगना can also be used with the oblique infinitive of the main verb to convey the meaning "to begin (doing something)."

In order to expose students to the subtle variations in the meanings of लगना, we will discuss the various ways in which लगना can be used and translated in the aforementioned categories.

(1) To be attached to, to be connected to, to adhere to (direct verb construction): This is one of the most direct translations of the verb लगना.

दीवार पर फ़िल्म का इश्तहार लगा था ।	*The film poster was attached to the wall.*
चोट पर पट्टी लगी थी ।	*There was a bandage on the wound.*

There are also a number of instances when the basic meaning of लगना as "to be attached to" can be better translated in English with other phrases, depending on its context:

(a) To be hit by or hurt by a physical object:

उसको दुश्मन की गोली लगी ।	*He was hit by the enemy's bullet.*
चिड़िया को शिकारी का तीर लगा ।	*The bird was hit by the hunter's arrow.*
मेरी आँखों में दवाई लग रही है ।	*Medicine is causing pain in my eyes.*

(b) To be burned: This literally means "to get stuck to/to adhere to." In the following examples, the milk and rice "adhere" to the pan on getting burned.

दूध लग गया है ।	*The milk got burned.*
क्या चावल लग गये हैं ?	*Is the rice burned?*

213

(c) To follow: This can also be seen as "to tail someone" or adhere in the sense of following someone very closely, as if attached.

बिल्ली रामू की बहू के साथ लग गई ।	*The cat followed Ramu's wife closely.*
तुम क्यों मेरे पीछे लगे हो ?	*Why are you following me?*
पुलिस उसके पीछे लगी है ।	*The police are following him.*

(d) To be engaged in (to be busy doing something): This connotation implies that the subject is attached to/engaged in the task at hand.

आजकल वह पढ़ने में लगा है ।	*These days he is busy studying.*
रामू की माँ अपनी पूजा में लग गई ।	*Ramu's mother got busy in (doing her) worship.*

(e) To be related to: Here the sense is of being attached/connected by blood or a close familial relationship.

वह मेरा भतीजा लगता है ।	*He is my nephew (brother's son).*
यह दोस्त मुझे भाई (के) जैसा लगता है ।	*This friend is like a brother to me.*

In the second example, a friendship is seen as a familial relationship.

(f) Some other expressions with लगना:

(i) X की नौकरी लगना *for X to be employed:*

मेरे दोस्त की नौकरी लग गई ।	*My friend got a job.*

This literally means that my friend's job has been attached to him.

(ii) X की आँख लगना *for X to fall asleep:*

दोपहर को मेरी आँखें लग गई ।	*I fell asleep in the afternoon.*

Here the connotation is that my eyelids got attached.

(iii) X में आग लगना *for X to catch fire:*

घर में आग लग गई ।　　　　　　*The house caught fire.*

(iv) X में कीड़ा लगना *for X to be eaten up by worms:*

अनाज में कीड़े लग गये हैं ।　*The grain got infested with worms.*

This usage implies that the worms adhere to something such as cloth, wood, or, as in the above example, grain.

(v) X का दिल / मन Y में लगना *for X's heart to be attached to Y:*

मेरा दिल / मन खाना पकाने में नहीं लगता ।
I don't enjoy cooking. (lit., *My heart is not attached to cooking.*)

आजकल मेरा दिल / मन किसी चीज़ में नहीं लगता ।
These days I don't enjoy anything. (lit., *My heart is not attached to anything these days.*)

संगीत में उसका दिल / मन बहुत लगता है ।
He/she really enjoys music. (lit., *His/her heart is very attached to music.*)

(vi) X को Y की आदत लगना *for X to get habituated to Y:*

उसको सिगरेट पीने की आदत लग गई ।
He got into the habit of smoking.

In other words, the habit of smoking got attached to him. Hence the postposition को is used with the subject "he," and unlike the first five examples, this particular use of लगना requires an indirect verb construction.

(2) To feel/to be felt/to be affected by (indirect verb constructions): This is used in a number of different ways. We will discuss each one in turn.

(a) To express physical sensations/feelings:

क्या आपको वहाँ धूप लग रही है ?
Are you feeling the sun there?

बच्चे को भूख लग रही है, उसे कुछ खाना दो ।
The child is hungry. Give him some food.

उसको कुत्तों से डर लगता है ।
He/she is afraid of dogs.

(b) To express judgment or one's opinion about something (in other words, "to seem," or "to appear"):

आपको हमारा देश कैसा लगता है ?	*How do you like our country?* *(How does our country seem/appear to you?)*
मुझे हिन्दुस्तानी कपड़े सुंदर लगते हैं ।	*I find Indian clothes to be beautiful.*
उसको तुम्हारी बात (बुरी) लग गई ।	*He felt hurt (bad) by your words. (Your words seemed bad/hurtful to him.)*

(c) To express a perception about someone/something ("it seems like," "it appears that"):

(मुझे) लगता है कि कल बारिश होगी ।
It seems [to me] that it will rain tomorrow.

(ऐसा) लगता है कि अगर यही हालत रही, तो देश में क्रान्ति हो जाएगी ।
It seems [to me] that if the same situation prevails, then there will be a revolution in the country.

216

(3) To require, to take (indirect verb constructions): In this particular use the verb लगना expresses the amount of something (e.g., time, money) that is required to perform some activity.

इस शहर में मकान ख़रीदने में बहुत पैसा लगता है ।
It takes a lot of money to buy a house in this city.

आपको वहाँ से मेरे घर आने में कोई आधा घंटा लगेगा ।
It will take you about half an hour to come to my house from there.

(4) For things to be arranged or set up (direct construction):

वहाँ फल की दुकानें लगी हैं ।	*Fruit shops are set up there.*
मेज़ पर आपका खाना लग गया है ।	*Your food has been laid on the table.*
कमरे में कुरसियाँ लगी हैं ।	*The chairs are arranged in the room.*
यहाँ शादी का मंडप लगेगा ।	*The wedding* mandap *will be set up here.*

(5) Oblique infinitive + लगना construction (to begin to do something) (direct construction):

वह अख़बार पढ़ने लगा ।	*He began to read the newspaper.*
संगीत सुनते ही वे लोग नाचने लगे ।	*As soon as they heard the music, they started dancing.*

The Verb लगना: Exercises

1. Transformation drill

He has put a note on his office door.
उसने अपने दफ़्तर के दरवाज़े पर नोट लगाया है ।

There is a note attached to his office door.
उसके दफ़्तर के दरवाज़े पर नोट लगा है ।

उसने अपने होंठों पर लिपस्टिक लगाई थी ।
उसने फटे कागज़ पर स्कॉच टेप लगाया है ।
उसने दीवारों पर सुन्दर तसवीरें लगाई थीं ।
आप इस लिफ़ाफ़े पर कितने पैसे के टिकट लगाएँगे ?
दुलहन ने माथे पर बिन्दी लगाई थी ।
पिताजी ने बच्चे को थप्पड़ लगाया ।
नौकर खाना मेज़ पर लगाएगा ।
उन्होंने पार्टी के लिये कमरे में गुब्बारे लगाये थे ।

2. Substitution drill

Various kinds of stalls have been set up at the fair.
मेले में तरह तरह की दुकानें लगी हैं ।
मेज़ पर प्लेटें
फूलदान में सुन्दर गुलाब
अलमारी में किताबें
कमरे में कुरसियाँ
दराज़ में कपड़े
कमरे के बीच में पलंग
मैदान में सरकस का तम्बू

3. Substitution drill

These days he is busy preparing for the elections.
आजकल वह चुनाव की तैयारी में लगा है ।

परीक्षा की तैयारी में

सरोद सीखने में

घर की मरम्मत करने में

मेहमानों की ख़ातिरदारी में

समाज सेवा में

आत्मकथा लिखने में

योगासन सीखने में

नौकरी ढूँढ़ने में

4. Answer the following questions

Why is the child crying?   Perhaps he has gotten hurt.
बच्चा क्यों रो रहा है ?   शायद उसको चोट लगी है ।

वह खाना क्यों माँग रही है ?

वह ठंडा पानी क्यों पी रही है ?

लड़के ने स्वेटर क्यों पहना है ?

किसान पेड़ के नीचे क्यों बैठा है ?

शिक्षक ने खिड़की क्यों बन्द की ?

कुत्ते को देखकर बच्ची क्यों चीखी ?

माँ ने बिजली का पंखा क्यों चलाया ?

5. Answer the following questions

I find Paris to be the most beautiful city. Which city do you find to be the most beautiful?
मुझे पेरिस सबसे सुन्दर शहर लगता है । आपको कौन-सा शहर सबसे सुन्दर लगता है ?

I find San Francisco to be the most beautiful city.
मुझे सैन फ़्रैन्सिस्को सबसे सुन्दर शहर लगता है ।

मुझे जापानी फ़िल्में दिलचस्प लगती हैं । तुम्हें कौन-सी फ़िल्में दिलचस्प लगती हैं ?
मुझे गणित मुश्किल लगता है । तुझे कौन-सा विषय मुश्किल लगता है ?
मुझे भाषाएँ सीखना आसान लगता है । तुम्हें क्या करना आसान लगता है ?
मुझे गरम मौसम अच्छा लगता है । तुम्हें कौन-सा मौसम अच्छा लगता है ?
मुझे चटपटा खाना मज़ेदार लगता है । तुझे कैसा खाना मज़ेदार लगता है ?
मुझे यह नेता पागल लगता है । आपको कौन पागल लगता है ?
मुझे यह रिवाज़ अजीब लगता है । आपको क्या अजीब लगता है ?
मुझे यह किताब नीरस लगती है । आपको कौन-सी किताब नीरस लगती है ?
मुझे शिकायत करना बुरा लगता है । आपको क्या बुरा लगता है ?

6. Substitution drill

It seems to me that he won't be able to return today.
मुझे लगता है कि वह आज नहीं लौट सकेगा ।

      that he will lose in this election
      that this war will cost a lot of money
      that this book will not be interesting
      that she will be married soon
      that this year a lot of snow will fall
      that he is angry with me
      that a lot of people will come to listen to his speech
      that the world's population will never decrease

7. Answer the following questions

How is he [formal] related to you?   He is my uncle.
वे आपके कौन / क्या लगते हैं ?   वे मेरे चाचा लगते हैं ।

आपका दिल / मन किस चीज़ में लगता है ?
बच्चे को चोट कैसे लगी ?
आपकी गाड़ी को किससे टक्कर लगी ?

तुम्हारे भाई की नौकरी कहाँ लगी है ?

वह लड़कियों के पीछे क्यों लगा रहता है ?

किसकी लापरवाही से घर में आग लगी ?

आपके बग़ीचे में कौन कौन से फूल लगे हैं ?

आज फिर किससे दूध लग गया ?

इन किताबों में दीमक क्यों लग गई ?

दोपहर को कितने बजे माँ की आँखें लग गईं ?

यह चाबी किस कमरे के ताले में लगती है ?

उसके पाँव में काँटा कैसे लग गया ?

हवाई जाने में कितना पैसा लगता है ?

क्या उसको पुलिस की लाठी लगी ?

आपका क्या करने में मन लगता है ?

किसको रोज़ सवेरे कॉफ़ी पीने की आदत लग गई है ?

इस साल आपके फलों में कीड़ा क्यों लग गया?

8. Translation exercise

(Use the appropriate लगना construction.)

1. Do you enjoy living in cities or in villages?
2. The little girl got hurt while playing.
3. I am afraid of living alone.
4. He got in the habit of telling lies.
5. She has a pretty flower in her hair.
6. That game seems dangerous to me.
7. It takes a lot of money to win an election.
8. Why are those boys always following her?
9. While she was busy talking on the phone, the rice got burned.
10. People say that she looks like my sister, but she is my mother.
11. I am feeling hungry because I haven't eaten breakfast this morning.
12. Every Sunday fruit and vegetable shops are set up here.
13. Her sari suddenly caught fire while she was cooking.
14. There are bugs in those tomatoes. Don't eat them.
15. These days he is busy preparing for his daughter's wedding.

23. INTERJECTIONS

Interjections are words or sounds that convey emotions such as joy, surprise, grief, or fear. They can also express approval, disapproval, and disgust, or they can be used to get someone's attention. Interjections are independent words that have no grammatical connection to the structure of the sentences in which they occur. Thus, they are invariable and act as if they are sentences in and of themselves. In written Hindi, interjections are almost always followed by an exclamation mark. However, in spoken Hindi, the intensity of a particular emotion can be expressed only through intonation.

The following is a list of commonly used interjections. Note that though translations have been given, they are only approximate, as many of these interjections are just sounds made in different emotional contexts.

To get someone's attention:

ए !	*Hey!*	ऐ / ओए !	*Hey!*
हे !	*Hey!*	ओ !	*Oh!*
अरे !	*Hey!*	अजी !	*Please listen!*
क्यों रे !	*Hey listen!*	सुनो !	*Listen!*
अबे !	*Hey you!* (derogatory)	सुनिये !	*Please listen!*
अरी !	*Hey!* (used only when addressing women)		

Note that since these interjections are used to get someone's attention, they are often followed by nouns in the vocative case (the case used to address people). For example, "हे लड़के !," "ओ बच्चो !," or "अरी लड़कियो !" (See Appendix I for further explanation of the vocative case.)

To express agreement:

अच्छा !	*Good!*	बहुत अच्छा !	*Very Good!*
ठीक !	*Correct! Right!*	ज़रूर !	*Certainly!*
जी !	*Yes!*	जी हाँ / हाँ जी !	*Yes!*
हाँ !	*Yes!*		

To express disagreement:

| नहीं ! | *No!* | कभी नहीं ! | *Never!* |
| जी नहीं / नहीं जी ! | *No!* | हरगिज़ नहीं ! | *Absolutely not!* |

To express approval, appreciation, or joy:

वाह !	*Wonderful! Excellent!*	वाह-वाह !	*Wonderful!*
कमाल !	*Wonderful! Miraculous!*	बहुत ख़ूब !	*Excellent! Well done!*
अहा !	*How wonderful!*	क्या बात है !	*How wonderful!*
ओहो !	*Oh! Great!*	बढ़िया !	*Excellent!*
बहुत अच्छा / बहुत अच्छे !	*Well done! Very good!*		
शाबाश !	*Excellent! Well done! Bravo! Splendid!*		
धन्य-धन्य !	*Well done! How fortunate!* (archaic)		

To express surprise, wonder, or doubt:

अरे !	*Huh! Oh!*	सच !	*Really! Truly!*
ऐं !	*Oh!*	वाक़ई !	*Really!*
अच्छा !	*Really!*	सचमुच !	*Really! Truly!*
वाह !	*Wow!*	क्या कहा !	*What did you say!* (disbelief)
हैं !	*Oh!*	क्या !	*What! Really!*
कमाल !	*Amazing! Incredible! Miraculous!*		
ख़ाक !	*Nonsense!* (disbelief) *Not a bit! By no means!*		

To express gratitude:

| धन्यवाद ! | *Thank you!* | शुक्रिया ! | *Thanks!* |
| मेहरबानी ! | *Very kind of you!* | | |

To express grief, sorrow, or regret:

हा !	*Oh!*	हाय !	*Alas!*
हाय-हाय !	*Oh no!*	ओफ़ / ओफ़्फ़ो !	*Oh!*
ऊह !	*Uh!*	आह !	*Alas!*
उफ़ !	*Oof!*	अफ़सोस !	*Alas!*
हे भगवान !	*Oh God!*	राम-राम !	*Oh God!*

223

To express contempt, disgust, or disapproval:

छि: !	*Gross! Dirty! Disgusting!*
थू !	*Dirty!*
दुर !	*Go away! Shoo!*
धिक् !	*Shame!*
धिक्कार !	*Shame!*
धत् !	*Cut it out!*
धत् तेरे की !	*You rascal, cut it out!*
हुश !	*Shoo! Shh! Go away! Be quiet!*
हट !	*Out of my way!*
चल चल !	*Come on! What nonsense! Move on!*
जा जा !	*Go on! What nonsense!*

To express fear or distress:

अरे !	*Oh!*	हे भगवान !	*Oh God!*
हाय / हाय रे !	*Alas!*	हाय मरा !	*Oh, I'm done for!*
दैया रे !	*Oh dear!*	हाय मर गया !	*Oh, I'm done for!*
बाप रे / बाप रे बाप !	*Oh dear! Oh my goodness!*		
मारे गये !	*I'm/we're done for! I'm/we're dead!*		

To give warning:

ख़बरदार !	*Don't you dare! Watch out!*
होशियार !	*Watch out! Be careful!*
सावधान !	*Watch out! Be careful!*
बचके / बचकर !	*Watch out! Be careful!*

Notes

1. As seen above, some interjections can convey more than one emotion, based on the context in which they are used. For example, "अरे !" can be used to articulate surprise or wonder or to get someone's attention, as well as to express fear or distress. Similarly, "हाय!" and "हे भगवान!" can be used to express grief, sorrow, or regret, as well as to express fear or distress.

2. Sometimes other parts of speech such as nouns, adjectives, pronouns, verbs, participles, and phrases are used as interjections. Thus, the conjunctive participles बचके and बचकर and the imperatives सुनो, सुनिये, चल चल, जा जा, and हट are also listed here as interjections.

Interjections: Exercises

1. Fill in the blanks

_____! ज़रा मेरी बात सुनिये । (to get someone's attention)

_____! राजू, यहाँ आ । (to get someone's attention)

_____! तो हम कल मिलेंगे । (to express agreement)

_____! आप बिलकुल ठीक कहते हैं । (to express agreement)

_____! मैं ऐसा कभी नहीं करूँगा । (to express disagreement)

_____! आप मेरी बात बिलकुल ग़लत समझे । (to express disagreement)

_____! मैं अपनी बेटी की शादी उस से कभी नहीं करूँगा । (to express disagreement)

_____! कितना सुन्दर दृश्य है । (to express joy)

_____! हमारी तो लॉटरी लग गई । (to express joy)

_____! अब हम सब साथ यूरोप जा सकते हैं । (to express joy)

_____! आपका गाना सुनकर मज़ा आ गया । (to express appreciation)

_____! तुमने कितनी अच्छी कविता लिखी । (to express approval)

_____! उसने इतनी छोटी उम्र में इतनी शोहरत पाई । (to express surprise)

_____! क्या ऐसा भी कभी हो सकता है ? (to express wonder)

_____! वह वापस आ भी गया ।   (to express doubt)

_____! तुम मुझे छोड़कर विदेश चले जाओगे ।   (to express doubt)

_____! आपने मेरी बहुत मदद की । (to express gratitude)

_____! आप ही की वजह से मुझे यह नौकरी मिली । (to express gratitude)

_____! अब मैं क्या करूँ ? (to express regret)

_____! मेरी तो तक़दीर ही फूट गई । (to express sorrow or grief)

_____! उसकी इतनी छोटी उम्र में मृत्यु हो गई ।(to express regret, sorrow, or grief)

_____! यहाँ कितना कीचड़ है । (to express disgust)

_____! ऐसी बातें मत कर । (to express disapproval)

तू मेरी मदद _____ करेगा । तू पहले अपनी मदद कर । (to express doubt/disbelief)

_____! मैं तो लुट गया । (to express distress)

_____! मेरे बच्चे कहाँ हैं ? (to express distress)

_____! यह हमारे घर में कौन घुस आया । (to express fear)

_____! वहाँ मत जाना । उनका कुत्ता ख़तरनाक है ।   (to give warning)

_____! जो मेरी बेटी के पास आने की हिम्मत भी की । (to give warning)

2. Translation exercise

1. Oh God! What is this that I have done?
2. Hey! Where did you put my glasses?
3. Good! We'll meet tomorrow at 10 o'clock sharp.
4. Watch out! Don't go in that room. There is glass on the floor.
5. Really! You didn't know about his marriage?
6. How wonderful! I didn't know she could sing so well.
7. Oh no! What have you done to my car?
8. Excellent! You came just in time.
9. Disgusting! Why don't you ever clean your room?
10. Absolutely not! I will never give him my vote.

24. PAIRING WORDS

Hyphenated compounds, echo pairs, and the reduplication of words are three ways of achieving linguistic and semantic variation in Hindi. While echo pairs bring together words that rhyme or share similar sounds, hyphenated compounds join words of similar, slightly different, or opposite meaning, and reduplication simply involves the repetition of a single word. These word pairs are very frequent, especially in colloquial Hindi, and they allow speakers to broaden, intensify, and/or change the meaning of a particular word or even to change the overall tone of a statement.

Hyphenated Compounds

Hyphenated compounds are very common in formal and informal Hindi. They generally combine two words (usually of the same part of speech) that are similar, slightly different, or opposite in meaning into a single hyphenated compound. In such word pairs the hyphen replaces a conjunction (e.g., और, या, etc.) that might otherwise be used to join the two words. While in some compounds the hyphen represents the conjunction और, (also व, तथा, एवम्, etc.), in other compounds it replaces या (also वा, अथवा, etc.). Though most hyphenated pairs have become fixed expressions that automatically imply the use of one conjunction or the other, there are some cases in which there is some ambiguity. In these cases, only context can clarify which conjunction is being replaced by the hyphen.

When words with similar meaning are joined with a hyphen to form compounds, they generally serve to intensify or generalize the shared meaning of both words. For example, उबड़-खाबड़ means "rough and uneven," दुबला-पतला means "lean and thin," and अच्छा-ख़ासा means "very good, fine." When a hyphen is used to join two words of opposite or different meaning, sometimes it functions as a replacement for the English "and" and sometimes for "or." For example, छोटा-बड़ा can mean either "big or small" or "big and small." However, a hyphen can also be used sometimes to form a compound that has a new meaning, one that is largely determined by the first word in the compound. For example, छोटा-मोटा means "small, smallish; ordinary" (not "small and/or fat"), and थोड़ा-बहुत means "a little; a small amount" (not "a little and/or a lot").

228

Examples:

पति-पत्नी	*husband and wife*
माता-पिता	*mother and father*
भाई-बहन	*brother and sister*
दिन-रात / रात-दिन	*day and night; day or night*
सुबह-शाम	*morning and evening; morning or evening*
कल-परसों	*tomorrow or the day after (tomorrow)*
इधर-उधर	*here and there; here or there*
अन्दर-बाहर	*inside and outside*
उलटा-सीधा	*right or wrong; wrong*
ऊँच-नीच	*ups and downs*
आना-जाना	*coming and going*
अच्छा-बुरा	*good and bad; good or bad*
हार-जीत	*defeat and victory; defeat or victory*
नफ़ा-नुकसान	*gain and loss; gain or loss*
लाभ-हानि	*gain and loss; gain or loss*
दो-तीन	*two or three*
दो-चार	*a few* (lit., *two or four*)
मौज-मस्ती	*joy and delight; fun and games; indulgence*
लड़ना-झगड़ना	*fighting and quarreling*
मिलना-जुलना	*to socialize* (lit., *meeting and mingling*)
नौकर-चाकर	*servants and attendants*
काम-काज	*work, business, and other tasks*
छान-बीन	*thorough search and investigation*

Echo Pairs

Though not usually found in literary or formal language, echo pairs are commonly used in colloquial Hindi to broaden or expand the meaning of a word, to include things of a similar type, to lighten up a conversation, and/or to add a touch of humor. They are also used to add emphasis or to intensify the meaning of a word. They consist of a main word plus a rhyming or echoing component and are almost always joined by a hyphen (e.g., चाय-वाय). The rhyming or echoing component can be a word that conveys the same meaning as the main word of the pair, or it may not convey any meaning at all. Note that even words that are borrowed from other languages may be used in echo pairs (e.g., सूट-बूट).

Formation

While there are no set rules for the formation of echo pairs, there are several common patterns to help students recognize and understand such pairs.

(1) The most commonly occurring echo pairs are formed by repeating the main word but changing its initial consonant to "व" to form the "echo." The main word is the first element of such compounds, while the echo word is the second. In such pairs, the echo word serves to broaden or expand the meaning of the main word. Thus, पानी-वानी means "water (or something else to drink)."

Examples:

गाड़ी-वाड़ी	*car (or some other form of transportation)*
शराब-वराब	*wine (or some other type of drink)*
रोटी-वोटी	*roti (or some other kind of bread)*
अचार-वचार	*pickle (or some other condiment)*
पार्टी-वार्टी	*party (or some other kind of gathering)*
पेंसिल-वेंसिल	*pencil (or something else with which to write)*
पालिश-वालिश	*polish (or something like it)*

Sometimes म is used instead of व to form an echo pair. Constructions with म are generally used to intensify the meaning of the main word.

Examples:

टेढ़ा-मेढ़ा	*crooked and/or twisted*
झूट-मूट	*lie (or false statement)*
गोल-मटोल	*fat and squat; flabby*

(2) Hindi speakers also form echo pairs by repeating the main word but changing its initial vowel sound in order to form the second element of the compound. Generally, the second element in these pairs simply intensifies or emphasizes the meaning of the main word.

Examples:

धूम-धाम	*pomp, show, or ostentatious display*
घूमना-घामना	*to wander about*
ठीक-ठाक	*all right, good, fine, okay*
छेड़-छाड़	*teasing, taunting, provoking*
चुप-चाप (से)	*quietly, silently*

(3) The verb stem of a conjunctive participle can also be modified and repeated to form an echo pair.

Examples:

ढूँढ़-ढाँढ़ कर	*having searched thoroughly*
धो-धा कर	*having washed thoroughly*
सोच-साच कर	*having thought thoroughly*
पीट-पाट कर	*having beaten thoroughly*

As seen from the above translations, these echo pairs generally convey a sense of thoroughness or intensity of an action.

(4) In some echo pairs the rhyming or echoing component precedes the main word. The first element of the echo word in such cases is usually the vowel अ or आ.

Examples:

अदल-बदल	*exchange, interchange*
अड़ोस-पड़ोस	*neighborhood and/or vicinity*
अता-पता	*whereabouts and/or address*
आलतू-फ़ालतू	*useless, unnecessary, dispensible*
आलथी-पालथी	*cross-legged posture*

Note that while the echo word in the first three pairs expands the meaning or scope of the main word, the echo words in the last two pairs do not add any additional meaning to the main word.

(5) Echo pairs can also be formed by combining two words of similar meaning. Here again, the echo pair serves to emphasize or generalize the shared meaning of both words.

Examples:

तोड़ना-फोड़ना	*to break into pieces, to shatter*
टूट-फूट	*breakage, fragmentation*
जान-पहचान	*acquaintance*
चमक-दमक	*glitter, shine, splendor*
सूझ-बूझ	*reasoning, common sense*

(6) In addition to the patterns discussed above, there are also echo pairs in Hindi that do not follow any observable patterns but maintain some similarity in sound.

Examples:

गाली-गलौज	*mutual (verbal) abuse; profanity*
अलग-थलग	*separate, aloof, isolated*
गंदा-शंदा	*dirty, filthy*
नोक-झोंक	*squabbling, mild rivalry*
अनाप-शनाप	*nonsense; confusion*
हट्टा-कट्टा	*sturdy, robust*
हेरा-फेरी	*change of order or position; manipulation*
चोरी-चकारी	*small-time theft/thievery*
बक-झक करना	*to chatter, to talk nonsense*
टाल-मटोल करना	*to put off, to defer, to make excuses*
हबड़-दबड़	*erratic haste, helter-skelter*

Reduplication

In Hindi, certain parts of speech (nouns, adjectives, adverbs, verb stems, interrogatives, etc.) may be reduplicated to indicate the following: to intensify the meaning of a word or phrase; to express the frequency or thoroughness of an action; to distribute an item, attribute, or quality throughout a group of people or things or across a specific time or space; to ask for specific details about someone or something, especially with the reduplication of interrogatives. Note that the meaning of each reduplicated phrase changes based on context.

Reduplication Using Nouns

दीवाली पर घर घर में दीपक जलते हैं ।	*On Diwali, lamps are lit in each and every home.*
देश के कोने कोने में उसकी शोहरत है ।	*His fame is well known in every corner of the nation.*
देश में जगह जगह पर पुरानी इमारतें हैं ।	*There are old buildings all over the country.*
यह हमारा जन्म जन्म का रिश्ता है ।	*This relationship of ours has lasted for a long time* (lit., *from one birth to the next*).
यहाँ बच्चे बच्चे को आपका नाम मालूम है ।	*Here each and every child knows your name.*
सच सच बताओ ।	*Tell me the whole/real truth.*

In the first three sentences above, nouns are reduplicated to indicate that the subject of the sentence is distributed across the space they designate. Thus, lamps, the subject of the first sentence, are distributed from home to home; fame, in the second sentence, is distributed from corner to corner of the nation; and old buildings, in the third sentence, are distributed from place to place across the country. The fourth sentence is an example of distribution across time. Hence, the reduplication of जन्म indicates that the subject of the sentence, the relationship, spans across many births. The subject of the fifth sentence, the name, is distributed across a group of children by the reduplication of बच्चे. Reduplication of सच in the final sentence indicates the thoroughness expected by the speaker in the act of telling the truth.

Reduplication Using Adjectives

(1) Reduplication using adjectives of quality:

मुझे गरम गरम चाय पसन्द है ।
I like very hot tea.

उसकी बड़ी बड़ी आँखें बहुत सुन्दर हैं ।
Her huge (very big) eyes are very beautiful.

मैं आपको मीठे मीठे आम दूँगा ।
I will give you very sweet mangoes.

तुम क्यों हमेशा महँगे महँगे कपड़े ख़रीदती हो ?
Why do you always buy expensive clothes?

Note that the reduplication of adjectives modifying an uncountable object, such as चाय, generally intensifies/amplifies a specific quality or attribute, such as the hotness of the tea. The reduplication of adjectives modifying countable nouns like आम or कपड़े can distribute a specific quality or attribute among a certain group of people or things, or sometimes, as with आँखें above, it simply intensifies a specific quality or attribute.

(2) Reduplication using adjectives of quantity/numbers:

सरकार सब बाढ़ पीड़ितों को दो दो हज़ार रुपये देगी ।
The government will give all flood victims two thousand rupees each.

भाई की शादी पर सब बहनों को एक एक साड़ी मिली ।
All the sisters got one sari each at (their) brother's wedding.

ये सब खिलौने बीस बीस रुपये के हैं ।
All of these toys are twenty rupees each.

तुम लोग जाने से पहले थोड़ा थोड़ा खाना खा लो ।
Each of you eat a little something before you go.

आपका बहुत बहुत शुक्रिया ।
Thank you very much.

Numbers and quantities can be reduplicated in Hindi to indicate that the nouns they modify are distributed among a certain group of people or things. In the first sentence above, the number two is repeated to show that each person in the specified group of flood victims will get two thousand rupees. Note that even though the amount to be distributed is two thousand, only the first numerical element is reduplicated. Similarly, in the second sentence, the number one is repeated to show that all the sisters got one sari each. In the third sentence the number twenty is repeated to indicate the distribution of price within a specified group (खिलौने); hence, the price of each toy is twenty rupees. In the fourth sentence above, a quantity (थोड़ा) rather than a specific number is distributed among a group (तुम लोग). In the final sentence above, the quantity बहुत is repeated to emphasize the thoroughness/intensity of the act of thanking.

Reduplication Using Adverbs or Adverbial Phrases

जल्दी जल्दी काम ख़त्म करो ।	*Finish your work quickly.*
वह बहुत आहिस्ता आहिस्ता बोली ।	*She spoke very softly/slowly.*
सीधे सीधे जवाब दो ।	*Give me a straight answer.*
मैं कभी कभी अपनी ही दुनिया में खो जाती हूँ ।	*Sometimes I get lost in my own world.*
कल कहीं कहीं बारिश हुई ।	*Yesterday it rained here and there.*

Reduplication of the adverbs जल्दी, आहिस्ता, and सीधे in the first three examples above emphasizes the intensity or thoroughness of the actions they modify. This intensity/thoroughness is generally difficult to convey in translation. In the last two sentences, the reduplicated adverbs कभी कभी and कहीं कहीं have specific idiomatic meanings.

235

Reduplication Using Verbs

मैं सोच सोचकर भी उसकी हरकत का कारण नहीं समझ पाया ।

Even after much thought, I could not understand the reason for his/her action.

भारत के बारे में माँ की बातें सुन सुनकर मैंने वहाँ जाने का फ़ैसला कर लिया ।

After repeatedly hearing Mother talk about India, I decided to go there.

ग़रीब बच्चों का हाल देख देखकर मुझे बड़ा अफ़सोस हुआ ।

I felt (became) very sad after repeatedly seeing the condition of poor children.

The reduplication of the verb stems सोच, सुन, and देख, used as conjunctive participles (the कर construction) in the three sentences above, expresses the frequency or the thoroughness of the action they indicate.

Reduplication Using Interrogatives

यूरोप में आप कहाँ कहाँ घूमे ?	*Where all (specifically) did you travel in Europe?*
अस्पताल के उद्घाटन में कौन कौन आया ?	*Who all (specifically) came to the inauguration of the hospital?*
आप मसालेवाली चाय में क्या क्या डालते हैं ?	*What all (specifically) do you put in masala chai?*
तुम किस किस मुहल्ले में होली खेलने गये ?	*To which (specific) neighborhoods did you go to play Holi?*
आपको कौन कौन-से फूल पसन्द हैं ?	*Which (specific) flowers do you like?*

Interrogatives that are reduplicated, such as कहाँ कहाँ, कौन कौन, क्या क्या, किस किस, and कौन कौन-से in the sentences above, are used to ask for specific details about someone or something. Note that in the final example, only the first element of the interrogative is repeated.

25. AFFIXES

As with many other languages, Hindi also uses affixes to enrich its vocabulary and allow for linguistic flexibility. Various words are formed in Hindi by adding prefixes and suffixes. These prefixes and suffixes are not words in and of themselves, but rather they are attached to the beginning or end of certain words in order to change their meaning and/or to change them from one part of speech to another.

Examples:

सत्य M *truth*	can become	असत्य M *untruth; a lie*
सरल A *easy, simple*	can become	सरलता F *simplicity, ease*

This chapter covers some commonly used Hindi prefixes and suffixes. Knowledge of these will help students to analyze and better understand new words they encounter in their readings and conversations. Since Hindi is influenced by many languages, including Sanskrit, Arabic, and Persian, we often find affixes that are also derived from these sources and that generally (but not always) augment words from the corresponding languages.

Prefixes

As their name indicates, prefixes come before the word to which they are attached. They are most often attached to nouns and adjectives to form new words. In this chapter, prefixes have been divided into two basic categories: the first group is prefixes of Sanskrit or Hindi origin, while the second group includes prefixes of Persian or Arabic origin.

Prefixes Derived from Sanskrit or Hindi

अ- [Sanskrit and Hindi] *non-, un-, in-, -less*
This prefix usually changes a noun or an adjective into another noun or adjective and denotes "not," "without," or "lacking."

Examples:

चूक F	mistake	अचूक A	unerring, unfailing
थाह F	bottom, limit	अथाह A	bottomless, limitless
न्याय M	justice	अन्याय M	injustice
सत्य M	truth	असत्य M	untruth, a lie

स्थिर A	stable	अस्थिर A	unstable
हिंसा F	violence	अहिंसा F	nonviolence

अन- [Sanskrit and Hindi] *un-*, *in-*, *im-*, *dis-*, *-less*

This prefix generally changes a noun or an adjective into an adjective and denotes "not," "without," or "lacking."

Examples:

जाना A	known	अनजाना A	unknown
ब्याहा A	married	अनब्याहा A	unmarried
मोल M	value, price	अनमोल A	invaluable, priceless, precious
होनी F	being, existence	अनहोनी A	improbable, impossible

अप- [Sanskrit] *dis-*, *in-*; *bad*

This prefix often changes a noun into another noun and denotes something bad or lacking.

Examples:

मान M	honor, respect	अपमान M	disgrace, insult
यश M	honor, glory, fame	अपयश M	dishonor, disgrace, infamy
शकुन M	omen (auspicious)	अपशकुन M	bad omen
शब्द M	word	अपशब्द M	bad word; term of abuse

कु- [Sanskrit and Hindi] *un-*, *ill-*, *mis-*; *bad*

This prefix often changes a noun into another noun or adjective and denotes something bad, defective, evil, or unworthy.

Examples:

कर्म M	deed, action	कुकर्म M	evil deed, bad action

चाल F	motion, pace, a move	कुचाल F	bad move, bad ways, misconduct
पात्र M	character (lit., vessel)	कुपात्र M	unworthy person, bad character, villain
पुत्र M	son	कुपुत्र M	bad son
रूप M	form, shape, appearance	कुरूप A/M	ugly, ill-formed; an ugly person

दुर्- [Sanskrit] *mis-, ill-, bad*

This prefix can change a noun or an adjective into another noun or adjective and denotes something bad, wrong, or lacking.

Examples:

गुण M	quality, virtue	दुर्गुण M	bad quality, vice
घटना F	incident, event	दुर्घटना F	accident, disaster
दशा F	situation, condition	दुर्दशा F	bad situation, bad condition
बल M	strength, power	दुर्बल A	weak
भाग्य M	fate, fortune, luck	दुर्भाग्य M	misfortune, ill-fortune, bad luck

निर्/नि- [Sanskrit and Hindi] *un-, -less*

This prefix generally changes nouns into adjectives and denotes "not having" or "without."

Examples:

डर M	fear	निडर A	fearless
धन M	wealth	निर्धन A	poor
भय M	fear	निर्भय A	fearless
मल M	dirt, impurity	निर्मल A	clear, pure
विघ्न M	obstacle	निर्विघ्न A	unobstructed

पुनर्- [Sanskrit] *re-*

This prefix generally changes a noun into another noun and denotes something done again or anew.

Examples:

जन्म M	birth	पुनर्जन्म M	rebirth
जागरण M	wakefulness, awareness	पुनर्जागरण M	renaissance, reawakening
निर्माण M	construction, building	पुनर्निर्माण M	reconstruction, rebuilding
मिलन M	union, meeting	पुनर्मिलन M	reunion
विवाह M	marriage	पुनर्विवाह M	remarriage

स- [Sanskrit] *with, full of, –ful*

This prefix can change a noun into an adjective and denotes "with" or "together with."

Examples:

जीव M	life, living creature	सजीव A	living, full of life
परिवार M	family	सपरिवार A	with family
फल M	fruit, result	सफल A	fruitful, successful
हर्ष M	happiness, joy	सहर्ष A	with happiness, with joy
हृदय M	heart	सहृदय A	compassionate, sensitive (lit., with heart)

सह- [Sanskrit] *co-*

This prefix generally changes a noun into another noun and denotes "with," "together with;" "same" or "similar."

Examples:

कार्य M	work	सहकार्य M	cooperation, collaboration

गान M	song	सहगान M	chorus
गामिनी F	one who goes	सहगामिनी F	co-traveler, companion
मति F	mind, understanding, thought	सहमति F	agreement
योग M	connection, union	सहयोग M	cooperation, collaboration

सु- [Sanskrit and Hindi] *good, well-*
This prefix can change a noun or adjective into another noun or adjective.

Examples:

कर्म M	deed, action	सुकर्म M	good deed, good action
गंध F	smell, odor	सुगंध F	good smell, fragrance
डौल M	shape, build	सुडौल A	well-built, strong; shapely, graceful
पुत्र M	son	सुपुत्र M	good son
रक्षित A	protected	सुरक्षित A	well-protected

स्व- [Sanskrit] *self-*
This prefix generally changes a noun into another noun and denotes something that is one's own.

Examples:

कर्म M	deed, action	स्वकर्म M	one's own deed/action
देश M	country	स्वदेश M	one's own country
धर्म M	religion; duty	स्वधर्म M	one's own religion; one's own/personal duty
भाव M	emotion, feelings, sentiment	स्वभाव M	one's own nature, one's own temperament
राज्य M	kingdom, state, rule	स्वराज्य M	self-rule

Prefixes Derived from Persian or Arabic

ख़ुश- [Persian] *good, happy*
This prefix generally changes nouns into adjectives.

Examples:

क़िस्मत F	fate, destiny, luck	ख़ुशक़िस्मत A	fortunate
दिल M	heart	ख़ुशदिल A	happy, content
नसीब M	destiny, fate, fortune	ख़ुशनसीब A	fortunate
मिज़ाज M	temperament	ख़ुशमिज़ाज A	of cheerful temperament
हाल M	condition, situation	ख़ुशहाल A	happy, prosperous

ग़ैर- [Arabic] *not, without*
This prefix changes an adjective or noun into another adjective or noun and can also denote something that is against, un-related, or foreign.

Examples:

क़ानूनी A	legal	ग़ैरक़ानूनी A	illegal
ज़िम्मेदारी F	responsibility	ग़ैरज़िम्मेदारी F	irresponsibility
मुमकिन A	possible	ग़ैरमुमकिन A	impossible
मुल्क M	country	ग़ैरमुल्क M	foreign country
सरकारी A	governmental, official	ग़ैरसरकारी A	nongovernmental, unofficial
हाज़िर A	present	ग़ैरहाज़िर A	absent

ना- [Persian] *un-, dis-, in-*
This prefix generally changes a noun or an adjective into another adjective and denotes "not" or "without something."

Examples:

क़ाबिल A	capable, worthy	नाक़ाबिल A	incapable, unworthy
ख़ुश A	happy	नाख़ुश A	unhappy
पसन्द F	liking	नापसन्द A	disliked

मुनासिब A	appropriate, proper	नामुनासिब A	inappropriate, improper
लायक A	worthy, able	नालायक A	unworthy, incapable
समझ F	understanding, intelligence	नासमझ A	unintelligent, naive

ब- [Persian] *with*, *by*, *according to*

This prefix generally changes nouns into adverbs.

Examples:

ख़ूबी F	excellence, virtue	बख़ूबी Adv	with excellence, excellently; thoroughly
दस्तूर M	custom, practice, rule, normal procedure	बदस्तूर Adv	according to custom, as usual
दौलत F	wealth, fortune	बदौलत Adv	by the good fortune of
नाम M	name	बनाम Adv	by the name (of)
हुक्म M	order	बहुक्म Adv	by the order (of)

बद- [Persian] *un-*, *in-*, *dis-*, *bad*

This prefix change a noun into an adjective or a noun and denotes something bad or unpleasant.

Examples:

क़िस्मत F	fate, destiny, luck	बदक़िस्मत A	unlucky
तमीज़ F	manners, courtesy	बदतमीज़ A	discourteous, rude
नाम M	name	बदनाम A	infamous, disgraced
बू F	smell, odor	बदबू F	bad smell, bad odor
सूरत F	form, face	बदसूरत A	ugly

बा- [Persian] *with*, *by*, *according to*

This prefix generally changes nouns into adjectives or adverbs.

Examples:

अदब M	respect	बाअदब A/Adv	respectful; respectfully
असर M	effect, influence	बाअसर A/Adv	effective, influential; effectively, influentially
ईमान M	faith, honesty	बाईमान A/Adv	honest, faithful; honestly, faithfully
क़ायदा M	rule, regulation, custom	बाक़ायदा A/Adv	regular, orderly; according to the rule, by the rule

बे- [Persian] *un-*, *-less*, *without*

This prefix generally changes nouns into adjectives and denotes not having something.

Examples:

अक़्ल F	wisdom, intellect	बेअक़्ल A	stupid, foolish
घर M	house	बेघर A	homeless
रोज़गार M	employment, livelihood	बेरोज़गार A	unemployed
शर्म F	shame, modesty, bashfulness	बेशर्म A	shameless
होश M	consciousness	बेहोश A	unconscious

ला- [Arabic] *in-*, *un-*

This prefix generally changes a noun into an adjective and denotes "not" or "without."

Examples:

इलाज M	medical treatment, remedy	लाइलाज A	incurable

244

जवाब M	answer; an equal	लाजवाब A	without answer, speechless; incomparable
पता M	address, whereabouts	लापता A	missing; of unknown whereabouts
वारिस M	heir; protector; owner	लावारिस A/M	stray; without heir; orphan

हम- [Persian] *co-, similar, equal*

This prefix generally changes nouns into nouns or adjectives and denotes "with," "together with," or "something in common or shared."

Examples:

उम्र F	age	हमउम्र A	of the same age
दर्द M	pain, sorrow	हमदर्द A/M	sympathetic; compassionate; a person who shows sympathy
राज़ M	secret	हमराज़ M	a person who knows someone's secret
राह F	path	हमराह M	fellow traveler, companion
वतन M	country	हमवतन A/M	of the same country; fellow countryman
शक़्ल F	face, form, appearance	हमशक़्ल A/M	of the same appearance; look-alike
सफ़र M	journey	हमसफ़र M	fellow traveler, companion

Suffixes

Suffixes can be attached at the end of a verb stem, noun, or adjective to create new words. As with prefixes, they are mostly derived from Sanskrit, Hindi, Persian, or Arabic.

Suffixes Derived from Sanskrit or Hindi

-आ [Hindi]

This suffix changes a verb stem into a masculine noun.

Examples:

घेर(ना) Tr	to surround	घेरा M	circle, encirclement
झगड़(ना) Intr	to quarrel, to fight	झगड़ा M	quarrel, fight
झूल(ना) Intr	to swing	झूला M	swing

-आई [Hindi]

This suffix changes a verb stem into a feminine noun.

Examples:

कमा(ना) Tr	to earn	कमाई F	earning
चढ़(ना) Intr	to climb	चढ़ाई F	ascent
पढ़(ना) Tr	to study	पढ़ाई F	studying, education
लड़(ना) Intr	to fight	लड़ाई F	fight

-आवट [Hindi]

This suffix changes a verb stem into a feminine noun.

Examples:

बन(ना) Intr	to be made	बनावट F	construction, structure, form, appearance
रुक(ना) Intr	to stop	रुकावट F	obstruction
लिख(ना) Tr	to write	लिखावट F	handwriting; penmanship

246

सज(ना) Intr   to be decorated   सजावट F   decoration

-इक [Sanskrit]

This suffix changes a noun into an adjective.

Examples:

दिन M	day	दैनिक* A	daily
धर्म M	religion, duty	धार्मिक* A	religious
वेद M	Veda	वैदिक* A	vedic
समाज M	society	सामाजिक* A	social
साहित्य M	literature	साहित्यिक A	literary

*Note the additional vowel changes.

-ईय [Sanskrit]

This suffix changes a noun into an adjective.

Examples:

भारत M	India	भारतीय A	Indian
रमण M	delight	रमणीय A	lovely, charming
शासक M	ruler	शासकीय A	governmental, official
स्मरण M	memory, remembrance	स्मरणीय A	memorable

-ता [Sanskrit]

This suffix changes an adjective into an abstract feminine noun.

Examples:

एक A	one	एकता F	unity, solidarity
महान A	great	महानता F	greatness
लघु A	small	लघुता F	smallness
सुन्दर A	beautiful	सुन्दरता F	beauty

-त्व [Sanskrit]

This suffix changes a noun or an adjective into an abstract masculine noun.

Examples:

अमर A	immortal, eternal	अमरत्व M	immortality
कवि M	poet	कवित्व M	poetic quality or insight
नारी F	woman	नारीत्व M	womanhood, femininity
पुरुष M	man	पुरुषत्व M	manliness
प्रभु M	lord, master, ruler	प्रभुत्व M	lordship, sovereignty

-पन [Hindi]

This suffix changes an adjective into an abstract masculine noun.

Examples:

अकेला A	alone, lonely	अकेलापन M	loneliness
कुँवारा A	unmarried	कुँवारापन M	bachelorhood
चिड़चिड़ा A	irritable	चिड़चिड़ापन M	irritability
छोटा A	small	छोटापन M	smallness
पागल A	insane	पागलपन M	insanity
रूखा A	dry, rough	रूखापन M	dryness, roughness
सीधा A	simple, straight, direct	सीधापन M	simplicity, directness

-पूर्वक [Sanskrit]

This suffix changes a noun into an adverb.

Examples:

आदर M	respect	आदरपूर्वक Adv	respectfully
आनन्द M	happiness, joy	आनन्दपूर्वक Adv	happily, joyfully
ध्यान M	attention	ध्यानपूर्वक Adv	attentively

-मान [Sanskrit]

This suffix changes a noun into an adjective.

Examples:

दीप्ति F	light, radiance, glow	दीप्तिमान A	illuminated, brilliant
बुद्धि F	intellect	बुद्धिमान A	intelligent
शक्ति F	strength, power	शक्तिमान A	strong, powerful

-वान्/वान [Sanskrit]

This suffix changes a noun into an adjective.

Examples:

गुण M	quality, virtue	गुणवान A	virtuous, talented
दया F	compassion	दयावान A	compassionate
धन M	wealth	धनवान A	wealthy
बल M	strength	बलवान A	strong

-हट [Hindi]

This suffix changes a verb stem into an abstract feminine noun.

Examples:

घबरा (ना) Intr/Tr	to be perplexed, to be agitated; to perplex, to agitate	घबराहट F	perplexity, agitation
चिल्ला (ना) Intr	to cry out, to scream	चिल्लाहट F	a cry, a scream
झुँझला (ना) Intr	to be irritable	झुँझलाहट F	irritability

Suffixes derived from Persian or Arabic

-आना [Persian]

This suffix changes a noun into an adjective or another noun.

Examples:

जुर्म M	crime, offense	जुर्माना M	fine, penalty	
मर्द M	male, man	मर्दाना A	manly; brave; related to man	
मेहनत F	hard work, labor	मेहनताना M	wages	
साल M	year	सालाना A	annual	

-ईन [Persian]

This suffix changes a noun into an adjective and denotes "having."

Examples:

नमक M	salt	नमकीन A	salty	
रंग M	color	रंगीन A	colored, colorful	
शौक़ M	fondness, liking, hobby	शौक़ीन A	desirous, fond (of); indulgent	

-ख़ाना [Persian]

This suffix changes a noun into another noun and denotes "abode/house of."

Examples:

कार M	work, occupation	कारख़ाना M	workshop, factory
ग़ुस्ल M	washing, bathing	ग़ुस्लख़ाना / ग़ुसलख़ाना M	bathroom
डाक F	mail, post	डाकख़ाना M	post office
दवा F	medicine	दवाख़ाना M	dispensary, pharmacy
पागल M	insane person	पागलख़ाना M	insane asylum
मै M	wine, liquor	मैख़ाना M	tavern, bar

-दान [Persian]
This suffix changes a noun into a masculine noun.

Examples:

फूल M	flower	फूलदान M flower vase
इतर / इत्र M	perfume	इतरदान / इत्रदान M container for perfume
क़लम M/F	pen	क़लमदान M penholder
पीक F	juice of a chewed *pan*	पीकदान M spittoon

-दार [Persian]
This suffix changes a noun into another noun or an adjective.

Examples:

दुकान F	shop, store	दुकानदार M shopkeeper
पहरा M	a turn of watch/guard	पहरेदार* M security guard; watchman
वफ़ा F	faithfulness	वफ़ादार A faithful, loyal
समझ F	understanding, intelligence	समझदार A intelligent

*Note the additional vowel changes.

-नाक [Persian]
This suffix changes a noun into an adjective and denotes "full of."

Examples:

ख़तरा M	danger	ख़तरनाक* A dangerous
ख़ौफ़ M	fear, fright	ख़ौफ़नाक A fearsome, frightful
दर्द M	pain	दर्दनाक A painful

*Note the additional vowel changes.

-बाज़ [Persian]

This suffix changes a noun into another noun or an adjective.

Examples:

चाल F	motion, a move; trickery	चालबाज़ A/M	deceitful, fraudulent; deceitful person
ठट्ठा M	joke; a laugh	ठट्ठेबाज़* A/M	jocular, facetious; joker
धोखा M	deception, deceit	धोखेबाज़* A/M	deceitful, fraudulent; deceitful person
पतंग F	kite	पतंगबाज़ M	kite flyer

*Note the additional vowel changes.

-मन्द [Persian]

This suffix changes a noun into an adjective and denotes "having."

Examples:

अक़्ल F	wisdom, intellect	अक़्लमन्द A	wise, intelligent
ज़रूरत F	need, necessity	ज़रूरतमन्द A	needy
दौलत F	wealth, prosperity	दौलतमन्द A	wealthy, prosperous

The Suffix ई

The suffix ई is very versatile; it can be used to change adjectives into nouns, nouns into adjectives, nouns into other nouns, and verb stems into nouns. Note that it is used with words of all origins, including words from Sanskrit, Hindi, Persian, and Arabic.

(1) The suffix ई can be used to change an adjective into a noun.

Examples:

अच्छा A	good	अच्छाई F	goodness
अमीर A	rich	अमीरी F	richness
कमज़ोर A	weak	कमज़ोरी F	weakness

ख़ुश A	happy	ख़ुशी F	happiness
ग़रीब A	poor	ग़रीबी F	poverty
तेज़ A	quick; sharp	तेज़ी F	quickness; sharpness
बुरा A	bad	बुराई F	evil, wickedness; vice, defect
संतुष्ट A	satisfied	संतुष्टी F	satisfaction
होशियार A	clever; skillful	होशियारी F	cleverness; skill

(2) The suffix ई can be used to change a noun into an adjective.

Examples:

ऊन F	wool	ऊनी A	woolen
क्रोध M	anger	क्रोधी A	angry
गुलाब M	rose	गुलाबी A	pink
जंगल M	jungle, forest	जंगली A	wild
दुख M	sorrow, grief	दुखी A	sad
देहात M	countryside	देहाती A	rural
नकल F	copy, imitation	नकली A	artificial; not genuine
पश्चिम M	the west	पश्चिमी A	western
बुनियाद F	foundation, basis	बुनियादी A	basic, fundamental
रेशम M	silk	रेशमी A	silken; made of silk
शाह M	king	शाही A	royal
सरकार M	government	सरकारी A	governmental, official
सुख M	happiness	सुखी A	happy
हवा F	air, wind	हवाई A	aerial

(3) The suffix ई can be used to change a noun into another noun or an adjective.

Examples:

मद्रास M	Madras	मद्रासी M/F/A	a person from Madras; Madrasi

जापान M	Japan	जापानी M/F/A	a person from Japan; Japanese
पंजाब M	Punjab	पंजाबी M/F/A	a person from Punjab; Punjabi
विदेश M	foreign country	विदेशी M/F/A	a foreigner; foreign

(4) The suffix ई can be used to change a noun into a feminine noun usually indicating a profession.

Examples:

डॉक्टर M/F	doctor	डॉक्टरी F	the medical profession
नौकर M	servant	नौकरी F	service, job, employment
पहरेदार M	watchman, guard	पहरेदारी F	the work of a watchman; guard/watch duty

(5) The suffix ई can be used to change a masculine noun into a feminine noun that is its diminutive form.

Examples:

घंटा	M	big bell; gong	घंटी	F	small bell
छुरा	M	large knife; dagger	छुरी	F	knife; small dagger
टोकरा	M	big basket	टोकरी	F	small basket
डंडा	M	big stick, staff	डंडी	F	small stick
पहाड़	M	mountain	पहाड़ी	F	hill
रस्सा	M	thick rope	रस्सी	F	thin rope

Note that with marked masculine nouns, the आ ending must be dropped before the suffix ई can be added.

(6) The suffix ई can be used to change a verb stem into an abstract feminine noun.

Examples:

चमक(ना) Intr	to shine, to sparkle	चमकी F	tinsel; foil
झड़(ना) Intr	to fall down; to be shed; to be poured	झड़ी F	continuous rain
बोल(ना) Tr	to speak	बोली F	speech; dialect
हँस(ना) Intr	to laugh	हँसी F	laughter; joke

Appendix I

MISCELLANOUS NOTES

(1) Variations in Colloquial Hindi

While the purpose of this book has for the most part been to provide a standard Hindi, students should be aware that colloquial speech is far more flexible and fluid in its observance of certain standards. Two phenomena that students may encounter in colloquial speech are the use of English in Hindi and the use of आप with तुम verb forms.

Hindi has incorporated vocabulary from many languages, including Arabic, English, Persian, Portuguese, and Sanskrit. These words have become a part of everyday speech, either in their original form or in a slightly modified form due to Hindi pronunciation. Thus Hindi has words like काग़ज़ and क़ानून from Arabic, वापस and कम from Persian, पेंसिल and प्लेटफ़ार्म from English, कमरा and मेज़ from Portuguese, and भाषा and भोजन from Sanskrit.

Recently, mixing English in Hindi sentences has grown in popularity due to the influence of satellite TV, films, and a variety of other media. Thus, Hindi speakers can often be heard saying sentences like "मुझे आजकल बहुत tension है" or "मैं आपका wait करूँगा." Advertising campaigns have also taken advantage of this trend, with slogans like Pepsi's "यह दिल माँगे more" and Coke's "Life हो तो ऐसी."

Another recent phenomenon in colloquial Hindi is addressing someone with आप but using तुम forms for verb agreement. For example, one might hear someone say, "आप आओगे न ?" instead of the standard Hindi "आप आएँगे न ?"

(2) More on Numbers

Fractions, cardinal numbers, and ordinal numbers were covered in *Introduction to Hindi Grammar*. Here we will focus on two commonly used numerical patterns in Hindi, the first based on the suffix -गुना and the second based on the suffix -ओं .

(a) गुना करना (also गुणा करना) in Hindi means to multiply. Thus, पाँचगुना means "five times" in the sentence "यह मकान उस मकान से पाँचगुना महँगा है ।" (This house is five times as expensive as that house).

Examples:

दुगुना / दुगना / दूना	*twice as much/many*
तिगुना	*three times as much/many*
चौगुना	*four times as much/many*
पाँचगुना / पचगुना	*five times as much/many*
छहगुना	*six times as much/many*
सातगुना / सतगुना	*seven times as much/many*
आठगुना / अठगुना	*eight times as much/many*
नौगुना	*nine times as much/many*
दसगुना	*ten times as much/many*

Note that some of these are irregular forms in that the cardinal numbers have undergone some minor spelling changes when combined with गुना.

(b) When the suffix -ओं is added to cardinal numbers representing a small quantity (e.g., दो, तीन), it signifies "both" or "all," as in दोनों *both* and तीनों *all three*. When used with larger numbers, it conveys an indefinite plurality. Thus सैंकड़ों and हज़ारों denote "hundreds" and "thousands."

(3) The Vocative Case

Vocative forms are the forms that are used when addressing someone. In Hindi vocative forms are similar to oblique forms. Thus, in the vocative case the -आ ending of singular marked masculine nouns changes to -ए while unmarked masculine nouns and marked and unmarked feminine nouns in the singular do not undergo any change. All plural nouns, when in the vocative case, take the -ओ ending. Note that here there is a difference between plural oblique forms, which take the -ओं ending, and plural vocative forms, which are not nasalized.

Examples:

अरे बेटे, जल्दी आ !	*Oh son, come quickly!*
अरी बेटी, क्या हुआ ?	*Oh daughter, what happened?*
ऐ रिक्शावाले, इधर आओ !	*Hey, riksha driver, come here!*
चलो बच्चो, अब घर जाओ ।	*Come on, children, now go home.*

257

भाइयो और बहनो, मेरी बात सुनो ।   *Brothers and sisters, listen to what*
                                        I have to say.

(4) The suffix -सा and the postposition के जैसा

The suffix -सा can be added to adjectives or nouns. In the case of adjectives, -सा denotes "-ish," "sort of," "rather," etc. and agrees with the following noun in number and gender. In other words, it indicates a similarity that is either approximate or somewhat diminished. However, with quantitative adjectives like बहुत and थोड़ा the addition of -सा intensifies the quantity.

Examples:

नीली-सी साड़ी	*a bluish sari*
छोटा-सा मकान	*a rather small house; a smallish house*
भोली-सी सूरत	*a rather innocent face*
बहुत-से फूल	*quite a few flowers*
थोड़ी-सी चीनी	*just a little sugar*

A noun or pronoun + सा functions as a marked adjective agreeing in number and gender with the following noun. In such cases the noun or pronoun will be in the oblique case. Here, -सा denotes "like" or "similar to" and functions much like the postposition के जैसा / जैसी / जैसे which also means "like" or "similar to."

Examples:

हीरे-सा बेटा	= हीरे (के) जैसा बेटा	*a gem of a son*
तुझ-सी छात्र	= तुझ / तेरे जैसी छात्र	*a student like you*
तोते-सी नाक	= तोते (के) जैसी नाक	*a parrot-like nose*
चाँद-सी बेटियाँ	= चाँद (के) जैसी बेटियाँ	*daughters like the moon*
		(daughters as beautiful as the moon)

Note that की तरह which also means "like," is used only when stating a similarity in the manner of an action.

Examples:

मैं भी आप की तरह गाना चाहती हूँ ।

I also want to sing like you.

वह मशीन की तरह काम करता है ।

He works like a machine.

Appendix II

ADVERBS AND ADVERBIAL EXPRESSIONS

अंत में	in the end, finally
अंदर	inside, within
अक्सर / अकसर	often, generally, usually
अचानक	suddenly, all of a sudden, unexpectedly
अच्छी तरह से	nicely
अति	very much, extremely
अधिक से अधिक	at most
अधिकतर	mostly, in most cases
अनजाने में	unknowingly
अपने आप (से)	by oneself, on one's own
अपने आप में	in itself
अपेक्षाकृत	comparatively
अब	now
अब से	from now onward, in the future
अब तक	up until now
अब की (बार)	this time
अब तो	now (as opposed to formerly)
अभी	just now, this very moment
अलग	separately
अलग-अलग	individually, separately
अवश्य	certainly, definitely, necessarily
असल में	in reality
आइंदा / आइन्दा	in future
आख़िर	at last, after all, finally
आख़िरकार	at last, after all, finally
आख़िर में / अंत में	in the end, finally, at last
आगे	in front; ahead; further

आगे से	in the future
आगे चलकर	further on, later on, subsequently
आज	today
आज रात को	tonight
आज शाम को	this evening
आज सवेरे / सुबह को	this morning
आजकल	nowadays, these days
आपस में	among themselves/ourselves/yourselves; mutually
आम तौर पर / से	generally
आराम से	slowly, gently, at leisure
आसपास	near, around, in the vicinity
आसानी से	easily
इकट्ठे	together
इतने में	meanwhile, at the moment, by then
इधर	here, this way
इधर-उधर	here and there
इस तरह (से)	in this way
इस बीच (में)	in the meantime
उधर	there, on that side, that way
ऊपर	above, upward
एक एक करके	one by one
एक साथ	together
एक हद तक	(up) to a certain extent
एक होकर	together, as one
एकदम	at once; completely
एकाएक	suddenly, all of a sudden
ऐसे	in this way, thus
कब	when, at what time
कभी	sometime; at any time
कभी-कभार	rarely, less often
कभी कभी	sometimes, now and then, occasionally

	कभी नहीं	never
	कभी न कभी	at one time or another
कम		little, few; less; seldom
	कम से कम	at the least
क़रीब		near, close by; nearly, approximately
	क़रीब-क़रीब	nearly, about, approximately, almost
कल		tomorrow; yesterday
कहाँ		where
कहीं		somewhere, anywhere
	कहीं और / और कहीं	somewhere else
	कहीं कहीं	here and there, in some places
	कहीं न कहीं	somewhere or other
	कहीं नहीं	nowhere
	कहीं भी	anywhere at all
	सब कहीं	evcrywhcrc
काफ़ी		quite
काफ़ी हद तक		to a great extent
किधर		where, which way
किसलिये		why, for what reason
किसी तरह		somehow
कुछ		somewhat
कुछ कुछ		somewhat
कुछ हद तक		to some extent
कुल		total
	कुल मिलाकर	in all
कृपया		kindly, please
केवल		only, merely; solely
कैसे		how, in what way
क्यों		why
क्यों कर		why, for what reason; how (could it be)
क्षण भर		for an instant

क्षण भर में	in a moment
ख़ास तौर पर / से	specifically, especially
ख़ासकर	specifically, especially
खुले आम	publicly, openly
खुल्लमखुल्ला	publicly, openly
ख़ुशी ख़ुशी	happily, cheerfully
ख़ुशी से	happily; gladly, with pleasure
ख़ूब	very much, lots (of); very well; splendidly
ख़्वामख़्वाह (ख़ाम ख़ा)	uselessly, without any purpose
चारों तरफ़ / ओर	everywhere, all around
चुपचाप	silently, quietly, stealthily
ज़बरदस्ती (से)	by force, forcibly, high-handedly (against one's wishes)
ज़रा	slightly, just, a bit
ज़रा भी नहीं	not at all
ज़रूर	certainly, undoubtedly
जल्दी (से)	quickly, urgently, immediately
जल्द से जल्द	as quickly as possible
जल्दी से जल्दी	as quickly as possible
जहाँ	where
जहाँ कहीं	wherever
जहाँ तक	as far as
जहाँ तहाँ	here and there
जहाँ का तहाँ	where it was before
जहाँ भी	wherever
जान-बूझकर	knowingly, deliberately, on purpose
जिधर	where, in what direction
जैसे	as, like; for example, for instance
जैसे तैसे	somehow, somehow or other
जैसे ही	as soon as
ज़ोर से	out loud; with force

263

ज़्यादा से ज़्यादा	at the most, maximum
ज़्यादातर	mostly, in most cases
ज्यों	in the way in which; just as; like
ज्यों का त्यों	unaltered, as it was (before), intact
ज्यों ही	as soon as
झट	at once
झूठमूठ	falsely
ठीक (से)	correctly, properly
ठीक-ठाक	all right, so-so
ढंग से	properly
X तक	even X; until or up to X
तक़रीबन	approximately, nearly; almost; about
तब	then, at that time, afterwards
तब तक	until then
तब से	since then
तभी	just then, just at that time; that is why
तुरंत	at once, immediately
तेज़ी से	quickly
थोड़ा बहुत	somewhat, a little
थोड़े ही	hardly, not at all, scarcely; by no means
दरअसल	in fact, in reality, as a matter of fact
दाएँ / दाहिने	to the right
दाएँ / दाहिने हाथ पर	to the right (hand side)
दिन भर	all day
दिन ब दिन	day by day
दुबारा	once again, for a second time
दूर	far (from), far off, far away
देर से	late (with delay)
दोपहर को	at noon; in the afternoon
धीरे (से)	slowly
धीरे-धीरे	gradually, slowly, by degrees

ध्यान से	attentively, carefully
नज़दीक़	near, close
निकट	near, close
नित्य	routinely, daily; always
निरन्तर	continuously
नीचे	below
परसों	the day after tomorrow; the day before yesterday
पल भर	(for) just a moment
पहले	at first, first of all, previously
पहले से	from the beginning; already
पहले-पहल	first of all; for the first time
पार	across, on the other bank / coast / side
पास	near, nearby
पीछे	behind, in back
पीछे से	from behind
पैदल	on foot
प्रायः	often, generally; approximately
फटाफट	at once
फिर	again; afterwards; furthermore
फिर भी	even so, nonetheless
फिर से	again, anew, afresh
फ़िलहाल	at present, for the time being
फ़ौरन	immediately, at once, instantly
बख़ूबी	excellently
बग़ल में	by the side, close by
बड़ा	very, exceedingly
...बजे (पर)	at ...o'clock
बतौर	as, like, on the pattern of
बमुश्किल	hardly; with difficulty
बराबर	constantly, continuously
बस	only, merely

बहुत	very, very much, too
बाएँ	to the left
बाएँ हाथ पर	on the left hand side
बाद में	later, subsequently
बार बार	repeatedly, again and again
बाहर	outside, out
बिलकुल / बिल्कुल	completely, absolutely
बीच में	in between; meanwhile
बीचोंबीच	in the very middle, exactly in the center
बीच बीच में	at intervals
बेतहाशा	very swiftly, recklessly, indiscreetly
बेशक	undoubtedly, no doubt, of course; certainly
भीतर	inside
भूलकर	by mistake
भूल से	by mistake
मन लगाकर	attentively, having fixed one's mind or attention (on)
मन ही मन	within one's mind, secretly
मिल-जुलकर	jointly, collectively
मुख्यतः	chiefly, mainly
मुश्किल से	with difficulty; hardly; scarcely
मेहरबानी करके	kindly, please
मोटे तौर पर	roughly speaking, in general
यहाँ	here, in/at this place
यहीं	at this very place, right here
यों / यूँ	thus, like this, in this way
यों ही / यूँ ही	just in this way; casually; for no special reason; by chance
रह रहकर	over and over again, repeatedly
रुक-रुक कर	haltingly
रोज़	daily, every day

रोज़ाना	daily, every day
रोज़-रोज़	day in and day out, day after day
लगभग	approximately, about
लगातार	continuously
वग़ैरह / वग़ैरा	etcetera (etc.)
वहाँ	there
वहीं	right there, at that very place
वाक़ई	really, truly, indeed
वास्तव में	in reality, in fact, as a matter of fact
विशेष तौर पर / से	especially
वैसे	thus, that way, in that manner; in fact
वैसे भी	even otherwise, otherwise
वैसे ही	in that very manner; casually, without a specific purpose, merely, simply
शाम को	in the evening
शायद	perhaps, maybe
शायद ही	hardly, rarely
शीघ्र	soon, quickly, promptly
सचमुच	truly, really
सदा	always
सब से ज़्यादा	most of all
सम्भवतः	possibly
सरासर	entirely, totally
सवेरे / सबेरे	in the morning
सहसा	suddenly
साथ	together
साथ-साथ	together; side by side; at the same time
साथ ही	simultaneously, together
साफ़-साफ़	clearly; frankly; openly
सामने	in front; opposite
सिर्फ़	only, merely

सीधे	straight ahead
सुबह (को)	in the morning
हमेशा	always
हर कहीं	everywhere
हरगिज़ नहीं	never at all, absolutely not, under no circumstances
हरदम	always, every moment
हाल में	recently
हूबहू	exactly the same as, exactly similar to
हो न हो	in all likelihood, most likely

Appendix III

POSTPOSITIONS

Simple Postpositions

का, के, की | postposition expressive of possession: belonging to, of, pertaining to, related to

को | postposition denoting to, etc.

तक | until, up to, as far as

ने | past tense agent marker

पर | on, on top of, at, upon

बिना | without

में | in, into, among, between

से | from; with; by; since; comparative postposition: than

Compound Postpositions with के / की

के अतिरिक्त | in addition to; apart from

के अनुकूल | in accordance (with); favorable to

के अनुसार | according to, in conformity with, in accordance with

के अंदर / अन्दर | in, inside, within

की अपेक्षा | in comparison with

के अलावा | in addition to; apart from

के आगे | ahead of, in front of, before

के आसपास | near, around, in the vicinity of

के उपरान्त | after

के ऊपर | on, upon, above, on top of, over

की ओर | towards, in the direction of

के क़रीब | near, close to

के कारण | because of, on account of, for the reason that

269

की ख़ातिर	for the sake of; out of consideration for
के ख़िलाफ़	against, opposed to
की जगह	in place of; instead of
के ज़रिये (से)	by, by means of, through the agency of
के जैसा	like, similar to
की तरफ़	towards, in the direction of
की तरफ़ से	on behalf of
की तरह	like, as, in the manner of
की तुलना में	in comparison with
के तौर पर	as, in the manner of
के दाएँ / दाहिने हाथ पर	on the right of, on the right side of
की दायीं ओर / तरफ़	to the right of, to the right side of
के दौरान	during, in the course of
के द्वारा	by means of; through, by the agency of
के निकट	close to, near
के नज़दीक	close to, near
के नीचे	under, beneath, below
के पहले	before; earlier than; ahead of
के पार	across, on the other side of, beyond
के पास	near, close to, by, in the vicinity of; owned by
के पीछे	behind, in the back of
के प्रति	towards, with respect to, regarding
के प्रतिकूल	against, counter to, contrary to
की बग़ल में	by the side of; adjoining
के बग़ैर	without
के / की बजाय	instead of, in place of
के बदले	instead of
के बदले में	in return for, in exchange for
के बराबर	equal to, on the same level as
के बहाने (से)	on the pretext of, with a pretense of

के बाएँ हाथ पर	on the left of, on the left side of
के बाद	after
की बायीं तरफ़ / ओर	to the left of, to the left side of
के बारे में	about, pertaining to, relating to
के बावजूद	in spite of, despite
के बाहर	outside of
के बिना	without
के बीच (में)	in the middle of; between, among; during
की भाँति	like, in the manner of
के भीतर	inside, within
की मारफ़त	through, by the means of; "care of" in postal addresses
के मारे	because of, on account of
के मुताबिक़	according to, in accordance with
के यहाँ	at the place or home of (someone)
के योग्य	worthy of, fit for, capable of
के लायक	worthy of, fit for, capable of
के लिये	for, on account of, in order to
की वजह से	because of, on account of, for the reason that
के वास्ते	for, for the sake of, in order to
के विपरीत	contrary to
के विरुद्ध	against, opposed (to)
के विषय में	about, in relation to
के संग	with, together with, along with
के सम्बन्ध / संबंध में	in connection with, with regard to, concerning
के समान	similar to, like, equal to
के समीप	near
के सहारे	with the help of, with the support of
के साथ	with, along with, together with
के साथ साथ	along with, alongside
के सामने	in front of

के सिलसिले में	in connection with
के सिवा / के सिवाय	except (for), apart from
के स्थान (में / पर)	instead of, in place of
के हेतु	for the sake of, because of
के हाथों	by the hands of

Other Compound Postpositions

को छोड़कर	excepting, except for, apart from
से दूर	far from
से पहले	before; earlier than; ahead of
से बढ़कर	more than, better than, superior to
से बाहर	outside of, beyond
में से	out of, from among; from inside of
से लेकर	from, starting with; beginning from (time and space)
से होकर	through, by way of, via

Appendix IV

CONJUNCTIONS

अगर...तो	if...then
अतः	so, therefore
अतएव	so, therefore
अथवा	or
अर्थात्	that is, that is to say, in other words
अन्यथा	otherwise, or else
इसलिये	so, therefore, for this reason
इसलिये कि	because, for the reason that
एवम् / एवं	and
और	and
कहीं .... न	lest
काश (कि)...	Oh that...! I wish that...! Would that...! Had God willed that...! If only …!
कि	that; or; when
किन्तु / किंतु	but
क्योंकि	because, since
चाहे	even if, whether
चाहे...चाहे / या	whether...or
चूँकि	because
जब कि	when, whereas
जब...तब	when...then
जब कभी... तब / तभी	whenever...then/right then
जब तक...तब तक	as long as…until then
जब भी...तब / तभी	whenever...then/right then
जब से...तब से	from (the time) when...since then
जहाँ...वहाँ	where...there
जहाँ कहीं...वहाँ / वहीं	wherever...there/right there

जहाँ तक… वहाँ तक	as far as…up until there
जहां भी… वहाँ / वहीं	wherever…there/right there
जितना…उतना	as much…that much
जिधर…उधर	in which direction…in that direction
जिधर भी…उधर (ही)	in whatever direction…in that (very) direction
जिस तरह का…उस तरह का	of which kind…of that kind
जिस तरह से…उस तरह से	in which manner…in that manner
जिस प्रकार का…उस प्रकार का	of which kind…of that kind
जिस प्रकार से…उस प्रकार से	in which manner…in that manner
जिससे (कि)	so that
जैसा…वैसा	of which kind…of that kind
जैसे	as if, as though; for example
जैसे कि	as, just as, for example
जैसे…वैसे	as…so, in which manner…in that manner
जैसे जैसे…वैसे वैसे	as (gradually)…so
जैसे ही…(वैसे ही)	as soon as…(then)
जो…वह / वे	who/which/what…he/she/that/they
जो भी हो	no matter what, in any case, whatever it might be, at any rate
ज्यों ज्यों…त्यों त्यों	as (gradually)…so
ज्यों ही …(त्यों ही)	as soon as…(then)
तथा	and
तब	then, at that time, afterwards
तब भी	even then, even so
तभी तो	for this reason, that is why
ताकि	so that, in order that
तो	then; therefore, moreover
तो भी	even then, in spite of this/that, nevertheless
न…न	neither...nor
नहीं तो	otherwise, or else, if not
पर	but, yet; still

परन्तु	but
फिर भी	nevertheless, even then, still, in spite of, yet
बल्कि	but also, but rather (not only X…but also/rather Y)
मगर	but
मानो / मानों	as if, as though; supposing
यदि…तो	if…then
यद्यपि…तथापि	although/even though…still/nonetheless
यहाँ तक कि	to the point where, so much so that
या	or
या (तो)…या (फिर)	either…or
यानी / याने	that is, that is to say, in other words
यों तो	while, whereas, though, although
लेकिन	but
व	and
वरना	otherwise, or else
वैसे	as it is, by the way
सो	so, therefore, hence
हालाँकि…फिर भी / तो भी	although/even though…still/nonetheless

Glossary

The Hindi-English glossary that follows covers new vocabulary words that have been introduced in this book. Vocabulary words are defined here based on their particular use in this text and therefore do not cover all possible meanings for every word. For further meanings and uses students should consult a dictionary. Note that the following categories of words have not been included here: (1) proper nouns; (2) onomatopoeic interjections; (3) words that were glossed in *Introduction to Hindi Grammar*, as they should already be a part of students' active vocabulary; and (4) words in Chapters 24 and 25 that are already listed in glossary format.

अ

अँगूठी	F	ring
अँधेरा	M	dark, darkness
अगर / यदि...तो	Conj	if ... then
अचानक	Adv	suddenly, unexpectedly
अजनबी	M	stranger
अजीब	A	strange
अतः	Conj	so, therefore
अतएव	Conj	so, therefore
अथवा	Conj	or
अध्यापक	M	teacher
अनाज	M	grain; food (in general)
अन्यथा	Conj	otherwise, or else
अफ़वाह	F	rumor
अफ़सोस	M	sorrow, regret
अब्बा	M	father
अभिनेता	M	actor
अभ्यास	M	practice
अमीरी	F	wealth
अर्ज़ी	F	application; petition

अर्थ	M	meaning
अर्थात्	Conj	that is, that is to say, in other words
अलग	A	apart, separate
अवसर	M	occasion; opportunity
अस्पताल	M	hospital
अहिंसा	F	non-violence

आ

आँसू	M	tear
आकाश	M	sky
आख़िर	Adv	finally, at last
आख़िरी	A	last, final
आग	F	fire
आज़ादी	F	freedom; independence
आज्ञा	F	permission; command
आत्मकथा	F	autobiography
आदत	F	habit
आदर	M	respect
आदरपूर्वक	Adv	respectfully
आदर्श	M/A	an ideal; ideal
आनन्द / आनंद	M	happiness
आनन्दपूर्वक	Adv	happily
आबादी	F	population
आम	M/A	mango; usual, general
आम तौर से / पर	Adv	usually, generally
आमदनी	F	income
आया	F	nanny
आयु	F	age; span of life
आराम	M	rest, comfort

आराम करना	Tr	to rest
आवश्यक	A	necessary
आवाज़	F	sound; voice
आशा	F	hope
आसमान	M	sky
आसान	A	easy
आसानी	F	ease
आसानी से	Adv	easily
आहिस्ता	A/Adv	slow; soft; slowly; softly

इ

इंतज़ाम	M	arrangement
इच्छा	F	wish, desire
इजाज़त	F	permission
इज़्ज़त	F	respect, honor
इतिहास	M	history
इरादा	M	intention
इश्तहार	M	poster; advertisement
इसलिए कि	Conj	because, for the reason that
इस्तरी	F	an iron

ई

ईष्र्या	F	envy, jealousy

उ

उगना	Intr	to sprout, to grow (crops)
उगवाना	Tr	to cause to sprout or grow (crops)

उगाना	Tr	to grow or sprout (crops)
उचित	A	appropriate; proper
उठवाना	Tr	to cause to lift or raise
उड़ना	Intr	to fly
उतरना	Intr	to get down
उतरवाना	Tr	to have an external agent take down
उतारना	Tr	to take down
उत्तर	M	answer; north
उत्तीर्ण	A	passed, successful (as in an examination)
उदार	A	generous
उदास	A	sad, dejected
उद्घाटन	M	inauguration
उन्नति	F	progress
उपन्यास	M	novel
उपस्थित	A	present
उपहार	M	gift
उबालना	Tr	to boil
उम्मीद	F	hope, expectation
उम्र	F	age; span of life

ऊ

ऊँचा	A	high, tall
ऊबना	Intr	to be bored

ए

एक एक करके	Adv	one by one
एवं / एवम्	Conj	and

कंजूस	A	miserly
कटना	Intr	to be cut
कटाना / कटवाना	Tr	to have an external agent cut
कठिनाई	F	difficulty
कठिनाई से	Adv	with difficulty
कथक	M	a style of dance
कभी	Adv	sometime, at any time, at one time
कभी कभी	Adv	sometimes, now and then, occasionally
कभी न कभी	Adv	sometime or other
कभी नहीं	Adv	never
जब कभी	Adv	whenever
कमज़ोर	A	weak
कमज़ोरी	F	weakness
कमाना	Tr	to earn
कमाल !	Interjection	Wonderful! Miraculous!
करवाना / कराना	Tr	to have an external agent do
करोड़पति	M	possessor of a crore of rupees or vast wealth
कर्त्तव्य	M	duty
कवि	M	poet
कवि-सम्मेलन	M	a gathering at which poets recite their work
कसरत	F	exercise
कसीदाकारी	F	embroidery
कहीं	Adv	somewhere, anywhere
कहीं और / और कहीं	Adv	somewhere else
कहीं कहीं	Adv	here and there, in some places

कहीं न कहीं	Adv	somewhere or other
कहीं नहीं	Adv	nowhere
कहीं भी	Adv	anywhere at all
जहाँ कहीं	Adv	wherever
सब कहीं	Adv	everywhere
काँटा	M	thorn
काँपना	Intr	to tremble, to shiver
काटना	Tr	to cut
काफ़ी	A/Adv	enough, sufficient; quite
कार्यक्रम	M	program
काश (कि)...	Conj	if only…
कि	Conj	that; or; when
किन्तु / किंतु	Conj	but
किराया	M	rent
किसान	M	farmer
की ओर	Post	towards, in the direction of
कीचड़	M	mud
कीड़ा	M	worm; insect
की तरह	Post	as, like, in the manner of
क़ीमती	A	expensive
कुत्ता	M	dog
कुली	M	coolie, porter
कूड़ा	M	garbage
कूदना	Intr	to jump
कृपया	Adv	kindly
कृपा करके	Adv	kindly
के अलावा	Post	in addition to; apart from
के द्वारा	Post	by, by means of; through; by the agency of
के पार	Post	across, on the other side of, beyond

के बग़ैर	Post	without
के बजाय	Post	instead of
के बिना	Post	without
के विरुद्ध	Post	against
के सिलसिले में	Post	in connection with
के हाथों	Post	by the hands of
को छोड़कर	Post	excepting, except for, apart from
कोहरा	M	fog
क्रांति / क्रान्ति	F	revolution

ख

खड़ा होना	Intr	to stand
ख़तरनाक	A	dangerous
ख़तरा	M	danger
ख़बरदार !	Interjection	Watch out! Be careful! Don't you dare!
ख़याल	M	thought, idea; opinion
ख़रीदवाना	Tr	to have an external agent buy
ख़ातिरदारी	F	hospitality
ख़ास	A	special, particular
ख़ासकर	Adv	especially
ख़ास तौर से / पर	Adv	especially
खिलना	Intr	to bloom, to blossom
खिलवाना	Tr	to have an external agent feed
खिलाना	Tr	to feed
खिलौना	M	toy
ख़ुदा	M	God
खुलना	Intr	to be opened, to open

खुलवाना	Tr	to have an external agent open
ख़ुश	A	happy
ख़ुशी से	Adv	happily
खेत	M	field(s)
खेती	F	farming
खोना	Tr/Intr	to lose; to be lost

ग

गंदा / गन्दा	A	dirty
गंभीर / गम्भीर	A	serious
गड़बड़	F	confusion; disorder; unrest
गणित	M	mathematics
गपशप	F	chitchat
गरजना	Intr	to thunder, to roar
ग़रीबी	F	poverty
गर्व	M	pride
गर्व से	Adv	proudly
ग़लत	A	wrong, incorrect
ग़लती	F	mistake, error
गाँव	M	village
गाना	Tr	to sing
गायक	M	singer
गायिका	F	singer
गाली	F	abuse, swear word
गाली देना	Tr	to abuse, to swear
गिरना	Intr	to fall, to fall down
गुना / गुणा करना	Tr	to multiply
ग़ुब्बारा	M	balloon
गुलाब	M	rose
ग़ुस्सा	M	anger

गूँजना	Intr	to buzz; to echo; to resound
गोद	F	lap
गोली	F	bullet; pill

घ

घंटी	F	bell
घटना	F	incident, event
घटना	Intr	to occur; to decline, to decrease
घड़ी	F	watch; clock
घनिष्ट	A	intimate
घमंड	M	pride, arrogance
घमंडी	A	proud, arrogant, vain
घाव	M	wound
घिरना	Intr	to be surrounded
घिरवाना	Tr	to have an external agent surround
घुमवाना	Tr	to have someone shown around
घुमाना	Tr	to show someone around
घुसना	Intr	to enter
घूमना	Intr	to wander; to tour around; to travel; to take a walk
घेरना	Tr	to surround

च

चटपटा	A	spicy
चढ़ना	Intr	to climb, to go up
चप्पल	F	sandal

चमकना	Intr	to shine
चमेली	F	jasmine
चलवाना	Tr	to have an external agent drive or move someone or something
चश्मा	M	eyeglasses
चहकना	Intr	to chirp
चाँद	M	moon
चाँदी	F	silver
चाबी	F	key
चाहे...चाहें / या	Conj	whether … or
चाहे...(लेकिन / फिर भी / तो भी)	Conj	regardless … still; no matter how … still; even if … still
चिंता / चिन्ता	F	worry; anxiety
चिड़िया	F	bird
चीखना	Intr	to scream
चीनी	F	sugar
चुटकुला	M	joke
चुनना	Tr	to choose, to select
चुनाव	M	election
चुप	A	quiet
चुपचाप	Adv	quietly, silently
चुराना	Tr	to steal
चुहिया	F	mouse
चूँकि	Conj	because
चोर	M	thief
चोरी	F	theft
चोरी करना	Tr	to steal
चौंकना	Intr	to be startled
चौराहा	M	crossroads, intersection

छ

छाता	M	umbrella
छिपकर	Adv	stealthily, secretly
छिपना	Intr	to be hidden; to hide
छिपाना	Tr	to hide, to conceal
छीनना	Tr	to snatch
छुड़वाना / छुड़ाना	Tr	to have an external agent set someone or something free
छूटना	Intr	to be free, to be released; to leave, to depart (a train, etc.)
छूना	Tr	to touch
छोड़ना	Tr	to let go, to release, to set someone or something free; to leave

ज

जगवाना	Tr	to have an external agent wake someone up
जगाना	Tr	to wake (someone) up
जनता	F	public
जन्म-दिन	M	birthday
ज़माना	M	time, period; the times, age
ज़मीन	F	ground; land
ज़रूर	Adv	certainly
ज़रूरी	A	necessary, important
जलना	Intr	to burn
जलवाना	Tr	to have an external agent burn something
जलाना	Tr	to burn something
जलेबी	F	a type of sweet

जल्दी	F	hurry, haste
जल्दी से	Adv	quickly
जागना / जगना	Intr	to wake up
जान-बूझकर	Adv	knowingly, deliberately
जानवर	M	animal
जायदाद	F	property
ज़िन्दगी	F	life; lifetime
जिस तरह का...उस तरह का	Conj	of which kind ... of that kind
जिस तरह से...उस तरह से	Conj	in which manner ... in that manner
जिस प्रकार का...उस प्रकार का	Conj	of which kind ... of that kind
जिस प्रकार से...उस प्रकार से	Conj	in which manner ... in that manner
जिससे (कि)	Conj	so that, in order that
जीत	F	victory
जीतना	Tr/Tr (non-ने)	to win
जीना	Intr	to live
जी भरकर	Adv	to one's heart's content
जीवन	M	life; lifetime
जीवन भर	Adv	entire life
जुआ	M	gambling
ज़ेवर	M	ornament
जैसे	Conj	as if, as though
जैसे जैसे...वैसे वैसे	Conj	as (gradually) ... so
जैसे ही...(वैसे ही)	Conj	as soon as ... (then)
ज़ोर	M	force
ज़ोर से	Adv	forcefully; loudly
ज्यों ज्यों...त्यों त्यों	Conj	as (gradually) ... so
ज्यों ही...(त्यों ही)	Conj	as soon as ... (then)

झ

झगड़ना	Intr	to quarrel
झूठ	M	falsehood, lie

ट

टक्कर	F	collision; knocking (against)
टक्कर खाना	Tr	to collide (with); to knock (against)
टक्कर लगना	Ind Intr	to collide (with); to knock (against)
टिकट घर	M	ticket booth, ticket office, booking office
टूटना	Intr	to be broken, to break

ठ

ठंडाई	F	a cold drink

ड

डरना	Intr	to fear, to be afraid
डराना	Tr	to frighten
डाँटना	Tr	to scold
डाकिया	M	mailman
डालना	Tr	to put in/down, to drop, to pour; to throw down
डूबना	Intr	to sink; to set (the sun, etc.)

ढ

ढाबा	M	a convenient roadside eatery
ढूँढ़ना	Tr	to search

त

तक़दीर	F	fate, destiny
तथा	Conj	and
तबियत	F	state of health
तम्बू	M	a large tent
तरक़्क़ी	F	progress
ताँगा	M	tonga
ताक़त	F	strength
ताकि	Conj	so that, in order that
तानाशाह़	M	dictator
ताला	M	lock
ताली	F	clapping of hands, applause
तीर	M	arrow
तुड़वाना / तुड़ाना	Tr	to have an external agent break something
तुरन्त / तुरंत	Adv	at once, immediately
तूफ़ान	M	storm
तेज़	A	sharp; quick, swift
तेज़ी	F	sharpness; swiftness
तेज़ी से	Adv	quickly
तैरना	Intr	to swim
तैयारी	F	preparation
तोड़ना	Tr	to break (something)
तोता	M	parrot

तौलिया	M	towel
त्यौहार	M	festival

थ

थकना	Intr	to be tired
थप्पड़	M	slap
थप्पड़ मारना	Tr	to slap

द

दक्षिण	M	south
दम	M	breath; life
दम घुटना	Intr	to be suffocated, to be choked
दराज़	M/F	drawer
दर्ज़ी	M	tailor
दर्द	M	pain
दवाई / दवा	F	medicine
दादा	M	paternal grandfather
दादी	F	paternal grandmother
दावत	F	feast; party
दिखवाना	Tr	to have an external agent show
दिल	M	heart
दिलचस्पी	F	interest
दिलवाना / दिलाना	Tr	to have an external agent give
दीपक	M	lamp
दीमक	F	termite, white ant
दुख	M	sadness, unhappiness
दुबला	A	thin
दुर्घटना	F	accident

दुल्हा	M	bridegroom
दुल्हिन / दुलहन	F	bride
दुश्मन	M	enemy
दुश्मनी	F	animosity
दूध	M	milk
दूरदर्शन	M	television
दूषित	A	contaminated
दृश्य	M	scene
देखभाल	F	care; supervision
देखभाल करना	Tr	to take care, to look after; to supervise
देर	F	delay
देर से	Adv	with delay, late
दोस्ती	F	friendship
दोहराना	Tr	to repeat
दौड़ना	Intr	to run

ध

धन	M	wealth; money
धर्म	M	religion
धुलाना / धुलवाना	Tr	to have an external agent wash
धैर्य	M	patience
धैर्य से	Adv	patiently
धोखा	M	deception, deceit
ध्यान	M	attention
ध्यानपूर्वक	Adv	attentively, carefully
ध्यान से	Adv	attentively, carefully

न...न	Conj	neither … nor
नदी	F	river
नमाज़	F	namaz (Muslim prayer)
नमाज़ पढ़ना	Tr	to perform namaz (Muslim prayer)
नहाना	Intr	to bathe
नहीं तो	Conj	otherwise, or else
नाक	M	nose
नाटक	M	drama, play
नानी	F	maternal grandmother
नायक	M	hero (as of a drama, play, or novel)
नायिका	F	heroine (as of a drama, play, or novel)
नाराज़	A	angry
निकट	Adv	near, close
निकलना	Intr	to come out, to get out
निकलवाना	Tr	to have an external agent take someone or something out
निकालना	Tr	to take someone or something out
नियम	M	law, rule, regulation
निवेदन	M	request
नींद	F	sleep
नीति	F	policy
नीरस	A	without taste; uninteresting
नुकसान	M	harm; damage; loss
नृत्य	M	dance
नेता	M	leader; politician

नौकर	M	servant
नौकरी	F	job
नौकरानी	F	servant

प

पंखा	M	fan
पकड़ना	Tr	to hold, to grasp, to catch
पकवाना	Tr	to have an external agent cook
पछताना	Tr	to repent, to regret
पट्टी	F	bandage
पड़ना	Intr	to fall; to lie (down), to lie around; to befall
पढ़वाना	Tr	to have an external agent teach
पढ़ाई	F	study; education
पता	M	address; information
पत्ता	M	leaf
पत्ती	F	leaf, petal
पत्रिका	F	magazine
पर	Conj	but
परन्तु	Conj	but
परिश्रम	M	hard work
पर्यावरण	M	environment
पलंग	M	bed
पश्चिमी	A	western
पाँव	M	foot; leg
पागल	A/M	insane, crazy; a crazy person
पाना	Tr	to get, to find, to obtain, to receive

पालन करना	Tr	to rear; to obey (a rule or command)
पालना	Tr	to rear
पिटना	Intr	to be beaten
पिटवाना	Tr	to have an external agent beat
पिलवाना	Tr	to have an external agent give someone something to drink
पिलाना	Tr	to give someone something to drink
पीटना	Tr	to beat
पीड़ित	A	suffering (from), afflicted (by)
पीढ़ी	F	generation
पीसना	Tr	to grind
पुछवाना	Tr	to have an external agent ask
पुराना	A	old (for inanimate nouns only); ancient
पूजा	F	worship
पूर्ण	A	complete, full
पूर्णतः	Adv	completely, fully
पूर्णतया	Adv	completely, fully
पूर्ण रूप से	Adv	completely, fully
पेट	M	stomach
पैदल	Adv	on foot
पैदल चलना	Intr	to walk
पैदा होना	Intr	to be born
पौधा	M	plant
प्यार	M	love
प्यार से	Adv	lovingly
प्याला	M	cup
प्रगति	F	progress
प्रतीक्षा	F	waiting

प्रधान मंत्री	M/F	prime minister
प्रयत्न	M	effort, attempt
प्रश्न	M	question
प्रसन्नता	F	happiness
प्रसिद्ध	A	famous
प्रेम	M	love
प्रेमपूर्वक	Adv	lovingly
प्रेमिका	F	beloved
प्रेमी	M	lover

फ

फंसना	Intr	to be stuck, to be entangled
फटना	Intr	to be torn
फड़वाना / फटवाना	Tr	to have an external agent tear something
फ़र्ज़	M	obligation, duty
फ़सल	F	harvest, crop
फ़साद	M	disturbance; riot; quarrelling
फाड़ना	Tr	to tear, to rip
फ़ायदा	M	benefit, advantage; profit
फिसलना	Intr	to slip
फुड़वाना	Tr	to have an external agent burst, break, or crack something
फूटना	Intr	to burst, to break, to crack
फूलदान	M	flower vase
फेंकना	Tr	to throw
फ़ेहरिस्त	F	list
फैलना	Intr	to spread, to be spread

फोड़ना	Tr	to burst, break, or crack something
फ़ौरन	Adv	at once, immediately

ब

बँटवारा	M	partition; division
बग़ीचा	M	a small garden
बचपन	M	childhood
बचवाना	Tr	to have an external agent save
बच्चा	M	child, baby
बजवाना	Tr	to have an external agent play (a musical instrument)
बटुआ / बटुवा	M	wallet
बढ़ना	Intr	to increase, to advance
बढ़ाना	Tr	to increase
बढ़िया	A	excellent, of good quality
बदनामी	F	bad reputation
बदलना	Intr/Tr	to be changed; to change something
बधाई	F	congratulation(s)
बनना	Intr	to be made
बनवाना	Tr	to have an external agent make
बरतन / बर्तन	M	(cooking) vessel
बरस / वर्ष	M	year
बल्कि	Conj	but also, but rather (not only X … but also/rather Y)
बस	Adv	only, merely
बहू	F	bride; daughter-in-law
बाँधना	Tr	to tie
बाग़	M	a large garden

बाढ़	F	flood
बादल	M	cloud
बालक	M	small boy
बालिका	F	small girl
बिन्दी / बिंदी	F	dot
बिकवाना	Tr	to have an external agent sell
बिखरना	Intr	to be scattered
बिजली	F	lightning; electricity
बिठवाना	Tr	to have someone seated
बिठाना	Tr	to seat someone
बिलकुल	Adv	completely, absolutely
बिल्ली	F	cat
बिस्तर	M	bedding; bed
बीतना	Intr	to pass (time), to elapse (time)
बीमार / बिमार	A	ill, unwell
बुद्धू	M	idiot
बुरा	A	bad
बूढ़ा	A	old, aged (for people or animate nouns only)
बेहतर	A	better

भ

भगवान	M	God, the supreme being
भतीजा	M	nephew
भयानक	A	fearsome, terrible; dangerous
भरना	Intr/Tr	to be filled; to fill
भरोसा	M	reliance, trust, confidence
भविष्य	M	future
भागना	Intr	to run
भाग्य	M	fortune

भाग्य से	Adv	fortunately
भाभी	F	elder brother's wife
भारी	A	heavy
भिगवाना	Tr	to have an external agent make someone or something wet
भिगाना	Tr	to make someone or something wet
भिजवाना	Tr	to have an external agent send
भीगना	Intr	to get wet
भुलाना	Tr	to erase from one's mind; to forget
भूकंप / भूकम्प	M	earthquake
भूलकर	Adv	mistakenly
भूलना	Tr (non-ने)	to forget
भेजना	Tr	to send

म

मंज़िल	F	destination; story/floor (of a building)
मंडप	M	*mandap*, a wedding pavilion
मगर	Conj	but
मच्छरदानी	F	mosquito net
मजबूर	A	helpless
मज़ा	M	pleasure, enjoyment; relish, taste
मज़ा आना	Ind Intr	to enjoy, to relish
मधुमेह	M	diabetes
मन	M	mind; heart
मना करना	Tr	to refuse; lit., to say "no"

मनाना	Tr	to celebrate (a festival, a holiday, etc.)
मरना	Intr	to die
मरीज़	M/F	patient, sick person
मर्ज़ी	F	wish, desire
मलना	Tr	to rub
मस्जिद	F	mosque
मस्त	A	exhilarated, delighted; carefree
महल	M	palace
माँग	F	demand
माँगना	Tr	to ask for
माथा	M	forehead
मानना	Tr	to accept, to agree, to listen to
मानो / मानों	Conj	as if, as though
माफ़ करना	Tr	to forgive
माफ़ी माँगना	Tr	to ask for forgiveness
मामला	M	matter, affair
मारना	Tr	to hit, to strike; to kill
मालिक	M	owner, master; possessor
माली	M	gardener
मिलकर	Adv	together, jointly
मिल-जुलकर	Adv	together, jointly, collectively
मिलाना	Tr	to connect, to unite; to mix
मील	M	mile
मुख्य	A	main, chief
मुख्यतः	Adv	mainly, chiefly
मुख्य रूप से	Adv	mainly, chiefly
मुनासिब	A	appropriate
मुबारक	A	blessed, fortunate
मुबारक !	Interjection	Blessings! Congratulations!

मुमकिन	A	possible
मुश्किल	A/F	difficult; difficulty
मुश्किल से	Adv	with difficulty
मुस्कुराना / मुसकराना	Intr	to smile
मुहल्ला	M	neighborhood
मृत्यु	F	death
मेहनत	F	hard work
मेहनत करना	Tr	to work hard
मेहमान	M/F	guest
मेहरबानी करके	Adv	kindly
मैदान	M	flat, open field; plain
मोटा	A	fat
मौक़ा	M	opportunity, chance; occasion

य

यद्यपि	Conj	although, even though
यद्यपि...तथापि	Conj	although/even though … still/nonetheless
या (तो)...या (फिर)	Conj	either … or
यात्री	M/F	passenger, traveller
याद	F	memory, recollection
याद आना	Ind Intr	to come to mind, to remember
याददाश्त	F	memory
यानी	Conj	that is, that is to say, in other words
योगासन	M	yogic posture

र

रंग	M	color

रखना	Tr	to put, to place; to keep
रसोई	F	kitchen
राक्षस	M	demon
राजनीति	F	politics
राज़ी	A	pleased, agreeable
राज़ी करना	Tr	to persuade
राज़ी होना	Intr	to be pleased; to consent
राय	F	opinion
रास्ता	M	path, road, way
रिवाज	M	custom
रिश्ता	M	relationship, relation
रिश्तेदार	M/F	relative
रिश्वत	F	bribe
रुकवाना	Tr	to have an external agent stop someone or something
रुलवाना	Tr	to have an external agent make someone cry
रुलाना	Tr	to make someone cry
रोकना	Tr	to stop someone or something
रोज़	M/Adv	day; every day, daily
रोशनी	F	light
रौनक	F	radiance; atmosphere of excitement/happiness; flourishing state

ल

लगभग	Adv	approximately
लगवाना	Tr	to have an external agent apply/attach/connect
लगाना	Tr	to apply; to attach, to connect
लड़ना	Tr (non-ने)	to fight, to quarrel

लड़ाई	F	fight, quarrel; war
लस्सी	F	*lassi*, a cold beverage
लाठी	F	staff, stick, cudgel
लापरवाही	F	carelessness
लिखवाना / लिखाना	Tr	to have an external agent write
लिटवाना	Tr	to have an external agent lay someone or something down
लिटाना	Tr	to lay someone or something down
लिफ़ाफ़ा	M	envelope
लुटना	Intr	to be robbed
लुटवाना	Tr	to have an external agent rob
लूटना	Tr	to rob
लेख	M	article
लेखक	M	writer
लेटना	Intr	to lie down
लोकगीत	M	folk song
लौटना	Intr	to return

व

व	Conj	and
वक़्त	M	time
वज़न	M	weight
वरना	Conj	otherwise, or else
वाकई	Adv	really, truly, indeed
वायदा / वादा	M	promise
विचार	M	thought, idea; opinion
विज्ञान	M	science
विशेष	A	special

विशेषकर	Adv	especially
विशेष तौर से / पर	Adv	especially
विशेष रूप से	Adv	especially
विश्वविद्यालय	M	university
विषय	M	subject; topic
वेतन	M	salary; wage
व्यवसाय	M	business; occupation, profession
व्यवहार	M	behavior, conduct
व्यस्त	A	busy

श

शक़	M	doubt
शक्तिशाली	A	powerful
शतरंज	F	chess
शरबत / शर्बत	M	sherbet, any sweet drink
शस्त्र	M	weapon
शादी	F	marriage
शानदार	A	splendid, gorgeous
शान्ति / शांति	F	peace
शान्तिपूर्वक	Adv	peacefully
शाबाश !	Interjection	Well done! Excellent! Bravo!
शास्त्रीय	A	classical (as in music)
शिकायत	F	complaint
शिकारी	M	hunter
शिक्षा	F	education; teaching
शीशा	M	mirror; glass
शेर	M	lion
शैतानी	F	naughtiness, mischief
शोर	M	noise

शोहरत	F	fame
शौक़	M	fondness

स

संभलकर	Adv	carefully
संभलना	Intr	to be careful
संभलवाना	Tr	to have an external agent take care of someone or something
संभव / सम्भव	A	possible
संभवतः / सम्भवतः	Adv	possibly
संभालना	Tr	to take care of someone or something
संस्कृति	F	culture
सच	M/A	truth; true
सचमुच	Adv	truly, really
सड़ना	Intr	to rot
सफ़र	M	journey, trip
सफल	A	successful
सफलता	F	success
सभ्यता	F	civilization
समझदार	A	intelligent
समझवाना	Tr	to have an external agent explain
समझाना	Tr	to explain
समझौता	M	compromise, agreement
समस्या	F	problem
समाज	M	society
समाज सेवक	M	social worker
समाज सेवा	F	social service
समोसा	M	*samosa*, an Indian snack
सम्बन्ध / संबंध	M	relation; connection

सम्मेलन	M	conference, gathering, assembly
सरकार	F	government
सलाह	F	advice
सहमत	A	agreeing (with)
सहमत होना	Intr	to agree (with)
सामान्य	A	general
सामान्यतः	Adv	generally
सामान्यतया	Adv	generally
सामान्य रूप से	Adv	generally
सारा	A	whole, entire
सावधान	A	careful, cautious
सावधानी	F	care, caution
सावधानी से	Adv	carefully, cautiously
सास	F	mother-in-law
साहित्य	M	literature
सिखवाना	Tr	to have an external agent teach
सिखाना	Tr	to teach
सिरदर्द	M	headache
सिर्फ़	A/Adv	only; merely, only
सिलवाना / सिलाना	Tr	to have an external agent sew
सीढ़ी	F	ladder; step (of a stair)
सीधा	A	straight; direct
सीधे	Adv	straight ahead, directly
सीना	Tr	to sew
सुखी	A	happy
सुनवाना	Tr	to have an external agent tell, relate, recite, or narrate
सुबकना	Intr	to sob

सुलवाना	Tr	to have an external agent put someone to sleep
सुलाना	Tr	to put someone to sleep
सुशिक्षित	A	well educated
सुसंस्कृत	A	cultured
सूखना	Intr	to dry up, to dry
सूना	A	desolate, empty
सूरज	M	sun
सूर्योदय	M	sunrise
से बढ़कर	Post	more than, better than, superior to
सेहत	F	health
से होकर	Post	through, by way of, via
सैर	F	a walk, stroll, trip
सो	Conj	so, therefore, hence
सोना	M	gold
स्नेह	M	affection
स्नेहपूर्वक	Adv	affectionately

ह

हँसी-मज़ाक	M	laughing and joking
हक़	M	right
हज़ार	A	thousand
हरकत	F	movement; action (a somewhat negative connotation)
हरगिज़ नहीं !	Interjection	Absolutely not!
हवाई जहाज़	M	airplane
हारना	Intr/Tr	to be defeated; to lose (as a battle, a match, etc.)
हाल	M	condition, state

हालत	F	condition, state
हालाँकि	Conj	although, even though
हालाँकि...फिर भी / तो भी	Conj	although/even though … still/nonetheless
हिंसा	F	violence
हिम्मत	F	courage
हीरा	M	diamond
होशियार !	Interjection	Watch out! Be careful!

ABOUT THE AUTHOR

USHA R. JAIN is Senior Lecturer in Hindi in the Department of South and Southeast Asian Studies, University of California at Berkeley, and is the author of *The Gujaratis of San Francisco* (1989), *Introduction to Hindi Grammar* (1995), *Intermediate Hindi Reader* (1999), and *Intermediate Hindi Reader* CD-ROM (2000).